SMARTER CRIME CONTROL

SMARTER CRIME CONTROL

A Guide to a Safer Future for Citizens, Communities, and Politicians

Irvin Waller

ROWMAN & LITTLEFIELD
Lanham • Boulder • New York • London

Published by Rowman & Littlefield
4501 Forbes Boulevard, Suite 200, Lanham, Maryland 20706
www.rowman.com

Unit A, Whitacre Mews, 26-34 Stannary Street, London SE11 4AB

British Library Cataloguing in Publication Information Available

Library of Congress Cataloging-in-Publication Data

The hardback edition of this book was previously cataloged by the Library of Congress as follows:

Waller, Irvin.
  Smarter crime control : a guide to a safer future for citizens, communities, and politicians / Irvin Waller.
    pages cm
  Includes bibliographical references and index.
  1. Crime prevention. I. Title.
  HV7431.W3265 2013
  364.4--dc23

2013037127

ISBN 978-1-4422-2169-7 (cloth : alk. paper)
ISBN 978-1-5381-0692-1 (pbk. : alk. paper)
ISBN 978-1-4422-2170-3 (electronic)

∞™ The paper used in this publication meets the minimum requirements of American National Standard for Information Sciences—Permanence of Paper for Printed Library Materials, ANSI/NISO Z39.48-1992.

Printed in the United States of America

CONTENTS

ACKNOWLEDGMENTS

This book builds on the extraordinary network of titans with whom I have worked for more than forty years, in and out of governments, across the world, but particularly in Canada, France, the United Kingdom, and the United States. I recognized each of their special contributions to my life and work in my previous books for interested readers, *Less Law, More Order* and *Rights for Victims of Crime*.

I felt a need to do more than those books because getting smart on crime had reached a critical moment—"Greater than the tread of mighty armies is an idea whose time has come." Political and police leaders were changing their discourse. They have started to use phrases such as "smart on crime," which were part of *Less Law, More Order*. They are admitting that they cannot arrest their way out of crime, and they want to match effective social prevention and smart enforcement. They are exercised by the failure of the war on drugs and mass incarceration.

My network of persons dedicated to using evidence to stop violence has been expanded by the extraordinary new world of social media, where like-minded professionals and advocates for victims can share and debate the latest developments. Some of them are referenced in this book, and others know that I learn from them. Three events brought to my attention on Twitter changed this book and my passion. The first was Michelle Alexander's *The New Jim Crow: Mass Incarceration in the Age of Colorblindness*, which caught the pulse of a nation (and the *New York Times* best-seller list) by demonstrating that mass incarceration is extraordinarily racially biased and counterproductive for their communities. The second was the Institute of Medicine's comprehensive analysis of the health gap for US young people, which showed the inability of extraordinary spending and cutting-edge health care (and hyperincarceration) to keep young men in America alive compared to other affluent democracies. The third was an initiative by a group of superstars and super change agents who took their view of mass incarceration and the war on drugs right to the president of the United States, who has already started to quote the irrefutable cost benefits of investing in preschool as a way to stop crime (seven dollars saved for every dollar invested) and lifeskills training to stop drug abuse (eighteen dollars saved for every dollar invested).

This book has benefitted immeasurably from the editorial skills and support of Elizabeth Bond. The figures and tables are the work of Pierre Bertrand. I hope the product justifies the sacrifices of those around me, particularly the patience and vision of my wife and partner.

So this book is dedicated to all those who have dedicated their careers to stopping the violence, sparing the lives of victims, and confronting the reality that more young men's lives are lost to violence because more young men's lives are lost behind bars—and not the reverse. But it is particularly dedicated to those in the generations that follow mine who are rekindling the torch to light a smarter way forward and persuading politicians to reinvest smartly in the number one right of victims of crime—to live in communities that are safe from violence.

Irvin Waller
Ottawa, Canada

PREFACE

"Safety is the first of our civil rights, and freedom from violence is the first of our freedoms."

—Connie Rice, Civil Rights Lawyer

The United States is the world's richest (and most medically advanced) nation. Among the affluent democracies (a term that I use to refer to the main nations of Western Europe, North America, and Australasia), it also has the highest rates of young men dying in homicides, traffic crashes, and drug overdoses. The United States has developed the most scientific knowledge about how to stop that violence—but it uses the least.

Smarter Crime Control confronts this extraordinary gorilla in the room and provides practical and affordable solutions that enhance public safety while saving taxes. It transforms the wealth of scientific knowledge on what stops violence—chapter by chapter—into precise actions on which legislators can act. And if the legislators acted on those reforms to reinvest a modest 10 percent of what is spent on law enforcement, courts, and corrections, they would spare innumerable victims a whopping $300 billion every year in loss of quality of life.

Further, the United States that believes in smaller government is spending more per capita on bigger government to react to crime than any other affluent democracy. While the United Kingdom has reacted to lower crime rates by cutting its more modest government expenditures by no less than 20 percent in the areas of policing and corrections, the United States has continued to spend more while benefitting from a similar unprecedented decline.

Smarter Crime Control shows how to reinvest to stop violence and so spare victims while saving money for taxpayers because crime is down. It shows how to save additional taxes by stopping the use of incarceration for offenses that do not incur harm to victims. While reinvesting 10 percent from what is spent currently on reaction to crime to get cost-effective prevention and smart crime control that spares victims, it also saves billions for taxpayers. So a 20 percent cut (as in the United Kingdom) would spare victims to the tune of $300 billion and provide a 10 percent tax rebate, while getting much more savings for taxpayers by cutting out what does not work.

Smarter Crime Control estimates annual savings to taxpayers as high as $100 billion, even after paying for the reinvestment in cost-effective public safety. This would be achieved while dropping crime rates further, but would require cutting mass incarceration to rates similar to periods in the United States when rates of violence were as low as today and ultimately to rates similar to other affluent democracies. The evidence shows that this can be done without increasing risk to crime victims.

Each chapter looks at the hard evidence of what would stop violence and then lists legislative actions. In part I, the book focuses on where police, courts, and corrections can safely regroup, cut actions that are ineffective, and retool to be more effective in sparing victims. In part II, it identifies legislative actions from the evidence that would not only stop youth from becoming chronic offenders but cut in half or more a range of major challenges for victims of crime, including gun violence, violence against women, traffic fatalities, and property crime.

The extraordinary rates of street violence in the United States are not new. They were so bad in the 1960s that no less than three presidential commissions produced pragmatic recommendations on how to stop the bleeding—one with the title of "The Challenge of Crime in a Free Society." Fifty years later, we have accumulated not only more experience of the limits of modern law enforcement, criminal justice, and corrections, but a wealth of scientific studies about what does and does not prevent violence and at what cost to taxpayers, most of which was developed in the United States.

The United States is the nation most proudly dedicated to civil rights and freedom. Even in the 1960s, while civil rights marched forward, the country incarcerated at rates double those of any other free democracy and already one third higher than the modest average rate of incarceration for the world today. But unfortunately for victims of violence, its various orders of government ignored the recommendations from those commissions on how to prevent violence and regrettably quadrupled its rates of incarceration in the name of justice, reinforcing racial biases so severely that a *New York Times* best-seller called it "The New Jim Crow."

But not only are blacks—the term I will use in this book because the major sources of statistics use it—incarcerated at rates much higher than whites. But these high rates of incarceration fail to eliminate the huge disparities in risk of homicide victimizations between blacks and whites and Hispanics—also the term I will use because it is used by the main statistical agencies.

Now, not only does the United States have the world's highest rates of homicides, traffic crashes, and drug overdoses, the population behind bars is also so vast that it is unimaginable in any other free democracy on the planet. Some say the country has operated like an incarceration addict: when the dose did not work, it was increased—over and over again.

Those operating this criminal justice complex (and their sociological apologists) justify the incarceration addiction as being what victims of crime advocated. But that is not most victims, and it is certainly not what protects most victims. Yes, a system that ignores the needs of victims rightly leads to anger. And yes, the United States does not have a monopoly on those victims—whose lives have been shattered by inexcusable violence—who cry out justifiably for draconian sentences. But that is not what modern justice is about and certainly not what stops violence.

Violence, though, is not inevitable; it is *preventable*. And what most victims really want is for the violence to stop. The scientists of the United States—the world's most powerful nation—one that is conquering outer space and finding cures for cancer—have not been asleep since the days of those commissions. A group of criminological titans has been exploring what prevents violence by using longitudinal studies, random control trials, and collaborative meta-analyses. Today there is an extraordinary arsenal of knowledge as well as programs that have earned a consumer seal of approval because there is scientific *proof* that they stop violence. So why is this arsenal not being used in the United States or in other affluent democracies?

This book is unique in many ways. It focuses on ways to stop violence, which disproportionally impacts young Hispanic and particularly black men, different from so many books that focus only on the racial bias in the use of incarceration. It focuses on what reinvestments prevent violence before victims are hurt in the first place, rather than headlining small shifts in reentry after incarceration. It focuses on what is cost-effective in pre-crime prevention rather than whether more costly repressive law enforcement can suppress crime. It puts trends in the United States in the perspective of trends in affluent democracies, rather than whether a US trend can be interpreted in isolation. But it uses US statistics and US knowledge, because they are the best in the world. As a result, its conclusions provide immeasurable hope for victims in the United States but also for other affluent democracies.

This book guides citizens, communities, and politicians to the proven actions that will stop violence, traffic crashes, and drug overdoses and so make communities safer. It proposes a pragmatic road map to stop waste—communities that are not as safe as modern science shows is possible, lives of young men warehoused in mass incarceration instead of contributing to communities, and taxes spent on what does not work rather than what is effective and cost-effective. Each chapter provides a short list of actions that politicians can take in the name of *citizens* to stop violence. If they act on this guide, they will provide smart public safety for ourselves and for the next generations, not only in the United States, but across the planet.

1

SMART PUBLIC SAFETY

Giving Priority to Victims and Taxpayers

INTRODUCTION

When we hear reports of the latest sensational and exceptional crime on the news, many of us react with fear and frustration. Often there is a reflexive cry of "Punish the criminals!" "If they do the crime, they must do the time." "Get them behind bars where they can do no more harm." And by this we mean have the police catch them, a judge sentence them, and the jailers incarcerate them. Without ever having given much thought to it, most people, and even our politicians, just assume that this system will somehow work to protect us from harm. It's always been that way, so it must work—right?

The answer is no, it doesn't always work. The United States, among affluent democracies, has the highest rates of young men dying in homicides, traffic crashes, and drug overdoses, despite having rates of incarceration five times those of England and Wales and seven times those of other major affluent democracies. Rates of property crime proportionate to the population have been declining in affluent democracies regardless of those levels of incarceration.

The sheer number of people in the United States who are still being victimized by crime every day—despite living with the most punitive system ever invented and at huge cost to taxpayers—adds urgency to finding a smarter way to control crime.

When this traditional system does work in the United States or elsewhere, even a little bit, it is extraordinarily repressive to young males, especially blacks and other minorities, who are the very persons who are still more likely to be killed or seriously injured despite the system.

It is also not cost effective for taxpayers. As we shall see throughout this book, the results that it gets are not as good (and often much worse) than what *could* have been achieved through smarter, less expensive means—particularly reinvestment in effective prevention. Ironically, those actions that are much more effective and cost effective have been identified because of the scientific acumen of researchers, many of whom are Americans. An accumulation of scientific research has found solutions that have been proven to reduce the numbers of crime victims, and at much lower costs to taxpayers. While these proven solutions are increasingly made available by the US government and so accessible for free on the web, they have not been presented as specific recommendations for legislative action, as will be done in this book, for the United States and other affluent democracies.

What continues to baffle me, however, is that the smarter way of doing things is *still* not being put into practice on a large scale in the United States nor in any other affluent democracies. Not when it comes to law enforcement, not when it comes to the court system, not when it comes to so-called corrections (which actually do little to "correct" the problem), and not when it comes to preventing crime *before* it happens—what smart people call "pre-crime prevention."

So it's time to ask our legislators in the United States and elsewhere, "Why aren't we doing it the smarter way?" Why aren't we acting based on the best knowledge out there? Why are we spending *exorbitant* amounts of taxpayers' money on methods that clearly don't work to spare victims? And why are our institutions still set up to allow people to be victimized *before* we act to "protect" them? Yes, we *do* have the right to hold our legislators' feet to the fire when citizens' safety and quality of life is being threatened by flawed thinking at the top of the food chain. So why aren't we asking our politicians these tough questions, demanding straight answers, and getting some significant actions?

Too often, books and academic articles about crime control are obscure and confusing. They are written in a way that seems to tell the average American or other citizen that solutions to crime are better left in the hands of professional law enforcement, lawyers, judges, and correctional administrators. So ordinary citizens and so politicians cannot understand the science, the legal principles, and the logic behind it without studying it in some advanced academic setting.

Well, this book is my response to that. I have been working in the field for over forty years, and I want to tell citizens of the United States and people around the world that crime control *is* their personal concern. It concerns them because it affects each and every one of them in a very personal way—either because they are victims of it (or may be soon), or because they work in a field where they see its devastating effects firsthand, or because they have unwittingly allowed politicians to give unwarranted portions of their hard-earned taxes to officials and lawyers to combat it.

This book will show that the knowledge about smarter crime control is not beyond the comprehension of the average taxpayer, voter, or politician. This book is written in plain English and means to share with citizens and politicians as well as police officers, justice workers, the media, and students what approaches *actually* work to stop crime and show them how these approaches can be implemented *today* to improve our collective public safety tomorrow. It intends to share this knowledge with those politicians who have the courage to make the changes that are so overdue—those legislators who genuinely have victims' (and would-be victims') interests at heart. It also offers this knowledge to members of the public, who have the basic civil right for their taxes to be used as wisely as possible—and who suffer the consequences when outdated and ineffective thinking prevails.

Yes, this book focuses on data, research, and evidence from the United States. In part, this is because the United States has more and better data, research, and evidence than any other affluent democracy on crime and their systems that react to it. But also this is because the challenges of violence on the street, in the home, and on the road (traffic) are so much more acute, while the measures and expenditures on reacting to these challenges are so much more extreme. So the potential to get conclusions based on science and basic data for the United States is clear, but many of these conclusions will be as relevant to other afflu-ent democracies who do not have the data and the evidence and have not taken crime control to such extremes.

It shows how the United States can retool its current systems of law enforcement, courts, and corrections through smarter thinking and pragmatic reforms. It shows how social agencies and organizations can be supported to bring about lasting solutions, often at much less cost and sometimes in combination with smarter law enforcement and courts that solve problems. It shows how these smarter approaches will spare potential victims from significant harm, save taxpayers money, and keep at-risk youth from misspending their years behind bars. Each chapter concludes with a succinct list of actions that legislators can take to improve their communities *today*. Those conclusions will be as rel-evant to the United States as to other affluent democracies.

It presents the results from hundreds of scientific studies on in-novative law enforcement, courts, and corrections projects—many of which were conducted by American researchers, in American neigh-borhoods, and with American innovations. It also offers some ex-amples from around the world that the United States can be inspired by. It points to proven programs that are already developed and just waiting to be implemented in any community across the country, and it tells readers exactly where they can go for more examples of approaches that are actually proven to work in stopping crime. Yes, the results of the new approaches might be more modest than the dazzling claims made by some politicians on behalf of the current institutions—but these results will be real, they will avoid harm to victims, and they will be affordable.

Importantly, this book focuses not on how we can punish offenders to a greater or lesser degree, but on how we can actually *stop* crime from happening in the first place so that we can reduce the numbers of victims. Here's some food for thought: our existing systems of law en-forcement, courts, and corrections all focus on *reacting to* crimes after they have happened—on putting the toothpaste back into the tube, so to speak. Well, doesn't anyone else think it's too little, too late to try to fix the problem *after* innocent people have already been victimized, espe-cially by violent crime? In effect, taxpayers are paying for cleanup crews when what they should be paying for are violence prevention specialists.

Now, if we were to shift our focus to proactively stopping crime by *preventing* it from happening in the first place, then we would save billions of dollars every year and spare millions of citizens and families the life-altering (and all too often devastating) experience of being victimized—harm estimated in the hundreds of billions of dollars. This thought was summed up nicely by the British prime minister in 2012 when he said, "Prevention is the most effective and cost-effective way to deal with crime; everything else is picking up the pieces." I hope that your picking up this book will help lead to a nationwide realization that simply picking up the pieces is no longer good enough.

THE CRIME PARADOX OF THE UNITED STATES

The United States is proudly the world's most affluent democracy. It is looked to around the globe as an example of a nation built on freedom, happiness, and personal entrepreneurship.

But of all the affluent democracies around the world, the United States continues to be the one with the highest rates of murder (see figure 1.1)—a title that it has held since before 1950. Its young men are killed at rates that are seven times those of other affluent democracies,

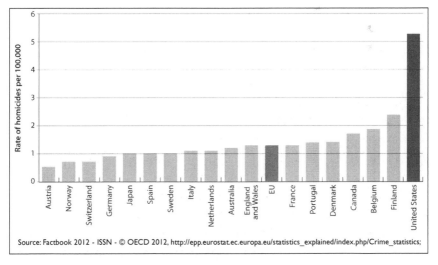

Source: Factbook 2012 - ISSN - © OECD 2012, http://epp.eurostat.ec.europa.eu/statistics_explained/index.php/Crime_statistics;

Figure 1.1   US Murder Rates: Much Higher Than Other Affluent Democracies

and it has *twenty times* as many murders committed with guns, usually handguns.[1] What's more, young black men are murdered at rates ten times those for young white men.

Further, the United States has rates of traffic fatalities that are at least double those of most other affluent democracies, and rates of drunk driving fatalities that exceed England and Wales by a factor of *eight* (see figure 1.2). In fact, the Institute of Medicine reports that young Americans are at far greater risk of dying earlier than their counterparts in other affluent democracies and suffer far higher rates of death not only from guns but also from automobile crashes (many of which involve drivers committing criminal offenses because they were impaired) and drug abuse.[2]

Yes, drug abuse is in that list, despite the country's pervasive and exorbitant so-called war on drugs. It is estimated that the United States consumes 25 percent of the world's illicit drugs but has only 5 percent of the population.[3] Further, the number of unintentional deaths from drug overdoses in the United States has *tripled* even as the drug war has intensified, and that rate now exceeds deaths from homicide and drunk driving accidents combined.[4]

Since before 1950, the United States has been the free world's champion jailer. Its back-to-back sentences to life and multiple decades of time in prison for violent crime were well known even then. In 1970, the United States already had incarceration rates roughly twice those of

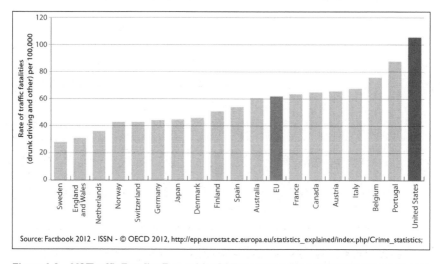

Source: Factbook 2012 - ISSN - © OECD 2012, http://epp.eurostat.ec.europa.eu/statistics_explained/index.php/Crime_statistics;

Figure 1.2   US Traffic Fatality Rates: Much Higher Than Most Affluent Democracies

countries such as Canada, France, Germany, and the United Kingdom, although they could not catch the USSR at that time.[5] Today, however, the United States has eclipsed every other major government in the world, democratic or not, with 20 percent of the world's inmates for 5 percent of that population. It exceeds England and Wales by a factor of five and most other affluent democracies by an alarming factor of *seven* (see figure 1.3). It also incarcerates at rates that are 50 percent higher than Russia and five times as high as China—the two countries usually thought of as the world's most oppressive societies.[6]

Curiously, the United States' response to traffic crimes has been much more restrained and has followed the successes of other affluent democracies and indeed international evidence by adopting laws to actually tackle the risk factors for fatalities (e.g., speed and drunk driving) instead of grasping at long prison sentences in a vain hope of solving the problem. "Smart," when considering traffic crashes, means designing roads and cars to keep people alive and enforcing speeding and drinking offenses with fines and judicious use of time behind bars. Still, rates of traffic fatalities in the United States are higher than in most advanced democracies—but this is likely because the United States is not enforcing these laws as much as other countries, as we shall see in chapter 8. The country is not making detection as certain as in Europe.

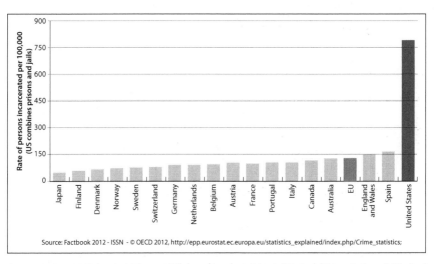

Source: Factbook 2012 - ISSN - © OECD 2012, http://epp.eurostat.ec.europa.eu/statistics_explained/index.php/Crime_statistics;

Figure 1.3 US Rates of (Hyper-)incarceration: Much Higher Than Other Affluent Democracies

I don't intend to paint the picture that the United States is failing beyond repair. The rates for most types of crime and traffic fatalities have actually been *falling* in the United States over the past thirty to forty years, just as they have been in other affluent democracies. The country has experienced a 50 percent drop in violent crime since 1990 and a 70 percent drop in property crime since 1970. In fact, the rates of most violent and property crimes have not been lower since 1970. Better still, when homicides and gun violence are taken out of the picture, the prevalence of crime in the United States today is roughly the same as it is in other affluent democracies. The United States has also achieved large reductions in deaths caused by road crimes such as drinking and driving—although still not to levels near those of other advanced democracies. Furthermore, it has focused as much as any country on responding to the needs of women who are victims of violence.

THE HIGH PRICE PAID BY VICTIMS

But these modest triumphs are not enough. A look at the statistics for crimes reported in the United States shows that the number of victimizations, while dropping over the past forty years, is still alarming from a victim perspective. And the annual National Crime Victimization Survey from the Bureau of Justice Statistics tells us that the *real* rate of victimization is nearly double what is known to law enforcement.[7] That's because many victims are disillusioned with the traditional ways that law enforcement, courts, and corrections go about their work, and so they do not report their victimization to the police.[8]

Let's have a look at the real rates of crime in a year. Even with the 50 percent drop in violent crime since 1990, for every thousand persons age twelve or older, there will still be close to three victims injured and five persons who are victims of serious violent crimes involving weapons.[9] There are five million assaults each year in the United States, including one million that were defined as serious (aggravated) crimes, for the 257 million persons age twelve or over— that's one for every fifty persons.

Similarly, even with the 70 percent drop since 1970 in the rate of property crime, for every thousand households, there will still be close to thirty households that will fall victim to household burglary and five that will suffer from motor vehicle theft. With the twelve million thefts that occur every year, that means there are an estimated seventeen million personal property victimizations for approximately 123 million households—that's one for every seven households. So while crime rates may have decreased significantly, victimizations have not gone away.

The picture is also disturbing in terms of violence against women. The long-term trends are not so clear because there were no reliable surveys until the past decade or so, but today we can look to the excellent surveys undertaken nationally. They show us that every year a million women are raped. That means that one in five American women have been raped in their lifetimes, most before the age of twenty-five.[10] One in five women will graduate after a college experience that includes a sexual assault. What's more, over a million women experience serious physical violence at the hands of an intimate partner every year.[11] We do not know whether the rates of these offenses are increasing or decreasing. What we do know is that we are now getting a reliable picture that shows disturbing rates of violence suffered by women.

It's much more difficult to gauge the numbers of young victims. Child-care authorities confirm that more than one in seven children has been abused, and the Child Welfare League confirms at least 800,000 cases of child abuse and maltreatment every year, usually perpetrated in the home. Of these children, 1,200 are murdered. The real number of children abused is likely much higher. Outside of the home, one in fourteen children is bullied in school with consequences that are increasingly being taken seriously, as they should.

We can now estimate in financially equivalent terms how much damage these violent and property crimes do to victims. The total exceeds $470 billion annually (or the equivalent of $1,500 per American). This amount has changed very little from the 1990s because most common crime rates have come down by about 50 percent, while the cost of living has increased by about the same amount.[12] The price tag in 1993 included medical costs ($18 billion); property loss, mental health care bills, and productivity losses ($87 billion); and a whopping loss of quality of life for (or pain and suffering lived by) victims ($345 billion).[13]

In figure 1.4, I have compared these estimated costs separately for three groups of offenses: homicides and drunk driving deaths ($108 billion), rapes/sexual assaults ($150 billion), and assaults ($90 billion).[14] Each of these groups of crimes came out to cost in the range of $90 billion to $150 billion a year—close to 1 percent of the GDP. The proportion of these costs that represents harm to victims is about six times the costs of police, courts, and corrections. I have added a column for child abuse—amounting to another $124 billion annually.[15] I have also added a column for drunk driving estimated at $135 billion.[16] There are different estimates of the total cost of traffic fatalities, including a cost used by the Centers for Disease Control and Prevention of $235 billion.[17] Illicit drug use is calculated in a different way as it does not directly lead to harm to victims. This cost I set at $195 billion, where less than $2 billion represents costs to victims, compared to $56 billion in costs to the court system and another $52 billion (not shown separately) in costs for lost productivity due to incarceration.[18] These estimates in dollars add to the far too many individual stories of tragedies and so reinforce the need to urgently refocus policies and budgets to succeed in reducing the numbers of victims and avoiding the devastating losses to their quality of life.

So clearly, the costs of victimization are high. But do they make any sense if the knowledge already exists to significantly reduce victimization and prevent violence from happening in the first place? In this book, you will see that the knowledge *does* exist—and that much of it has been developed in the United States. Part II of this book discusses the promising programs that *prevent* losses such as those discussed above, rather than merely reacting after the fact.[19] In fact, this book has a dedicated chapter looking at pre-crime prevention, with an emphasis on ways to reduce child abuse and avoid youth growing up to become persistent offenders and so perpetrators of a broad gamut of violence on the streets, in the homes, and on the roads (behind the wheels of cars). It has chapters focusing on gun homicides (which amount to about 80 percent of all homicides in the United States), a chapter on traffic fatalities (about 30 percent of which involve drinking and driving), a chapter on violence against women, and a chapter on preventing property crime.[20]

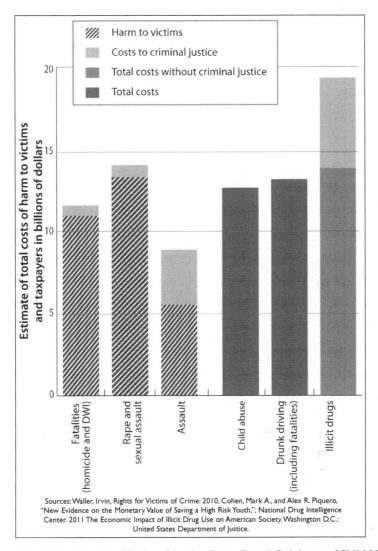

Sources: Waller, Irvin, Rights for Victims of Crime: 2010, Cohen, Mark A., and Alex R. Piquero, "New Evidence on the Monetary Value of Saving a High Risk Youth,"; National Drug Intelligence Center. 2011 The Economic Impact of Illicit Drug Use on American Society. Washington D.C.: United States Department of Justice.

Figure 1.4   Crime Costs for Victims: Murder, Rape, Drunk Driving, and Child Abuse

THE UNEASY LINK BETWEEN INCARCERATION AND CRIME

As you read earlier, the United States has much higher levels of murder, traffic fatalities, and drug abuse than other affluent democracies. Sadly, there is a huge racial divide for homicides, where per capita ten times as many young black men are murdered as white men.[21] The reduction of these deaths—and the racial bias—must become a focus for policy.

You also saw that the United States is the world's most overzealous jailer, with a prison population at least five times greater per capita than any other affluent democracy. But these other democracies generally have rates of common crime (excluding homicides and gun crime) that are basically the same as the United States. Therefore, American-style mass incarceration (what I refer to as "hyperincarceration") is clearly not as effective as some people would like us to believe. If it *were* highly effective, then the United States should have common crime rates that are much lower than other advanced democracies—but that's not the case. Still, politicians are allowing budgets that rack up enormous bills in the belief that mass incarceration is a cure-all for the violence and crime problem—and these bills are being paid by taxpayers, who are getting a terrible rate of return on their investment.

In the three decades from 1980 to 2010, the rate of adults incarcerated per capita skyrocketed by an astronomical 350 percent—a phenomenon unique to the United States. Today, more than 2.2 million Americans are behind bars on any given day. If this population were gathered together, this number would make it the fourth-largest city, smaller than Chicago but larger than Houston and, equally shockingly, larger than the populations of fifteen states. Many of these prisoners are black. Today, the rate of incarceration for black males (4,347 per 100,000 black males) is six times higher than that for whites (678 per 100,000 white males).[22] Indeed, mass incarceration seems to represent a new type of Jim Crow law—a sort of judicially mandated system of racial control based on inequality in the supposed age of colorblindness, as noted in the *New York Times* best seller by Michelle Alexander.[23] The result is that blacks are murdered at ten times the rate of whites, and seemingly the failed response leads to blacks being incarcerated at six times the rate of whites.[24]

This racial divide has existed since at least the 1970s[25] but has been exacerbated by America's war on drugs, which too often focuses on the easy-to-catch black males on the streets rather than on the more active users and sellers of drugs at schools and colleges, who tend to be white. And all the while, these black inmates who are being held for drug offenses that do no harm to victims are gaining many insurmountable "collateral consequences" from their time behind bars: they may be banned from voting, and it becomes difficult for them to hold down a job, to maintain a healthy relationship with loved ones, and to be there for their children, their families, and their communities. Some of these collateral consequences are mandated by the law after conviction for a felony, and others are the natural result of being warehoused for a long time behind bars. In fact, with such sizeable postrelease consequences, it is surprising that any young black men released from behind bars succeed at all.[26]

The racial divide is only one manifestation of the complex social situations that we must consider when it comes to controlling crime and reducing crime rates. There are life experiences that predispose some people to crime; there are problems with addictions that come into play; there is the factor of getting and keeping a job. While a person can always make the choice not to commit a crime, some people have an easier time making that choice than others. As Anatole France said, "In its majestic equality, the law forbids rich and poor alike to sleep under bridges, beg in the streets, and steal loaves of bread."

It is a complex and delicate problem that warrants a complex and delicate solution—nothing as simple as just clamping down with brute force and hoping for the best. Besides, it's clear that the clamp-down approach is not working. As a result, the same faces are returning again and again to police cells, courtrooms, and incarceration facilities. Astonishingly, more than three quarters of people charged with felonies in 2006 had a prior history of arrest, and 69 percent had *multiple* prior arrests.[27] What's more, 40–60 percent of men released from "corrections" will get caught again within three years of their release from behind bars. These statistics are not surprising, because there is very little rehabilitative focus—actual "correcting"—built into corrections systems; even though there is no better captive audience for rehabilitation programs, such programs are generally not being delivered. Too many prisoners aren't getting help with their addictions, they aren't getting counseling for their issues, and they aren't getting treatment for their mental illnesses. Instead, they are simply being warehoused with other offenders, many of whom have similar problems. So, in many ways, imprisoning offenders may actually be *worsening* the problems that put them behind bars in the first place.

I'm not saying that incarceration *never* works to stop crime. The research shows that when incarceration rates were skyrocketing, every 10 percent increase in traditional incarceration correlated with a 2 percent reduction in crime rates.[28] But that's a huge investment for not much gain! And we already know, as I share in this book, that drops in incarceration coincide with drops in crime rates, and much larger reductions in crime rates can be achieved if we use *smarter* strategies—and these better results will also be much less expensive for the taxpayer and much better for citizens who would otherwise become victims.

A lot of these smarter strategies involve investing in pre-crime prevention, as we will see in part II. We know that a vast majority of crimes happen in certain "problem places" and that a vast majority of prisoners come from these places. Fortunately, there are proven solutions to the problems that plague these places, and by investing in these community-based solutions (instead of simply funneling people into the prison pipeline en masse), we have a real shot at actually "correcting" what is wrong.

Perhaps the National League of Cities said it best: "We can't arrest our way out of this." Instead, we have to *strategize* our way out of this, one problem community at a time. And if that sounds daunting, it shouldn't. Community-based solutions are proven to work and to work *well*. Better still, they can be implemented today to save victims tomorrow. We already have blueprints for cost-effective programs that we know work. Now all we need is the political will to make it happen.

THE PRICE OF "CONTROLLING" CRIME THE OLD WAY

Not surprisingly, mass incarceration does not come cheap. The annual bill for corrections to taxpayers reached an astronomical $80 *billion* per year in 2010. Even accounting for inflation, this still represents a growth of 250 percent, just since 1980. This increase is primarily due to the increased numbers of prisoners. Today, taxpayers collectively spend $36,000 per inmate per year at just the state prison level, not including local jails. And this doesn't reflect the costs of prison facility construction; when additional cells are built, they cost between $50,000 and $100,000 each. And the Department of Justice is rapidly expanding the federal prison system, to which it allocates $6 billion annually, or a quarter of the Department of Justice budget[29]—all for systems that were one-seventh of their current size back in 1970, when rates of violent crimes were much what they are today.

The expenditures on law enforcement, courts, and corrections have grown inexorably over the past thirty years.[30] In fact, what American families spend on law enforcement, courts, and corrections is at least 30 percent more than what their counterparts spend on these measures in other advanced democracies such as the United Kingdom or Canada. At election time, the politicians are actually *increasing* our tax burden when they promise to be "tougher" on crime by hiring more law enforcement officers, enacting minimum sentences, and keeping repeat offenders behind bars longer. Figure 1.5 shows just how tough it has become on American taxpayers. Even if you adjust the figures for inflation by using what economists call "constant dollars," the direct expenditures on law enforcement have more than doubled, and the expenditures on corrections have more than *tripled* since 1980.

Here is what US taxpayers are paying more for. They are paying $124 billion a year for 750,000 or more full-time sworn law enforcement officers and another 350,000 civilian employees at the state and local levels.[31] From 1980 to 2010, their numbers grew by about 54 percent. However, the United States was catching up, and today the number of law enforcement officers per capita in the United States is little different from the number in Canada or the United Kingdom.[32] The taxes allocated to the courts (i.e., judicial and court-appointed legal services) now exceed $56 billion per year, and mass incarceration costs $80 billion annually. The grand total for law enforcement, courts, and corrections in the United States was $261 billion in 2010—the latest year for which expenditures are publicly available—and they must be even more today.[33]

As to whether or not these increases (particularly for corrections) did indeed impact the drop in crime rates on some level, they did not do so in any major way, as shown by comparisons with other affluent democracies that are also experiencing similar drops in crime without the exorbitant increases in expenditures. And, more importantly for this book, these increases have nevertheless left the United States with much higher levels of murder and gun violence than other affluent democracies.

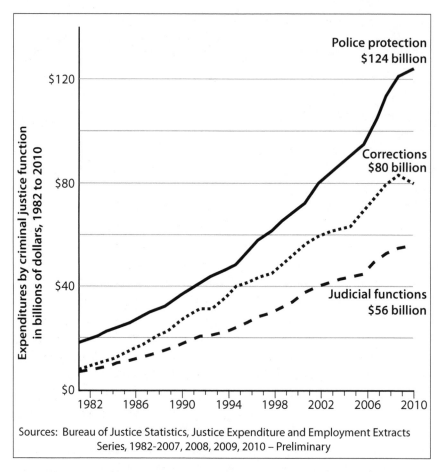

Figure 1.5   Growing Taxpayer Expenditures on Police, Courts, and Corrections

But this is not the end of the costs for US taxpayers, some of whom are paying for private security as homeowners or business owners. There are more than two million employees in the private security industry in the United States, and their services are likely costing Americans another $100 billion. Americans are also paying for alarms and other security gadgets, as well as insurance against theft and other crimes, but these costs will measure yet another $100 billion or more. Unfortunately, there are no reliable estimates of these totals.

Despite all this, many Americans still own handguns so that they can feel "protected." So Americans pay 30 percent more taxes for law enforcement, courts, and corrections as compared to other affluent democracies such as Canada and the United Kingdom, and then they pay for private security, and then many (30 percent) still feel the need to arm themselves for their protection.[34] So why are American taxpayers footing such enormous bills for inflated systems in which they clearly don't have any real confidence?

PREVENTION: A SOLUTION THAT AMERICANS CAN HAVE CONFIDENCE IN

Crime is *not* inevitable. Crime rates have come down, and they can come down much more by using proven solutions. A major part of these solutions involves prevention. Part I of this book shows how the usual *reactive* responses to crime are short-term, surface-level solutions. Having so many of our law enforcement officers to react to 911 calls and possibly chase down offenders *after* a person has been victimized is just not the smartest use of our resources—particularly when the offenders come back like in a game of whack-a-mole but with far more serious consequences for them, for victims, and for taxpayers.

Curiously, prevention is almost never mentioned in political debates on crime policy.[35] It's almost as if politicians are afraid of coming off as being "soft on crime" as compared with the advocates for mass incarceration and police clampdowns, who like to boast that they are "tough on crime." I like to think of prevention as being *"smart* on crime" because it stops citizens from suffering the harm caused by victimization and saves taxpayers money.

We should not blame the politicians entirely for the widespread lack of focus on prevention. With a few important exceptions that you will see in this book, the United States research industries that are fixated on the current law enforcement, courts, and corrections systems, rarely mention prevention. However, the country's public health research industry is a world leader when it comes to violence prevention, as are the Centers for Disease Control and Prevention. But for the moment, even these organizations talk more to public health departments and doctors than to chiefs of police and politicians, so I suppose it is no wonder that much of their good research is not yet being implemented in the communities that need it most.

When we think of other epidemics that lead to fatalities, we think of prevention. Cholera and typhoid were eradicated through cleaning up the drinking water and thereby preventing the spread of disease. Polio can be prevented through a vaccination. We already accept in principle that traffic fatalities can be prevented through using seat belts and enforcing speeding and alcohol laws. Prevention just makes sense, and I am not alone in this thinking.

Violent crime is a recognized public health concern worldwide. As such, the respected public health physicians at the World Health Organization (WHO) have worked hard to provide evidence on ways to reduce injuries, trauma, and fatalities from violence as well as on how to implement that knowledge. They emphasize that violence is produced by social forces. So the solutions to violence are to tackle those social causes—what is called pre-crime prevention. The WHO continues to see a role for law enforcement and the courts in this process, but the evidence also points to important roles for schools, housing, social services, and other stakeholders.

Importantly, the cost savings associated with crime prevention are huge, and so the taxpayers could reap the benefits. Good research has shown that when using the traditional reactive systems of law enforcement, courts, and corrections, more than $200 in tax increases per family is needed to achieve a 10 percent reduction in the overall crime rate. Now, consider that an investment of $50 per family in helping at-risk kids complete school and a $35 investment in parent training would achieve the same reductions—and cost less than half as much.[36]

THE SCIENCE OF WHY YOUNG MEN GROW UP TO BE OFFENDERS

The current systems of law enforcement, courts, and corrections have developed out of the legal thinking of the eighteenth and nineteenth centuries, when we had no better way to approach crime than to punish offenders with vengeance one at a time. This way of thinking has come back with a vengeance (*sic*) in the past forty years. Meanwhile (and luckily for this book), we've learned a lot about what works to reduce the number of victims and even about its cost-effectiveness. The bad news for victims and taxpayers is that little of this knowledge has been put into practice. But today's science shows that crime is not simply the compulsive evil act of one individual against another. It is a predictable outcome for groups of people growing up with particular negative life experiences. Knowing this, we can now set out to change the outcomes—that is, we can stop crime.

The evidence for what predisposes young persons to become persistent offenders is strong and clear. Large-scale research projects (called "longitudinal studies") have followed the personal development of males from birth through adolescence to adulthood. As the youths grew up, the researchers recorded data about their life experiences such as inconsistent and abusive parenting, behavioral difficulties in primary school, abuse of alcohol and drugs, and skipping school as a teenager. These are known as "risk factors." For instance, today we know that offenders are more likely to

1. Be born into a family in relative poverty and inadequate housing;
2. Be brought up with inconsistent and uncaring parenting, including violence;
3. Show limited social and cognitive abilities;
4. Show behavioral problems identified in primary school;
5. Be excluded from or drop out of secondary school;
6. Live with a culture of violence on television and in the neighborhood; and
7. Be frequently unemployed and have a relatively limited income as a young adult.

When they considered the males with negative life experiences such as these, researchers found that there was a much higher probability that these individuals would be involved in persistent offending as compared to those with fewer such experiences.[37] What's more, they can now use this knowledge of risk factors to predict later involvement in crime to a degree that is about as accurate as epidemiological predictions about who will get lung cancer based on their weight, income, and smoking habits.[38] This is by no means meant to excuse offenders' behavior. Many people grow up with all these disadvantages and still choose not to victimize; it's just that when these factors are present, making the right choice becomes a lot harder (and a lot less likely).

Another important factor in contributing to persistent offending is *place*. One recent large-scale study conducted in Chicago under Felton Earls of Harvard University tracked these risk factors and found that the "protective" factors of community ties and interpersonal relationships can make up for some of these risk factors and can affect expected outcomes in a positive way. Certainly, communities play a large role in determining outcomes for youth at risk of offending.

Analysis of 911 calls by police researchers and data analysts working for police departments has confirmed that most common crimes are concentrated in particular parts of cities with persistent poverty (called "problem places" by the researchers). That's why cities and community-based organizations are so important to many of the smart solutions advocated in this book. Nobody knows these places better than the municipal politicians and planners, and nobody can direct solutions to problem places more effectively than cities—with the financial and practical support of higher levels of government, of course.

The most important finding from the longitudinal surveys is that a small group of children born each year will account for a disproportionate number of the offenses committed in the future. Indeed, a mere 5–10 percent of all children will account for 50–70 percent of offending.[39] This small subgroup is often referred to as "chronic offenders" since their behavior puts them in conflict with law enforcement, courts, and corrections frequently.[40] The children who become chronic offenders tend to grow up with the presence of many of the risk factors mentioned above. However, these studies do *not* show that arrest or incarceration reduces offending. In fact, the more a person is arrested, the more likely he or she is to be arrested again in the future. With this evidence, it becomes clear why hyperincarceration is just as ineffective as it is expensive. Once again, we can see the stark contrast between low-cost prevention and high-cost reaction.

For effective results, therefore, we need to look for smarter solutions. That means considering all this information about risk factors and problem places so that we can begin to do what public health professionals have been doing successfully for decades: targeting initiatives meant to help reverse, reduce, or mitigate these risk factors, in order to actually stop crimes before they create victims—and to do so in the most cost-effective way possible.

THE PROOF BEHIND PREVENTION

Never before have we known so much about how to stop crime before it happens. Using the knowledge we've gained about which negative life experiences predispose some people to offend, we have accumulated a hoard of scientific knowledge about what works to tackle these risk factors. This knowledge is compelling, remarkably strong, and surprisingly accessible on the websites of some respected authorities in the field such as the US Department of Justice and the World Health Organization.[41]

Some of this knowledge suggests ways to reform and retool the existing *reactive* systems of law enforcement, courts, and corrections to stop reoffending. A lot of it supports a compelling case for taking crime prevention programs—not police officers—right into schools and the community in order to stop at-risk people from starting a life of crime in the first place. By "program," I am referring to a systematically delivered service with clear steps and goals. The most effective of these programs focus on innovations that promote remedies for the risk factors listed above. For instance, a crime prevention program might send public-health nurses into the homes of drug-addicted young moms once a week to help mitigate trends toward inconsistent and uncaring parenting. Another example is a program that goes into high schools and teaches teenage boys about why and how to avoid perpetrating sexual violence in order to prevent rape by combating a culture of sexual violence that may have been reinforced by television and in the neighborhood.

The body of evidence on prevention has been held to rigorous scientific standards. Many of the studies are based on random control trials, which compare the crime-reduction results achieved through an experimental program with the outcomes of similar groups of individuals who did not participate in the new program; this is the same testing method that the Food and Drug Administration (FDA) uses before allowing pharmaceuticals to advertise their effectiveness on the market. The crime reduction program's results are then written up and scrutinized by independent experts before being published in scientific journals. We now have many of these articles on similar projects, so experts can now review the lessons learned from the most scientifically sound articles. These reviews are known as meta-analyses, and they provide a compelling basis for the conclusion that many preventive strategies are effective and cost-effective ways to reduce the number of (and the harm to) crime victims.

In 2009, the WHO released a succinct and accessible report on evidence for the effectiveness of various interventions to prevent violence. The report makes it clear that violence *is* preventable, not inevitable. I strongly agree with the report's conclusions, and politicians should take them seriously as well. The report divides the preventive approaches to violence into six main categories that have influenced this book: (a) nurturing the relationships between children and their parents (discussed in chapter 5 of this book); (b) developing life skills in children and adolescents (chapter 5); (c) reducing access to guns (chapter 6); (d) promoting gender equality to prevent violence against women (chapter 7); (e) reducing the harmful use of alcohol (chapter 8); and (f) changing cultural and social norms that support violence (chapters 5, 7, and 8).

So the science of crime and violence prevention is sound, and so is the certainty that many crime prevention programs work. A lot of these proven programs are veritable road maps for stopping crime, and they are just waiting to be implemented. The Center for the Study and Prevention of Violence vigorously reviewed over one thousand programs before identifying its top eleven Blueprints-certified programs and many other programs with promising status.[42] Their ratings are all based on scientific evidence that the programs work, and they are a wonderful starting point for smart politicians. Similarly, in 1996, a group of criminologists at the University of Maryland completed a review of more than five hundred evaluations of projects funded by the US federal government. It came to important conclusions about what had succeeded and what had not. Sadly, it also showed how little investment was being made in what worked.[43] In the 2000s, reviews were also conducted by such respected organizations as the WHO,[44] the Centers for Disease Control and Prevention,[45] and the US National Research Council.[46]

In 2011, the US Department of Justice released its own website promoting proven solutions to stop crime (crimesolutions.gov), although it has unfortunately not acted on its own advice.[47] This website showcases 256 programs in its database, of which 72 are confirmed as being effective and 157 are certified as promising. Of those that are certified as effective, forty-four are social-prevention oriented.

All of the above resources are good starting points for any smart politicians who are looking for what one commentator called "well-scrubbed lists of projects where a legislator could invest $1 to save $10."[48] The good news—and there is lots of it—is that the evidence is strong, and it proves that some specific programs that tackle the identified risk factors have reduced victimizations from both violent and property crime. Most of that evidence points to a need to invest in a radically different way of dealing with crime—that is, in *preventing* it—as opposed to continuing with the same old *reactive* way that the politicians have been spending our taxes in a mad dash to "pick up the pieces." The best news is that this knowledge is now becoming available to the general public through avenues such as this book, which is written in plain English and intended for a general audience.

MORE THAN JUST LIP SERVICE: THE CHALLENGE OF IMPLEMENTATION

Never before have we known so much about how to prevent violence but used so little of it. It seems that most politicians and their networks have not taken the time to access the evidence that is now available on what will reduce the number of victims and save money for taxpayers. They do not learn about it in political science class or in their careers leading up to political life. They do not discuss it with their partisan cronies because seeming to be "tough on crime" has somehow come to mean being soft on knowledge. The public is also in the dark for the most part since the science of crime prevention is not taught in civics or law classes in school or highlighted in the media. Most of us do not read newspapers or watch YouTube videos about it. As a result, we continue to allow politicians to misspend our taxes on allowing more crime than is necessary.

This book shares the knowledge about what is proven to stop crime. It shows how it is much more cost-effective and affordable than the status quo of clamping down with traditional law enforcement, courts, and corrections. It looks at ways to *proactively* implement youth programs targeted to problem places, to provide support for parents where it is needed, to target education to problem attitudes, and much more. It rolls these approaches into a comprehensive crime-stopping strategy that will reduce violence before it makes a victim and shows why these approaches should no longer be limited to the existing *reactive* systems of law enforcement, courts, and corrections.

The book also looks at ways to shift away from misspending on reactive policing and move toward law enforcement that is smarter on crime; it looks at using courts to get offenders into effective treatment and off the conveyor belt of offending; and, particularly, it looks at ways to cut the exorbitant costs of incarceration to be proportionate to current crime levels and to match what is strictly necessary to be smart on crime control. All of this calls for a shift toward spending taxes in much more cost-effective ways that save victims as well as our hard-earned tax dollars.

But smart solutions require more than just the knowledge contained in these pages. Smart solutions demand that the knowledge be *used* by policy makers, who must allocate sustainable funds and modernize legislation and who must question why they are settling for the expensive status quo when they have the ability to really implement great strides forward in reducing victimization and making a real difference in the quality of life for many would-be victims.

CONCLUSION: THE CRISIS OF OVERREACTION AND THE OPPORTUNITIES FOR SMARTER CRIME CONTROL TO GIVE PRIORITY TO VICTIMS AND TAXPAYERS

Even though reported rates of many common crimes have been falling in most affluent democracies (including the United States), young Americans are still at dramatically greater risk of having their lives cut short by gun homicide, drunk driving, and drug overdoses than citizens in any other affluent democracy.

The United States went from its relatively harsh level of incarceration in the 1970s to a system of hyperincarceration without equivalent anywhere else in the world. This system has not done significantly better or worse than other affluent democracies at reducing common crime, but it has clearly failed to save lives among those who are also most likely to be incarcerated for violence and for possession of drugs—young disadvantaged males, particularly black males.

Even today's reduced rates of victimization still inflict a level of pain and suffering on citizens that is unacceptable and account for severe losses in quality of life that can never be recouped. The economic costs of victimization suggest a need to focus on better solutions to road and homicide fatalities, violence against women, and child abuse. From a crime victim's and taxpayer's perspective, such solutions put into question the expensive use of incarceration to combat drug abuse and drug-related deaths.

Our existing systems of law enforcement, courts, and corrections react too often to the same problem places. They leave too many young black men dead and seriously injured as well as many more incarcerated. Luckily, the research is ahead of these traditional reactive systems. We know what negative life experiences (or "risk factors") predispose some people to offend, and we know where the majority of crimes are concentrated. We also know how to break the vicious cycle and stop crime by investing in youth in problem places.

This book shares that knowledge and puts it in the form of key actions for legislators. Part I shows how pragmatic reforms can make problem places safer and problem persons less likely to become problem offenders, and it shows how decriminalization that avoids the use of the courts as well as investments in effective treatment programs, particularly in the community, would reduce crime and save taxpayers significant costs. Part II uses the compelling knowledge available to show how to invest in pre-crime prevention—that is, how to stop crime from happening rather than just reacting to it. It focuses on preventing youth from becoming repeat offenders, preventing gun violence, preventing violence against women, preventing traffic crashes, and even preventing property crime further. Part III looks at how to reinvest over five or ten years from overreaction to effective and smart crime control—true "public safety"—that saves lives and spares pain to victims, all while cutting the taxes wasted in the current system. It shows that smart crime control isn't being "soft" on crime—it's about getting tough on stopping wasted taxes and on stopping crime from ruining so many lives.

I

ACTIONS FOR
SMART CRIME CONTROL

2

POLICING

From Overreaction after the Fact to Stopping Crime before It Harms

INTRODUCTION

Law enforcement is a multibillion-dollar-a-year industry. $124 billion of US taxpayers' money was spent on law enforcement in 2010. It accounted for 1.1 million jobs with federal, state, and local governments; to put this in perspective, this is approximately twice the number of jobs that Apple has created.[1]

Of the 1.1 million jobs, 765,000 are sworn officers (i.e., officers with the power to make arrests).[2] There is one sworn law enforcement officer for every four hundred persons, which is similar to a number of affluent countries. The rate of police officers per one hundred thousand of the population is presented in figure 2.1 for the affluent countries that were used in chapter 1. This shows the United States with rates similar to countries such as Canada and England and Wales, but lower than countries in Southern Europe, where police are more numerous but are paid less.

In general, police officers and law enforcement officials are well-paid professionals, with the cost to taxpayers for one sworn officer, when including costs of civilian personnel and equipment, averaging $160,000 a year and climbing. Despite these costs, their numbers have increased by more than 30 percent over the past twenty years. Some of this growth

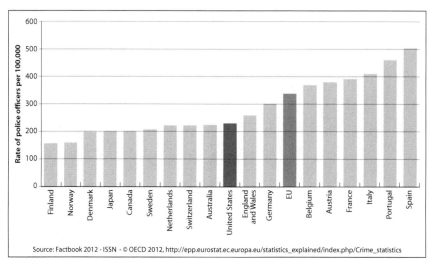

Source: Factbook 2012 - ISSN - © OECD 2012, http://epp.eurostat.ec.europa.eu/statistics_explained/index.php/Crime_statistics

Figure 2.1   US Rates of Police per Capita: Similar to Other Affluent Democracies

accompanied an increase in arrests for drug offenses because the war on drugs offered financial incentives to police departments that demonstrated enforcement against drug offenses.

While the numbers and salaries of police officers have had an impact on budgets, it is not so clear that the way the officers are used has had a consequential impact on stopping persons from being victims of crime.[3] The national statistics on policing show a decline in crime known to the police and a continuing low proportion of those crimes that result in an arrest. Also, considerable new knowledge has accumulated on policing, questioning effectiveness as budgets pay for significant reaction to crime in responding to 911 calls and limited effectiveness of basic patrol, but also confirming the positive impacts on crime of policing that is proactively targeted to problem offenders and places.

Despite the new knowledge, there seems to be a wide gap between the knowledge of what works in policing and budgeting decisions about policing and an even wider gap between decisions about balancing the distribution of funds between cost-effective policing and the many highly cost-effective ways to reduce crime that will be discussed in part II of this book.

The first section of this chapter uses statistics and scientific evidence to show why several long-held "truths" about law enforcement are ill informed and why the current strategies are not using the positive talents and abilities of today's law enforcement officers and so misspends taxes. The second section will look at law enforcement actions that have reduced the numbers of victims, mostly by targeting problem places. In table 2.1, I have set out a road map of the pragmatic actions that will be discussed in this chapter. These are grouped around what will not reduce the numbers of crime victims and additionally those that are proven to reduce crime and those where more knowledge is needed. This table refers only to policing on its own—in isolation—as much of the practice of policing and its budgeting is regrettably happening today without serious consideration to the alternative and more cost-effective ways of reducing crime that either do not involve policing or involve policing as one source of data and one partner. I will show in later chapters that smart policing, in combination with investments in targeted pre-crime prevention, can achieve much more than in this table and so this chapter. It is important to note that even policing that stops violence is not necessarily the best investment as policing is often repressive against racial minorities rather than stimulating for personal development. It is expensive and so often not the most cost-effective or sustainable way to reduce crime. This will become clear only once we have reviewed the comparative cost-effectiveness of pre-crime prevention in part II of the book.

SOURCES OF KNOWLEDGE ABOUT PROVEN WAYS FOR POLICE TO STOP CRIME

So first, let's look at the sources of knowledge on which kind of policing does or does not stop crime. Of the global leaders in this research field, the

Knowledge, mapping, and Compstat facilitate added focus on problem places and effective tactics		
What law enforcement strategies DO NOT stop crime?	What law enforcement strategies DO stop crime?	What areas need more knowledge to determine what strategies work?
Too much focus on reaction (e.g. 9-1-1 response)	Problem-oriented policing	Domestic violence
Equating "crime reduction" to "law enforcement"	Focused deterrence (gang crime)	"Hot spots" policing (when focus on retail drug markets without violence)
Random patrol	Stop-and-frisk (gun crime)	Police role in schools
DARE and public relations projects (misleadingly labeled prevention)	Focusing on repeat offenders	Law enforcement response to victims
	Focusing on stopping repeat victimization	
	Policing not in isolation (see Part II)	

Table 2.1   What Law Enforcement Strategies Stop Crime?

United States is the largest producer of good scientific knowledge about which policing strategies *really* stop crime and violence without swelling the numbers of law enforcement personnel. The good news is that we have accumulated considerable knowledge about what does not work but also about what does work in law enforcement to reduce the number of crime victims. This has come from an accumulation of basic statistics about the limits to policing, where so many victims do not report crime to police, so many cases do not result in an identified perpetrator, and so many arrests do not result in a conviction. It has also come from pioneering innovations and research done in collaboration with progressive law enforcement leadership, and it has been brought together by leading authorities such as the US National Research Council and the UK Inspectorate of Constabulary.[4]

Some of this knowledge is not only available across the world but is easily understandable on easy-to-access websites such as popcenter.org (funded in part by the Department of Justice) and crimesolutions.gov (organized by the Department of Justice). So there is little excuse for it not being used in budgeting decisions except that old (and expensive) habits die hard. Interestingly, the UK report was developed to educate candidates for a new political role pioneered in 2012 with oversight for crime and policing policy decisions in the forty-two regions of England and Wales.

Much of the law enforcement research and knowledge comes from random control trials that test whether standard practices (e.g., random preventive patrol) or particular innovations (e.g., focusing on "hot spots," or what I and others call "problem places") really stop crime. Other information comes from expert analysis of certain innovations as well as informed debates over new law enforcement methods (e.g., stop-and-frisk strategies in New York City).

In 2004, the National Research Council (NRC) completed a review of the law enforcement research to that date.[5] The review concluded that there is only weak or mixed evidence that the standard policing model on its isolated own reduces crime; it follows that adding more officers to work in the same isolated manner is not likely to be cost-effective. In contrast, the NRC pointed to a body of carefully conducted research that provides abundant evidence for the effectiveness of the focused model of law enforcement (what this book calls "smarter" policing).

Overall, the NRC concluded that more law enforcement is not better—but *smarter* law enforcement is.[6] Unfortunately, politicians, legislators, and, importantly, police leaders at the federal, state, and local levels are not yet choosing enough to put those smarter and evidence-based solutions into practice and are still not acting to stop crime (which is vitally important to would-be victims of crime) or to reduce the number of priority calls for service (which is important to taxpayers).

The other persuasive review of the law enforcement research to date comes from a prestigious law enforcement oversight board in the United Kingdom, Her Majesty's Inspectorate of Constabulary (HMIC). HMIC is made up of the crème de la crème of recently retired British police chiefs, and together with crime experts they produced an informed and comprehensive guide for ways that law enforcement *can* reduce crime—and ways that elected officials can usher in better law enforcement practices.[7]

Like the NRC study, HMIC reached the sober conclusion that there is little evidence to support the notion that large increases or decreases in standard, isolated law enforcement practices actually stop crime—and this came from police chiefs who were evaluating their own forces, so their conclusions on the limits of traditional law enforcement are particularly persuasive and worrisome in terms of the use of taxes. HMIC cited more value for money when law enforcement is "problem oriented" and tackles a particular risk factor to stop crime before it can happen (e.g., taking away illegal handguns to reduce murders).[8] Their brief guides for politicians are easily accessible and in plain English, and they should be mandatory reading for politicians charged with decisions on police budgets before wasting more tax money on what does not work.

THE LIMITS OF STANDARD POLICING

Only a limited proportion of the crimes that involve victims are actually reported by those victims to the police. For instance, the National Crime Victimization Survey undertaken for the Department of Justice's Bureau of Justice Statistics shows that approximately 60 percent of all assaults or threats to do harm and 40 percent of robberies are *not* reported to law enforcement. The reasons for not reporting are not simple, but they include a loss of confidence in many cases that law enforcement can do something to recover property or prevent further violence.[9]

An even more sobering fact is that most crimes recorded by law enforcement do not result in an arrest and are often met with very little optimism that law enforcement even has a chance of proving the identity of the perpetrator. Each year, the FBI publishes statistics on the actions that law enforcement was able to take following a crime recorded by the police. In instances where an arrest is made, the case is considered to be "cleared." Therefore, "clearance rates" represent reported crimes where arrests are made versus reported crimes that go unsolved.

As figure 2.2 shows, one-third of all murder/manslaughter cases in the United States remain uncleared; what's more, nearly two-thirds of forc-

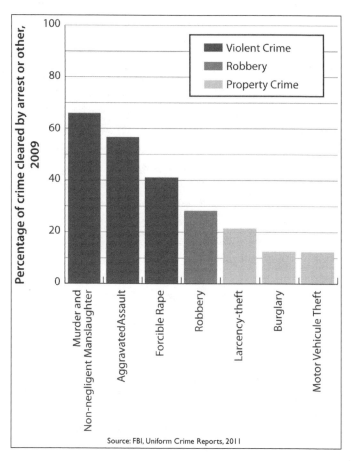

Figure 2.2   Rates of Uncleared Crimes: Many Offenses Known to Police Do Not Lead to Arrest

ible rape cases go uncleared—and that's not taking into account the vast majority—82 percent—of forcible rapes that go unreported by victims. Sometimes, even though the identity of the perpetrator is known, the case remains uncleared by law enforcement because of a low probability of conviction, because the perpetrator has already been arrested for another crime, or for other reasons.[10]

As figure 2.3 shows, more than 50 percent of the over ten million arrests that *are* made in the United States are for just four offenses—drugs, theft, assault, and driving under the influence (DUI). Each category accounts for more than 1.2 million arrests.[11] All the crimes involving theft and assault become known to the police where the victims called the police after they were victimized and so reflect harm to victims. DUI arrests are typically initiated by law enforcement and will, in fact, reduce the risk of potential victimization. The more than 1.5 million arrests (12 percent of total arrests in 2011) for drug-abuse violations are generated by the police themselves as part of their own war on drugs, and these arrests (like other arrests) generate a significant cost for law enforcement agencies, courts, and corrections—even though they have arguably little benefit for crime victims and take away precious resources from solving uncleared violent crime cases, or enhancing safety on the road, or indeed any role that the police can play in reducing intimate partner violence.

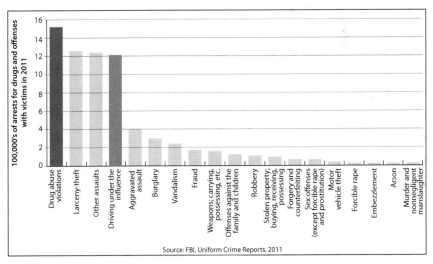

Source: FBI, Uniform Crime Reports, 2011

Figure 2.3   Arrests for Drugs Outnumber Arrests for Many Offenses with Victims

Policing That Is Reactive Is Not Preventive

Policing today is dominated by response to the universal emergency number 911. From the 1980s forward, police managers began to pull resources away from walking beats to solve problems and instead put more of those resources toward responding to calls from citizens for service. The result was that a larger and larger portion of police budgets goes for more and more cars to respond to calls for service, thereby reinforcing isolated, reactive policing. According to the report by the National Research Council (NRC) on the effectiveness of policing, over 60 percent of law enforcement budgets today are allocated to reacting to 911 calls on a case-by-case basis, with another 20 percent dedicated to further reaction via detective units.[12] With this shift to responding to calls for service came more investment in dispatch cars and the latest in communications technologies, from car radios to cellphones, to laptops, and to tablets.

But if a crime has already happened, it's too late to spare the victims the pain and loss associated with that crime. Let's compare the idea of law enforcement to big oil. What if more than two-thirds of a company's operating capital was spent on cleaning up oil *after* it spilled into the environment? Wouldn't we hope that some smart industry bigwigs would say, "Let's put more money into *stopping* the oil from spilling in the first place. That would be better for the environment, and cheaper, too." Smart, huh?

So why doesn't this same concept carry over to modern law enforcement? And why is so much focus placed (and often ill placed) on catching the criminals only *after* a victim's life has been ruined—instead of preventing that crime *before* it happens and saving taxpayers all the associated costs of courts and incarceration? The key is that politicians and law enforcement culture need to start responding to the scientific evidence we have about preventing crimes—and stop working based on "the way it's always been" and knee-jerk reactions about criminals and crime.

Policing in Isolation

Although today's police chiefs sometimes make speeches about working with the community, it seems clear that the approachable, problem-solving bobby of the mid-1900s street beat is long gone from mainstream law enforcement. Today's police officers communicate mostly with other police officers and via the latest technology. They carry handguns and electric stun guns to use against offenders. They use advanced science to confirm the identities of criminals and to learn the physics of weapons fired. They have acquired military technologies as part of their war on drugs, and they've set up SWAT teams to arrest drug users and other offenders. They go about these activities in isolation and rarely work with nonpolice entities.

Too often, law enforcement is based on the false premise that the best and most important way to stop crime is to hope that arrests of violent and property offenders will deter those offenders and the general public. Thirty years of mass incarceration in the United States without better results than other affluent countries that do not have mass incarceration certainly puts that belief in question.[13] The premise is also based on ensuring that the bad guys get what they deserve. Generally, however, more policing in isolation doesn't actually stop crime or spare victims.

Picture a medieval castle. For the most part, today's isolated law enforcement systems are operated in a top-down manner from behind castle walls. Most officers are dispatched from their fortresses to react to crimes on a case-by-case basis and are tasked with catching offenders. A few are engaged in problem-oriented policing, and some others are into proactive (even *hyper*active, Rambo-style) stop-and-frisk policing.

Politicians Confuse Crime Reduction with Policing

Probably the largest waste in our taxes and missed opportunities to protect potential victims from harm is the continuing confusion among politicians that law enforcement equals crime reduction. It does not. Unfortunately, when politicians decide how to use our taxes, they focus on how much to increase the police budget, comparing with other police agencies and salaries rather than whether that increase is a *cost-effective* use of taxpayers' money. After all, those within the isolated policing world (or those who are politically above it) often believe—without evidence—that *more* of the same law enforcement is *better* safety and more cost-effective for the public. The politicians and bureaucrats tend to see law enforcement not as part of an overall crime reduction strategy but rather as *the* crime reduction strategy. The notion of stopping citizens from being victims of crime has somehow been replaced with a focus on 911, "boots on the street," and numbers of arrests, regardless of their real contribution or possible comparative advantage to achieving safer communities.

It can sometimes be challenging to hold a real, informed discussion about law enforcement policy due to the politically (and ideologically) charged nature of the police role in crime control. One good example of where political messaging has skewed the discussion is crime rates for New York City. The claims made in the media and by politicians such as New York's former mayor Rudy Giuliani have been accepted without reflection elsewhere in the United States and around the world.

In the 1960s, crime and violence in US cities such as New York were so bad that a presidential commission was launched to find solutions. However, the following two decades saw the violent crime problem get even worse. History was therefore made in the mid-1990s, when the rates of violent and property crime in New York City were on their way down in 1990—yes, 1990, four years before Giuliani was elected as mayor[14]—and had started to drop rapidly, crashing from a spike in the late 1980s by more than 81 percent in the ensuing two decades.[15] In fact, many cities experienced large crime drops that started in different years and that show New York City to be not that different.[16] And while New York City's murder rate still remains scary to anyone living in any other affluent democracy, this city's crash in the rates of violent crime does deserve applause.

However, politicians have an unfortunate tendency to automatically equate drops in crime rates only with law enforcement efforts. Giuliani himself claimed that CompStat, the NYPD's use of records to manage law enforcement actions, was primarily responsible for his "success" by holding law enforcement accountable for reducing crime in the city. However, in New York City, it is clear that several players other than law enforcement deserve credit for the drop—and probably the lion's share thereof.

Starting in the mid 1990s, the media hyped this drop in crime as a New York miracle. Columnists and commentators pilloried experts who used basic facts to cast any doubt on whether the drop was due to anything other than Giuliani's demands for "tough and accountable policing."[17] Despite a cool reception, Andrew Karmen is an expert who undertook careful scientific analyses of all the explanations for the drop in crime in New York City in the 1990s.[18] In one study, he quotes the work by George Kelling, one of the originators of New York's broken windows strategy, in saying that the increases in misdemeanor arrests in New York City during the broken windows period of 1989 to 1998 were responsible for only 5 percent of the reduction in violent crimes.[19] Indeed, there is strong evidence that when law enforcement uses misdemeanor arrests to tackle an established risk factor, crime rates *will* be somewhat reduced—but in New York's case, several non–law enforcement factors were also at play. Karmen demonstrated the importance of the economic recovery that provided hope for disadvantaged young men to go to college as there would be jobs. He pointed to increases in the price of liquor that reduced abuse of alcohol. He identified the role played by the decrease of young men in the population, and so on.

But people still hold up Giuliani's zero-tolerance strategies as an example of why the strength of law enforcement should be increased and zero-tolerance policing should be engaged in. Even the next mayor, Michael Bloomberg, celebrated an all-time low in index crimes recorded by the NYPD in New York City in 2013 and then credited only the law enforcement tactics for the reduction in crime rates.[20] Indeed, many politicians talk as if law enforcement were crime reduction in and of itself rather than an important single component of a wider (and smarter) crime control policy.

While optimizing the role of law enforcement *is* important, policing on its own and so in isolation (even at its best) is only one contributor to stopping crime. Perhaps the mayor of London said it best when, in regard to making London the safest big city in the world, he stated that law enforcement cannot stop crime on its own.[21] This reality, however, is all too often whitewashed over by politicians and the media, who unfortunately are not yet focused on what actually works to stop crime in cost-effective ways and therefore on policing as only one tool in the tool box.

USING EVIDENCE TO AVOID WHAT DOESN'T WORK

The concept of using evidence—"smart policing"—is not new. The government already has a useful definition of smart policing as "building evidence-based, data-driven law enforcement tactics and strategies that are effective, efficient, and economical."[22] There are two points to high-light here. First, to be "smart," law enforcement must be cost-effective. Second, it means that the strategies and methods must be proven to *actually work* to stop crime and promote safer communities. And why would taxpayers and their politicians continue to settle for anything less?

It's hard to imagine paying for expensive medical care that is proven to be ineffective. It's equally hard to imagine having a health care strategy in the twenty-first century that is based only on waiting until a major crisis ensues in order to call for an ambulance. So why should taxpayers continue to pay exorbitant costs for reactive policing strategies that aren't based on evidence, that don't really work, and that don't ef-fectively spare victims?

The Misconception That Random Preventive Patrols Work

One long-held misconception about law enforcement is that random preventive patrols deter crime. The idea is that if officers regularly drive through neighborhoods in marked patrol cars, even without any specific target in mind, they will deter criminals from committing a crime. In the 1970s, the Police Foundation in Washington, DC decided to test the actual effectiveness of random preventive patrols using Kansas City, Missouri, as a backdrop.[23]

In the one-year experiment, law enforcement management withdrew preventive patrols from one group of neighborhoods, doubled the num-ber of patrols in a second group of neighborhoods, and left the number of patrols at the standard level for a third group of neighborhoods. The public was not informed about the changes in levels of patrol.

Researchers then assessed whether there were any changes in rates of crime, as determined by crime victimization surveys that were conducted at the beginning and end of the twelve months. Like all crime victimization surveys, these surveys were conducted independently of law enforcement and measured the proportion of residents who had been victims of crime, regardless of whether they had reported the crime or not.

The results of this important experiment proved that random pre-ventive patrols had no impact on the frequency of crime. That is, it was scientifically proven that random preventive patrols do not work. This was a dramatic indictment of the way the majority of law enforcement resources were being used at the time, in the United States and in many other affluent democracies. Politicians and law enforcement representatives put up enormous resistance to the findings, largely due to the huge investment in preventive police patrols and in doing what they had always been doing.

Today, we do not know what proportion of law enforcement resources are still devoted to random preventive patrols, but we do know that most police patrols respond to 911 calls rather than patrolling at random.

"Public Relations" Strategies (Misleadingly Confused with Crime Prevention) Are Not Crime Prevention

Random preventive patrols are not the only popular law enforcement initiative that has been scientifically proven to be ineffective. Some police departments still have a small crime prevention section that doubles as its public relations office. These sections are responsible for programs such as Neighborhood Watch and Child Print, which bring the section's police officers into interaction with the public. Unfortunately, many of these programs are misleadingly called crime prevention but they do not have the necessary resources and are often replicating actions that have been proven not to stop crime. For instance, the evaluations of Neighborhood Watch as implemented by these sections show that they do not stop crime, even though the original program run out of a city hall did.[24]

The Los Angeles Police Department (LAPD) developed the DARE drug prevention program, where officers talk in school classrooms about the dangers of illicit drug use—again, an attractive way of getting support for policies where policing operates in an isolated manner. However, evaluations have not shown any beneficial impacts in terms of reduced drug use.[25] In contrast, life skills training, to be discussed in chapter 5, shows a return of eighteen dollars for each dollar spent because it uses trained teachers who are already in the classroom and a program that has been proven to be effective.

Importantly, a Department of Justice website, crimesolutions.gov, does not include any of the typical programs run by these sections as effective. However, it does include some problem-oriented projects, which are sometimes run by these sections and which will be discussed among those programs that are effective.

USING EVIDENCE TO FOCUS POLICING ON WHAT WE KNOW STOPS CRIME

Focusing Law Enforcement on Problem Places

It was the proven failure of random preventive patrols that slowly led to a search for what *would* be effective in law enforcement. This renewed focus brought on a shift toward positive innovations that actually *do* give the public value for its taxes—and several law enforcement approaches that are largely isolated from the public and other agencies fall into this category. For instance, according to one recent review, there is good evidence that some crime is stopped through problem-oriented policing (POP), hot-spots policing, and gun seizure efforts, as well as focused deterrence approaches and using DNA in property cases.[26]

These innovations have been brought about by a combination of mapping and law enforcement management. Most urban residents will cite "inner-city" areas as the most dangerous and crime-ridden parts of a city and will anecdotally say that young men in street gangs are the most frequent perpetrators. And indeed, violent street crime by men between the ages of fifteen and twenty-five tends to be concentrated in areas of disadvantage, social exclusion, and relative poverty—places known as "hot spots" (or what I and others call "problem places" since, like all problems, these places' problems *do* have solutions).[27] As discussed in chapter 1, extensive studies in many countries have identified the specific life experiences that predispose some young men (especially those concentrated in these areas) to become persistent violent offenders.

Focusing on problem places has become one of the best scientifically established ways for law enforcement to reduce crime—a tactic which Anthony Braga and David Weisburd have called "policing problem places" and have devoted a whole book to.[28] In large cities, problem places are identified and mapped, primarily through the computer analysis of 911 calls, which are typically coded geographically. Experts have long hypothesized that this coded information can be used to inform smarter law enforcement practices.

In one seminal analysis of all dispatched calls for service in Minneapolis during a one-year period in the early 1990s, Lawrence Sherman and David Weisburd showed that the vast majority of addresses never made an emergency call—but that 3.5 percent of addresses accounted for a staggering 50 percent of the calls, and that these addresses tended to be concentrated in certain problem places. An analysis in Seattle showed that a city's hot spots tend to persist over time and remain hot spots for decades. Statistics like these are now common knowledge and have been demonstrated from different perspectives. For instance, the British Crime Survey showed that only 4 percent of respondents accounted for 44 percent of victimizations. These statistics indicate that there is a high proportion of addresses that suffer more than one victimization a year—what the British have termed "repeat victimization."

With the research they'd gathered, Sherman and Weisburd persuaded the Minneapolis police to engage in a random control trial to test whether increased police patrols in these problem places had an impact on these areas' high call volumes for service. The study confirmed that *targeted* police patrols in problem places (which are the opposite of *random* preventive patrols) led to a modest but clear reduction in crime rates, as measured by a decrease in calls from the public for police services.[29]

The arrival of mapping technology, along with an understanding that crime was often concentrated around a few problem addresses and offenders, was combined with ways to focus law enforcement action proactively on these problems.

Problem-Oriented Policing

The most important law enforcement innovation of the past few decades is called "problem-oriented policing" (POP) because it looks at the risk factors that create the crime problem in the first place. Once the risk factors are identified, law enforcement services can use their resources in a smarter way, which often means working with other partners such as housing and parking design to tackle those risk factors and consequently reduce crime. The original concept in its most effective incarnation is ascribed to Wisconsin University professor Herman Goldstein.[30]

Today, many examples of successful problem-oriented policing have been brought together at popcenter.org, the Center for Problem-Oriented Policing, an important website for politicians and police leaders who want to reinvest in strategies that actually stop crime.[31] However, most of the examples of problem-oriented policing on this website are localized efforts by one or two police officers rather than citywide efforts to stop crime, which is what we really need.

One of the original examples of effective problem-oriented policing by law enforcement was organized in Newport News, Virginia, in the early 1980s.[32] Essentially, an enlightened police chief removed twenty police officers from responding to calls so that they could analyze a high-crime area—a problem place—that was rife with car thefts and break-ins, and then he tasked them to find a solution. In the end, the officers recommended that the city enforce its bylaws to improve physical environment issues such as lighting and the quality of the houses' doors. The result was a 30 percent reduction in burglaries—and so 30 percent fewer victimizations. Smart.

Chicago also used smart problem solving to gain a reduction in crime rates recorded across the city in the 1990s, largely due to launching its Chicago Policing Alternatives Program in 1993.[33] This program was a concerted effort to bring law enforcement, citizens, and community agencies together to actually prevent—rather than just react to—crime. The program included assigning certain law enforcement officers to particular areas of the city so that they got to know local community residents and vice versa. The program included community meetings where officers would discuss law enforcement priorities (e.g., robberies, street drug sales, and prostitution) with citizens, essentially asking for their buy-in to find solutions. This strategy brought communities into *partnership* with law enforcement, and prototype districts showed reductions of 50 percent or more in gangs and drugs.[34]

While problem-oriented policing is an important tool, it is not clear that officers trained to be law enforcement officers are necessarily the most cost-effective at implementing it, particularly as the research suggests that it is not always well implemented by them.

Focused Deterrence: Targeting Gang Crime Another proven "smart policing" strategy comes from a well-known project in Boston that reduced gang violence in the 1990s. This strategy is referred to as "focused deterrence." In simple terms, the Boston Police Department focused deterrence techniques on persons known to the department as being involved in street gangs and violence. They made certain individuals in certain problem places aware that law enforcement was watching them and would do everything possible to get them behind bars with severe punishments if they were caught for a crime. This action was a key component to the sudden drop in homicides in that city. One scientific estimate put this reduction at a whopping 66 percent.[35] Though proven effective, it is not clear how much of this reduction came from the policing component and how much from a youth outreach component. This will be discussed further in chapter 6.

Importantly, the concept of focused deterrence is targeted and so different from general deterrence, which simply hopes that the general threat of arrest and punishment will deter citizens at large from committing crimes. In fact, the evidence shows that general deterrence, unlike focused deterrence, is *not* effective in reducing rates of street crime and gang violence.

Focused deterrence has been the subject of an impressive scientific review to assess whether there is reliable evidence to support the belief that it actually stops crime.[36] The review agreed that Boston, along with four other cities, had all successfully reduced homicide rates by 34 percent to 44 percent due to the use of focused deterrence strategies. These positive results were achieved within their existing law enforcement budgets, and they reduced not only the loss of life (and likely many serious injuries) but the number of cases going through to the courts and corrections systems, thereby saving taxpayers' money.

The reviewers were cautious about generalizing the results because they were based on nonrandomized quasi-experimental designs (that is, the methodology was not as scientifically sound as the reviewers would have liked). The reviewers still asserted that focused deterrence contributed to these sizeable drops in crime rates, but they were not sure by how much, as there may have also been an investment in offering social services to these young men to get them back into school or to get them jobs. Still, these examples of focused deterrence did achieve important results, and so focused deterrence strategies must be on the list of actions for smart crime control—even if only as one part of a combined approach where law enforcement steps outside its parameters of acting in its own isolated way and acts in cooperation with other community agencies, which we will discuss more in chapter 6.

Stop-and-Frisk: Targeting Gun Crime

Stop-and-frisk is a crime-stopping tactic that is an offshoot of hot-spots policing. The tactic is used by many large law enforcement agencies, generally in problem places. It involves officers targeting an individual or set of individuals that they deem to be suspicious and then frisking them. To legally stop a person, a law enforcement officer must have a reasonable suspicion that the person has committed, is committing, or is about to commit an unlawful act. To legally frisk someone, law enforcement must "reasonably suspect" that the person has a weapon that might endanger officer safety. The main problem with stop-and-frisk is that law enforcement officers tend to base their "reasonable suspicions" on stereotypes.[37] This will be further discussed later on in the chapter.

Hot-spot analysis can assist in directing stop-and-frisk to problem places. One example is its use in targeted actions to get guns off the street. It's a known and obvious fact that taking away illegal handguns reduces rates of gun crime. For example, in Kansas City, one targeted law enforcement effort increased the number of guns seized by 65 percent—and achieved a 49 percent decrease in gun-crime rates. The law enforcement techniques used in this effort also included searching the property of individuals under arrest on charges other than gun crimes, plain-view searches of cars, and safety frisks of individuals who had been stopped in their cars for traffic violations.[38]

One Jersey City law enforcement program, called Problem-Oriented Policing at Violent Places, is a successful example of smart policing in problem places. The program was an early 1990s initiative of the Jersey City Police Department's violent crime unit and was the subject of a scientific study. After identifying the city's problem places based on 911 calls, the unit looked at what scenarios for violence existed in those areas and which of those scenarios could be influenced by a situational approach to law enforcement—that is, they looked at how law enforcement could *influence* a situation to reduce the chances of a violent outcome. The unit then instituted a combination of measures that included focused enforcement (e.g., foot and radio patrols, breaking up groups of loiterers, issuing tickets for public drinking, and using stop-and-frisk on suspicious persons) and situational measures (e.g., securing vacant lots, cleaning the streets of trash, increasing lighting in problem areas, and removing graffiti).[39] Situational measures are similar to problem-oriented policing but tend to reduce opportunities for crime by changing lighting or the design of buildings or property.[40] The results were impressive, with large reductions in 911 calls relating to street fights, property crimes, and narcotics. There was a spillover effect to the neighboring areas, where street fights and narcotics calls were also reduced (although there was no spillover effect that reduced property crimes).

Without a doubt, the limitations of stop-and-frisk tactics must be recognized to ensure fair law enforcement. And although other less contentious hot-spot strategies (such as those used in Jersey City) are scientifically proven to make communities safer from violent crime, they do have limited scope because they work within the limits of what law enforcement can do in isolation. In particular, they don't address the many social determinants of why some individuals, families, and groups cluster in problem places and generate high rates of crime to begin with. Chapters 5 and 6 of this book take a closer look at the research on these issues and will illustrate several very real ways that law enforcement services and community agencies can work together to focus on social services to eliminate crime hot spots altogether.

The most important project to date to deal with inner-city gun crime has been Project Safe Neighborhoods. It grew out of the outstanding reductions in street homicides achieved in Boston in the mid-1990s, where gun crime was reduced by 60 percent through a combination of smart policing and effective social prevention.[41] This inspired a National Institute of Justice project called the Strategic Approaches to Community Safety Initiative (SACSI), which focused on targeting law enforcement on problem places in ten cities, with some resulting reductions in violence. Then the law enforcement component was used in Project Safe Neighborhoods, implemented in all ninety-four US attorney districts nationwide to respond to high gun-crime rates.

Though Project Safe Neighborhoods referred to collaboration with community partners, the primary focus was on getting different law enforcement agencies to tackle gun crime from their existing isolated standpoint. An estimated $3 billion was pumped into these programs over several years. And while Project Safe Neighborhoods did accomplish some reductions in homicide rates in a handful of participating cities, overall these drops were not large. In chapter 6, you will learn how these projects could have been smarter had they succeeded in moving out of the all-too-typical isolated policing mentality to invest as much in the targeted problem solving of social problems, as was originally done in Boston.[42]

Focusing on Repeat Offenders

Unfortunately, the number of offenders returning to courts and to the correctional system for the second or third time (or more) is extraordinarily high. So there are good grounds for focusing law enforcement attention on offenders who are already known for offending, since there is a good chance they may revictimize.

Law enforcement units known as "repeat offender units" continue to be used by law enforcement agencies in an effort to reduce the number of crimes committed by focusing on repeat offenders for a small deterrent effect, and also by incapacitating persistent offenders by getting them off the streets through misdemeanor arrests for violating bail, probation, and parole conditions.[43] Curiously, the number of studies on the effectiveness of repeat offender units is limited, and the results from studies in the 1980s show only marginal reductions in crime rates—mostly through doling out slightly longer prison sentences for an incapacitation effect rather than by bringing about clear reductions in crime or improvements in rates of conviction.

Focusing on Repeat Victimization

Important successes in stopping crime can happen by focusing on those victims who are victimized more than once within a period as short as a year—what is referred to as "repeat victimization." An analysis of the locations of 911 calls is one of the simplest ways to identify repeat victimization and is a strategy that any law enforcement agency can easily undertake. But the actions to reduce repeat victimization have to be based on actions by agencies other than policing. So this is discussed further in chapter 9.

IMPORTANT ISSUES WHERE SMART POLICING NEEDS MORE WORK

Smarter Ways to Reduce Domestic Violence

Responding to domestic violence calls is a challenge that can be both dangerous and difficult. The research on the effectiveness of policing alone is not clear. The role of police, problem-solving courts, and social agencies are all important. This is discussed further in chapter 7.

Smart Ways to Put Victims at the Zenith of Law Enforcement

The focus on taking action to enforce the law against perpetrators has led to overlooking the victims of crime in terms of support and protection. Generally, victims are voting with their feet by not going to law enforcement. Instead of blaming victims for not reporting, police must reconsider ways to put victims at the zenith of law enforcement. The International Association of Chiefs of Police in cooperation with the Office for Victims of Crime has provided impressive leadership by developing strategies for whole police departments to make the shift. With so many victims choosing to not report crime to the police, action to implement these guidelines would help law enforcement get more information on victimization and thereby focus law enforcement's contribution to stopping crime.[44]

Fairness and Drugs

As discussed above, the evolution of 911-centered law enforcement has naturally led to a large body of geographic information about hot spots for crime. Expert reviews have also confirmed that focused deterrence has been successful in reducing the number of cases of illegal possession of drugs in two cities, but these studies did not show any reduction in harm to crime victims. While some good hot-spots policing tactics have emerged and should be applauded (as discussed earlier), another offspring of hot-spots policing is the marked increase in stop-and-frisk tactics in inner-city areas—particularly of young males in New York City. In many ways, stop-and-frisk takes the smart idea of hot-spots policing and turns it into an *un*smart hybrid of new scientific information and old-school policing methods.

Stop-and-frisk can be exaggerated so that the interference with innocent men does damage that far outweighs the benefits to public safety. It is this vigorous, disproportionate targeting that deserves a critical eye. Indeed, young black and Hispanic men are the targets of a hugely disproportionate number of stop-and-frisk stops. For example, although they account for only 4.7 percent of New York City's population, black and Hispanic males between the ages of fourteen and twenty-four accounted for 41.6 percent of stops in 2011. In fact, the number of stops of young black men exceeded the city's entire population of young black men that year (168,126 stops versus 158,406 residents). More than 50 percent of the stops were made because the persons "looked furtive."[45]

Importantly, close to 90 percent of the young black and Hispanic men stopped in New York City in 2011 were innocent. Furthermore, the exaggerated use of stop-and-frisk tactics has not provided any additional benefit in terms of fewer gun-crime victims. For example, in New York City in 2002, there were 1,892 victims of gun violence and 97,296 stops. In 2011, there were still 1,821 victims of gun violence, although there were a record 685,724 stops—almost seven times as many.[46]

At this point, smart politicians should be asking themselves, "What are the actual proven benefits of stop-and-frisk? What are the more cost-effective and fairer ways to stop inner-city gun violence (as will be discussed in chapter 6)? And are our communities better and more cohesive for it—or worse off than they were before?" Indeed, this can be a steep trade-off, for as you will see in chapter 5, social cohesion contributes a fair amount to stopping crime and increasing public safety.

Policing in Schools

Another area that requires some attention is the role of law enforcement—typically known as "resource officers"—in schools. There is no evidence that the presence of a police officer solves the problems of violence and bullying in schools, although there is evidence that these problems can be solved in other ways. However, there is a concern that the police presence may contribute to the school-to-prison pipeline—that is, more youth being incarcerated.[47]

SHIFTING LAW ENFORCEMENT'S FOCUS TO MISDEMEANORS REDUCES INCARCERATION WHILE STOPPING CRIME

One important but unintended effect of the shift toward favoring misdemeanor arrests in 1990s New York City is that some offenders who would otherwise have gone behind bars for a long period of time with a felony conviction were instead sentenced for a shorter time based on a misdemeanor conviction. Indeed, as the NYPD focused on arrests for less serious offenses, it devoted fewer resources to felony arrests. At the same time, the additional factor of a reduced crime rate meant that fewer people were committing felonies.

An important and sound analysis by leading experts showed how the shorter sentences and reduced rates of incarceration were a significant contributor to the 1990s crime drop in New York.[48] In basic terms, crime rates came down and incarceration rates came down. So taxpayers can save costs on incarceration without increasing risk of harm to potential victims. Smart policing is the gatekeeper to this benefit. Unfortunately, it is not clear whether this benefit still continues today, as stop-and-frisk is often used to charge persons with felonies for lesser crimes such as drug possession, regardless of their danger to potential victims.

CONCLUSION

Points to Note: Smarter Strategies That Use Effective Law Enforcement to Reduce Crime

Law enforcement is a significant industry in the United States, with a turnover of $124 billion a year—much of which is paid for by local taxes. The number of police officers per capita in the United States is not that different proportionately from many other affluent democracies, though they are often better paid.

The good news is that scientific research, combined with pioneering law enforcement leadership, has provided an important core of knowledge about what is wasteful and what works in law enforcement to stop crime, reduce the number of victims of crime, and save taxes. This knowledge is easily accessible but still infrequently put to use.

Standard policing is limited in its ability to reduce crime for several fundamental reasons, such as victims who do not report to police and the difficult realities of identifying perpetrators. Law enforcement resources are too often used to *react* to crime, particularly to 911 calls. Random patrols and public relations projects misleadingly labeled as crime prevention have been shown not to reduce crime.

For policing to play a greater role in stopping victimization, actions must focus on problem places and problem people, which have actually been proven to stop crime. These actions include problem-oriented policing, focused deterrence, and stop-and-frisk (when used carefully), as well as a focus on repeat offenders and repeat victims. The ensuing reductions in crime rates are significant, reaching 30 percent or more. Law enforcement might get more information about crime if it put victims at the zenith of law enforcement. Finally, law enforcement can help reduce costs to taxpayers by using the least serious penalty that is still effective; in many cases, this will mean placing misdemeanor charges, which are effective at stopping crime and are more cost-effective than overuse of felony convictions.

Some law enforcement strategies target the possession and low-level trafficking of marijuana and so contribute both to costs to taxpayers as well as to racial bias in the courts and correctional systems but do little to reduce harm to victims.

Politicians too often treat policing at budget time as if it equates with stopping crime, which it does not. Ultimately, the litmus test of sound political and law enforcement leadership must include shifting resources smartly to what *actually* stops crime and prevents victimization in a cost-effective manner, but this must be done without mistakenly assuming that expenditure on law enforcement is the only contributor to reducing the number of crime victims.

Actions for Politicians to Reduce Crime through Policing That Stops Crime before It Harms

1. Politicians and police leadership must:
   a. get to know what police and nonpolice strategies are proven and insist on their use rather than allow law enforcement budgets to grow without the benefits from crime reduction and savings to taxpayers that outweigh increased law enforcement costs;

    b. avoid ways of thinking and actions that assume that law enforcement is the only contributor to crime reduction; and

    c. hire advisers with knowledge of what works in policing and what is cost-effective in prevention to inform the public debate and their policy decisions.

2. Law enforcement must apply promising problem-oriented and proven policing strategies across cities to reduce rates of violence and property crimes at the neighborhood level (see popcenter.org and crimesolutions.gov); it must also recognize that sometimes misdemeanor charges are just as effective while being less costly.

3. Law enforcement must not waste resources on strategies known not to stop crime, such as random preventive patrol, project DARE, and public relations exercises (misleadingly called crime prevention).

4. Law enforcement must use geographic analysis of 911 calls for service to:

    a. identify hot spots and problem places where further analysis and solutions using problem-oriented policing (and pre-crime prevention) can be used to stop crime; and

    b. analyze repeat victimization of both violent and property crimes with a view to introduce focused and problem-oriented solutions.

5. Law enforcement must use enforcement in problem places to stop urban gun violence and other crimes through:

    a. focused deterrence such as call-ins, likely combined with other social prevention;

    b. stop-and-frisk, undertaken in moderation with support of the affected neighborhoods; and

    c. enforcing traffic violations, as violent offenders disproportionately commit traffic offenses (to be discussed in chapter 8).

6. Police leaders and researchers must focus on identifying effective ways to apply law enforcement and social and court strategies to stop repeat offending, both by domestic violence offenders and by potential violators of bail, probation, and parole conditions, as well as persons released without any support or supervision.

Shifting law enforcement from reactive crime control to smart prevention within its isolated parameters is a big job. More successful and cost-effective reductions in crime rates will require law enforcement to move away from regarding law enforcement in its isolated form as *the* crime reduction action.

Chapters 5 and 6 include law enforcement as a partner in planning strategies with other community services and agencies to prevent violence. Chapters 7 and 8 look at the role of law enforcement in preventing violence against women and reducing traffic fatalities. Ultimately, the major contributions of law enforcement toward smarter crime control are brought back in chapter 10.

Waller

Chpt 1:

- US highest crime rates
- money spent on crimes
- Need to work on preventing crimes rather than trying to fix them later after they occur.

Chapt 2:

- police tactics
- gangs
- Drugs
- Detterance crime
- stop & frisk

2018 Scholarship Recipients

olar Reflections
eet Kaur

mily Address
esident, of AKT Investments

g Remarks
President, Student Retention and Academic Success

olar Reflections
or Victoria

p Photos

t Reception

i Xiong for his musical presentation.

AMENTO
TATE
e the Possible

3

JUSTICE

Courts That Stop Crime or Do Not Unnecessarily Interfere

INTRODUCTION

Our image of justice is one of a case being tried in front of a criminal court with a judge in a gown (and maybe a wig), defense counsel and prosecutor, and probably a jury. Trial day is the day for smart lawyers to duel with the life of the accused. But this only happens in Hollywood.

Astonishingly, more than three-quarters of felony defendants in front of courts reporting to the Bureau of Justice Statistics in 2006 had a prior history of arrest, with 69 percent having *multiple* prior arrests.[1] Felonies are serious offenses, such as murder, manslaughter, rape, robbery, or burglary. Each year, an estimated 1.1 million people are convicted of a felony. Of those convicted, an amazingly high proportion—94 percent—pleaded guilty, and seven in ten were sentenced to incarceration, with the average sentence being almost five years.[2] As in figure 3.1, a whopping 34 percent of those were convicted for drug offenses, not dangerous crimes of personal violence or theft that did harm to victims.[3]

Something is seriously wrong with a system that has a 75 percent failure rate. This is clear proof that what the courts did last time did *not* stop future crimes from happening. In place of punishing the same

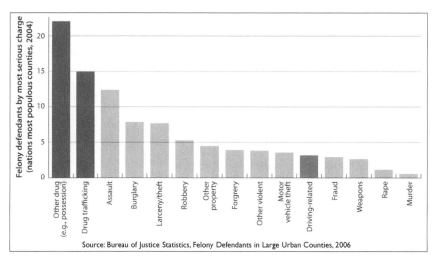

Source: Bureau of Justice Statistics, Felony Defendants in Large Urban Counties, 2006

Figure 3.1   Felony Defendants for Drugs Outnumber Felony Defendants for Offenses with Victims

criminals again and again—a revolving door—courts must be focused on actions that stop reoffending at affordable prices or wherever possible get out of the way and let others do it better.

Today, many prosecutors (and some politicians) see their role as being to get justice for the victim, often through a lengthy prison sentence. However, this is a bit of a one-size-fits-all goal. After all, not all victims are looking for punishment and vengeance. The data from the national crime victim survey show that many victims of property crime are looking for reparation and compensation, and many victims of violent crime are looking for real actions that will stop similar violence from happening to themselves and to others in the future—that is, they want prevention. Only a few want punishment as such.[4] So how do we get justice for those victims who want to stop the vicious reoffending cycle? We'll explore that question in this chapter.

Why Not Use Sentencing That Is Results Oriented to Bring About Less Crime?

Why shouldn't we look to retool our court system from antiquated institutions that punish offenders to modern-day organizations that protect public safety through the firm use of smart strategies that are *proven* to stop future crime? In some cases, incarceration will be part of those smart strategies, but so will court-controlled rehabilitation programs, community involvement, restorative justice, and decriminalizing what does no harm to victims.

In the real world, judges do not have explicit control over what is a "fair" punishment. The legislature also plays a role in determining what punishment (generally) fits what crime (generally). It passes laws that may set minimum and maximum penalties, although these laws rarely reflect any real understanding of what reduces reoffending or what the accumulated costs of incarceration will be. Judges then decide sentences for particular offenders based on these laws, again without any real concern for public safety or taxpayers' money. But it doesn't have to be this way. The court system can become much smarter to stop reoffending, and it can direct more concern to avoiding a waste of our tax dollars—and, indeed, to the waste of offenders' lives—provided there's a will to make it so.

One thing is certain: our courts need a critical look, and not only because they are not meeting their full potential in terms of stopping future crime. There is also a racial bias embedded in American criminal justice systems at all levels—not solely in the federal system, where blacks receive sentences 20 percent longer on average than whites and where 37 percent of those incarcerated are black.[5]

This chapter focuses on some pragmatic reforms for courts that would follow the science to reduce reoffending and control costs. In particular, it looks at: (1) "problem-solving" courts combined with community treatment centers that work with communities to effectively tackle the *causes* of offending in order to reduce *re*offending in a cost-effective manner—an approach that is proven beyond any reasonable doubt; (2) some smart innovations to sentencing to control and reduce wasted costs for taxpayers; (3) diverting people out of the court system if there is a better way to serve the community, thus saving lots on taxes; and (4) some promising innovations that still need more work, although in all likelihood they are better than the current system. It also looks at decriminalizing drug offenses that relate to possession and storefront retailing (not capos from Colombia or Mexico) when they do no harm to victims. I have listed the main ideas that we will cover in this chapter in table 3.1.

What court reforms DO stop reoffending?	What reforms to criminal justice would save costs to taxpayers without increasing harm to victims?	What needs more work?
Community courts and services Alcohol and drug courts (where linked to violence) Community Drug Treatment (Prop. 36) Mental health courts and treatment Sentence planner in courts or DA office	Sentencing Commissions to stop reoffending and deficits Diversion to community programs Restorative justice with proven reoffending reduction Legalization of marijuana	Domestic violence Problem analysis courts Engaging victims Decriminalization of illicit drugs
All areas can benefit from better data on accused, treatment, costs, restitution, and reoffending		

Table 3.1   What Court Actions Stop Crime and Overspending?

DOING MORE THAN JUST PUNISHING: HOW SMART COURTS ARE *STOPPING* REVICTIMIZATION

Surprisingly, there is no substantial body of research on the effectiveness of courts at stopping crime—at least none equivalent to those that have grown around prevention, law enforcement, and corrections. However, there are innovators. In New York City, the Center for Court Innovations is an independent research and development agency that looks for ways to improve on traditional courts that too often operate in isolation. In particular, it focuses on ways to use judicial powers and courts to *solve problems* and thereby stop future crime. The center believes that "if given the right tools, the justice system can aid victims, change the behavior of offenders, and improve public safety."[6] While there's no mention of saving on taxes, nothing can be as expensive as the current system of mass incarceration. The center's projects include drug courts and mental health courts, which have strong evidence to support them, as well as domestic violence courts and community courts, which are promising but need more work to get evidence on their effectiveness.[7] Importantly, these problem-solving courts seek to promote outcomes that will stop reoffending, as well as look for ways to meet some of the needs of victims and society. They are an important step toward making our communities safer by targeting reoffending *before* it happens.

Courts too often operate in isolation, with an insular and top-down frame of mind. To succeed in reducing reoffending, therefore, problem-solving courts step out of this isolationist mentality to combine the power of the court with the influence of local social service programs.

To do so, they engage several key components: (1) judges who take a more hands-on approach to addressing problems and changing the future behaviors of defendants; (2) collaboration with local social services agencies; and (3) processes that are not common in traditional courts (e.g., being less adversarial than traditional court proceedings are). The overall result is a smarter, more results-based approach to dealing with offenders, but as yet the approach is not sufficiently used. Typically, these courts are created in problem places, where crime rates are high and social problems remain omnipresent.

Community Courts

Community courts look for community-based solutions when it comes to dealing with minor offenders. They focus on stopping crime to reduce harm to future victims as well as on cost savings and enhanced engagement between offenders and the community. Today, there are more than thirty community courts in the United States and a handful in other countries.[8]

The precursor for New York City's Center for Court Innovation was the very first community court, Midtown Community Court, which was created in 1993 to address less serious offending around Times Square. Like all community courts today, the Midtown Community Court combines two key concepts: sanctions and help. It finds placements for offenders to perform community service and to receive social services, with the possibility of a sanction if the offender does not follow through.[9]

The initial impact evaluation of the Midtown Community Court showed notable reductions in reoffending rates as measured over time (i.e., by comparing the reconviction rates of the program with the reconviction rates before the program). However, some of this drop could have been associated with the general drop in crime that was occurring in New York City and across the United States at that time.[10] It could also have been part of the urban regeneration that was simultaneously occurring in the Times Square area. Regardless, the Midtown Community Court's commitment to social services rather than incarceration is logical, and this focus enabled it to thrive in the neighborhood. What's more, it has shown some cost savings when compared to traditional court systems.

The results from Midtown were so promising that community leaders in Red Hook, a particularly poor and violence-ridden area of New York City—a classic problem place—were motivated to follow suit. They established the now famous Red Hook Community Court, where judges have an array of sanctions and services at their disposal. These sanctions include community restitution projects, short-term psychoeducational groups, and long-term treatment (e.g., drug treatment, mental health treatment, and trauma-focused psychotherapy). Red Hook also features an on-site clinic (the Red Hook Community Justice Center) that is staffed by social service professionals who use trauma- and evidence-informed approaches to assess and connect individuals to appropriate services. The clinic also works to connect court-involved youth with strengths-based programming that will increase their options in the future (i.e., encourage them to make choices other than crime), including art projects and peer education programs.

At this point, there are no evaluations of Red Hook, not because it is not promising but because for evaluators, its holistic methods make it technically hard to isolate for objective measurement. Still, the logic of what it does justifies more interest in the model. Likely, some improvements in effectiveness could be achieved by a more explicit focus on using proven methods such as those I discuss in the next chapter, but we also know that community ties, such as keeping a person with his or her family or in a job, can be more important than any particular therapies in terms of reducing the likelihood of reoffending and causing harm to another victim.

While all this is important for reducing reoffending rates, the benefits for victims still depend on whether restitution is paid and, importantly, whether there is adequate investment in these services. Without question, smart crime control requires investment in what works in the community to avoid future harm to potential victims and to avoid the high cost of recourse to incarceration.

Drug Courts

When it comes to problem-solving courts, perhaps none have been more proven as effective than so-called drug courts.[11] The first modern drug court was launched in Florida's Miami-Dade County in 1989. It was the innovation of a group of criminal justice professionals who were tired of seeing the same faces coming back to court again and again— the common and disastrous problem for traditional courts. They did not need statistics to realize that the system was broken and needed fixing, and they set about finding a smart way to do so.

Essentially, drug courts use the power of the court to enforce drug abstinence and open up space in treatment programs in which the offender must participate. If an offender gets reinvolved with drugs, the court will sanction the offender with "flash" sanctions such as a weekend in jail, but importantly not with a lengthy blunderbuss of a prison sentence, as could have followed the original offense in a traditional court. The result is that some offenders become (and stay) drug free. Drug courts are typically used in instances where the offender is arrested on a drug use charge. In some cases, it is used prior to a formal charge, and in other cases, it is used after conviction but before sentencing. In some drug courts, successful completion of the treatment program means that the court does not record a conviction, saving the offender from multiple disadvantages in getting jobs and staying out of prison.

By 1993, the judges and lawyers working in drug courts had established their own nongovernmental association. Today, the National Association of Drug Court Professionals boasts more than 2,600 drug courts. By 2012, there had been no less than ninety-two evaluations of adult drug courts. One large-scale scientific review of the results— a meta-analysis—concluded that adult drug courts are effective at stopping reoffending, as shown by a drop in reoffending rates from 50 percent to 38 percent for the three years following completion of drug court programs.[12] Another meta-analysis by one of the best-known correctional researchers, Doris MacKenzie, comes to similar conclusions[13] and points to the effectiveness of combining aspects of rehabilitation and enforcement.

Other reviews show the cost benefits of drug courts as compared to probation and criminal justice sanctions; the return on every one-dollar investment is at least two dollars in savings from traditional court costs. But when other benefits are calculated, estimates put the rate of return at four dollars saved for every dollar invested and could even be higher if the offenders going through drug courts did less harm to themselves— although they do significantly less harm to victims.[14]

The success of drug courts has inspired other innovations to stop reoffending and thereby reduce harm to would-be victims. Project HOPE has become the poster project for this in the media. Its full name is Hawaii Opportunity Probation and Enforcement. It is a probation system that uses some of the same swift sanctions that drug courts use to enforce abstinence from drugs. The program uses a behavioral modification technique to punish violations of probation agreements (mostly relating to meetings with a probation officer and abstinence from drugs). If an offender misses a meeting with a probation officer and results show positive on a drug test, he is immediately put in jail for a night or two.[15] The results from a random control trial of Project HOPE show an impressive reduction in rearrests from 47 percent for those not in the program down to 21 percent for those in the program.[16]

Many drug courts succeed by threatening and then imposing a heavy sentence on an offender who does not complete the treatment. Sometimes, these sentences can turn out to be more expensive than the traditional court process and the ensuing incarceration. Therefore, my support for using the criminal powers of drug courts is limited to those offenders who have engaged in violence or in a serious property crime and therefore avoid harm to victims if there is no reoffending. I do not advocate for the use of drug courts to deal with basic drug use, which on its own does no harm to victims and which, I believe, has no place in any criminal court system.[17]

Even though the overall outcomes for drug courts are impressive at reducing reoffending, it is clear that some drug courts do much better than others by following key components that include proven treatments,[18] urine testing at least twice a week, graduated sanctions, and an interdisciplinary team. Likewise, positive results have been shown from twenty-eight evaluations of similar problem-solving courts for drunk drivers, but more work is needed.[19]

An Even Smarter and More Popular Approach to Sentencing: California's Proposition 36

In 2000, 61 percent of the California electorate voted to adopt Proposition 36 (the Substance Abuse and Crime Prevention Act, or SACPA, not to be confused with the Proposition 36 initiated in 2012 relating to three strikes). The original Proposition 36 forced legislators to invest $120 million a year in (and subsequently sentence convicted offenders to use) a proven treatment program for nonviolent drug users.[20] Leading up to the 2000 vote, proponents brought several facts to the attention of voters: (1) a 1994 California Drug and Alcohol Treatment Assessment (CALDATA) study showed that community treatment reduced criminal activity by 72 percent—which meant savings of seven dollars for every one dollar needed for the program;[21] (2) it would save $100 million annually and would delay building a new prison that would cost taxpayers half a billion dollars; and (3) 59 percent of police chiefs supported the program. It is important to note that the California voters were influenced by *evidence*, which is unfortunately not yet true of many legislators.

So the legislature invested the $120 million in the community treatment centers, and offenders started to participate. In 2006, an evaluation was completed after six years of the program. It showed large reductions in costs because of the reduced use of prisons and jails. Every $1.00 invested in the program saved $2.50—savings that increased to $4.00 for those offenders who completed the program.[22] The evaluation made a number of suggestions, including the use of courts to supervise and force offenders to take part in treatment.[23] An offender treatment program (OTP) was added in 2006 to enhance the outcomes and accountability of the program.[24] But sadly, a shortsighted budget cut the funding to this smart approach, and despite these clear cost benefits and targeted strategies for improvement, funding for Proposition 36 was eliminated by legislators effective July 1, 2009. Sadly, legislators prefer to use taxpayers' money to pay for mass incarceration, regardless of the facts.

Mental Health Courts and Community Treatment Centers

In the 1960s and 1970s, mentally ill persons were released from institutions in droves and sent out into the community. Indeed, over those two decades, about five hundred thousand mentally ill persons were decarcerated, at huge savings to taxpayers. Unfortunately, funding did not come through for the community treatment centers and programs necessary to fulfill the promise of the research and enable mentally ill persons to be managed within the community. So the result is that many mentally ill persons are left to get into difficulties, which some of them do and which sometimes require the intervention of law enforcement. Unfortunately for victims and for taxpayers, the courts do not know where to put these offenders other than to incarcerate them.[25] One very sad statistic is that the three largest facilities that house the mentally ill today are actually jails.[26]

In 2012, a major study looked at the mental health status of twenty thousand adults booked into five jails in New York and Maryland. It found that more than 14 percent of male and 31 percent of female inmates had a serious mental illness—about three times the rate of that found in the general population.[27] The true proportions may be dramatically worse. For instance, the Bureau of Justice Statistics estimates that more than 50 percent of those incarcerated have mental health problems.[28] Sadly, neither of these estimates includes those with alcohol- and drug-related disorders, which are themselves exhibited by well above 60 percent of the incarcerated population.[29]

Among the innovations to cope with mentally ill offenders was the development of mental health courts. Today, there are more than 250 of these courts, and the number is growing. They share many of the characteristics of drug courts: they offer a way to avoid the costs of incarceration, they open up opportunities for treatment, and they combine treatment with possible sanctions to keep the person in treatment.

Overall, the general evaluations of the impact of mental health courts on rates of reoffending are positive but tentative; because these courts are a recent invention, there are relatively few good evaluations of them. On average, these meta-analyses suggest that mental health courts can bring about a 30 percent reduction in reoffending for those who complete the program. That's a reduction from an average 40 percent reoffending rate to a 28 percent reoffending rate for those who complete the treatment.[30] The evidence shows benefits to victims and taxpayers of seven dollars for each dollar invested, which is an impressive return and justifies much wider reinvestment into these courts.[31]

Even so, it must be considered only one tool in efforts to stop mentally ill persons from harming victims. Ultimately, it must be accompanied by investment in community mental health treatment centers and diversion from incarceration. A British review of what to do about the mentally ill and criminal justice proposes a portfolio of actions, including community treatment centers (that have nothing to do with criminal justice), diversion from the courts to such treatment centers, and enriched programs for cases when offenders return to the criminal justice system. The two key components of the UK plan are (1) adequate funding and (2) a health and criminal justice board to spearhead the implementation of the pragmatic reforms.[32] Maybe we need to take a leaf from the United Kingdom and reinvest expenditures on incarceration into community mental health centers and set up a board to spearhead this action nationwide.

Alternative Sentence Planners

Another impressive innovation to stop reoffending and thereby reduce harm to future victims was introduced by the San Francisco district attorney in 2013. He wanted to use the moneys allocated by the California Realignment Act to focus on effective programs that were known to reduce reoffending rates. He created a position in the courthouse for an alternative sentence planner, whose job is to make case-specific recommendations about what sentence would most reduce the likelihood of reoffending. This appointee is also responsible for assessing what local programs are most likely to help stop reoffending.[33] This is one example of how taxpayers' money can be smartly used to make real strides toward building communities with less crime. Every court should have one.

A *SMART* LOOK AT OUR EXISTING COURT SYSTEMS

Is there enough social will to demand that courts get smart about sentencing and begin to ration their use of expensive incarceration so that funds are available for the prevention of crime and reoffending?

Some ideologues believe, without scientific basis, that putting even minor offenders behind bars is the "right" thing to do—no matter what the cost to taxpayers. But in reality, criminal justice is often about getting justice for the accused, not the victim. Unfortunately, taxpayers pay the price of being victimized as well as the price of bringing (or *trying* to bring) the accused to "justice" and then helps pay for incarceration through taxes until the offender is out on the streets again—without undergoing any proven programs to prevent reoffending and stop revictimization.

Improved Sentencing Commissions

A growing consensus among experts is that courts need to be held more accountable for their outcomes. Some experts have proposed that judges should be given a budget like any other professional and then be held accountable for the results. This budget would enable judges to trade off a certain number of hours in community treatment programs and a certain number of years of incarceration so that the taxpayers funds are allocated optimally, and so victims are protected by programs that stop reoffending. For instance, violent, dangerous, and serious offenders would be given longer sentences, while less serious offenders would be given a combination of shorter sentences and community rehabilitation. The chief justice would have an emergency fund for exceptional circumstances, but the use of this money would have to be justified. Judges would then set priorities on the use of their budget.

In a system like this, accountability would be measured by the number of persons rearrested within a certain period of time following the sentence, as compared to the rearrest rate of previous years. In this way, judges would have a real interest in ensuring that reoffending rates were as low as possible. Their attention would turn from following reactive procedures to focusing on strategies that stop future crime and spare future victims.

In terms of reforming sentencing, the main effort in the United States thus far has been to establish sentencing commissions. Essentially, sentencing commissions are intended to introduce greater consistency and proportionality (fairness) in sentencing. After all, sentencing is in fact a subjective human process, and different judges may come to different conclusions about what a "fair" punishment would be in a particular situation. Therefore, sentencing commissions provide somewhat objective guidelines for judges to follow during the sentencing process.

One of the first sentencing commissions in the United States was the Minnesota Sentencing Guidelines Commission, established in 1978.[34]

The commission, which still exists today, comprises a Supreme Court justice, the commissioner of corrections, two trial court judges, a prosecutor, a defender, a law enforcement representative, a parole agent, and two citizen members. The role of the commission is to develop guidelines so that sentencing is fairer.

Like most sentencing commissions, the Minnesota Commission integrates two principles. The first is about consistency of sentencing among different judges. The second is the seriousness of the offense and the offender's criminal history. Using the second principle, the commission developed a matrix that sets out the offender's criminal history on one axis and the seriousness of the offense on the other axis in order to calculate a fair and consistent sentence. This matrix was approved by the legislature in 1980. In the first year of its application, there was a 72 percent decrease in property offenders with moderate criminal histories going to prison and an equivalent increase in violent offenders with little criminal history going to prison. This makes some sense, as it protects potential victims from the more serious harm committed by violent offenders.

In terms of prison sentences, Minnesota tackled the additional task of coordinating sentencing practices with the availability of incarceration space. In effect, they modified the sentencing matrix/guidelines in order to avoid overcrowding. This prediction strategy also provides information to the legislature so that it does not adopt new bills that will result in overcrowding and the need to build new prisons.[35] Again, it makes sense because the legislators can decide how much they are willing to pay for incarceration rather than have to find the money because they had not thought about the fiscal consequences of giving judges freedom to sentence as they saw fit. This makes sense to taxpayers, as the total need for incarceration remains steady under these guidelines.

Since the 1980s, about half of US states have sentencing commissions, many of which resemble that in Minnesota. While they do go some way in imposing fairness of sentencing, there is still a lot of room to leverage the use of sentencing commissions to make smarter decisions about what sort of sentences will actually stop certain offenders from committing further crime—and from hurting additional victims. Fortunately, we already have the scientific knowledge we need to enhance the sentencing guidelines to reduce reoffending (as is discussed in chapter 4), and it would be a small innovation to provide commissions with the science on risk and how to reduce it.[36]

SOLVING CRIME PROBLEMS OUTSIDE OF THE COURTS

One smart discussion to have in regard to improving the justice system so that it *solves* crime problems instead of just punishing crime is to consider how to deal with matters of justice *outside* of standard criminal courts. For instance, diversion from the courts, the use of targeted cautioning, and the decriminalization of marijuana are all pragmatic ways to solve crime problems without engaging expensive court systems.

Diversion

Since the 1960s, justice system reformers in affluent democracies have argued that it is best to avoid getting nonviolent offenders involved with the court system at all. The result has been the diversion of offenders from the courts, often informally but also following official guidelines. In the United States, diversion has taken many forms—most often involving law enforcement or prosecutors diverting mentally ill and drug- and alcohol-addicted offenders away from courts and into community treatment programs.

One major benefit of diversion is the enormous cost savings to the public. Indeed, the results from a random control trial of one diversion-based treatment program in California saw less incarceration, greater outpatient contacts, and fewer hospital stays. Savings exceed $18,000 per offender but have varied from study to study because of sizeable differentials in costs; for instance, community-based treatment services may cost only $12 a day for adults, as opposed to a night behind bars at $137 or an emergency room visit at $986.[37]

Importantly, an assessment of the outcomes of diversion programs for the seriously mentally ill and those with alcohol and drug problems shows that diversion programs achieve these cost savings *without* increasing the likelihood of reoffending.[38] One recent study in Wisconsin that followed offenders with drug and alcohol problems showed that only 24 percent of those referred to diversion programs were rearrested within three years, as compared to a 38 percent rearrest rate for those coming out of incarceration.[39] This study also showed two dollars of savings in court costs for each dollar spent on diversion.

New York State has been at the leading edge of diversion programs. Its Classification/Alternatives to Incarceration Act was established in 1984 to provide funding for an array of alternatives to incarceration, and it has the largest network of alternatives to incarceration programs in the United States. For instance, the Drug Treatment Alternative to Prison program, established by the Brooklyn District Attorney's Office to divert thousands of prison-bound defendants into treatment programs, has ultimately expanded to prosecutors' offices statewide. What's most impressive about New York's diversion programs is that, unlike other large states such as California, Florida, and Texas, New York has seen crime and incarceration rates plummet *simultaneously*, thereby showing that improving public safety and reducing the numbers of victims can also save much-needed revenue.

Other regions in the United States have taken notice of how New York's programs to divert offenders from jails and prisons seem to effectively stop crime. For example, one San Diego diversion program's goal is to offer positive and more cost-efficient programs to *prevent* further risky behavior such as gang involvement.[40] Referrals to diversion programs such as this can also come from schools, courts, probation departments, child protective services, or even parents.[41]

One sophisticated study of the economic benefits of diverting non-violent offenders with substance problems from incarceration to community treatment has identified nationwide net benefits in savings on criminal justice costs (primarily incarceration) of $12 billion when 40 percent of these offenders are diverted. The reduced crime rates that would result also mean cost savings to society—primarily costs to would-be victims—of $22 billion.[42]

Studies such as these provide good reason for reinvesting the moneys saved from the overuse of mass incarceration into the diversion of nonviolent offenders. It is likely that similar results would be gained by diverting some violent offenders as well, but more improvements in treatments and extensive outcome evaluations would be needed before any widespread use could be justified.

Formal and Informal Cautioning by Police

Another way to keep less serious offenders out of the expensive criminal justice system is to have law enforcement caution them as a warning not to reoffend. In the 1960s, the United Kingdom legislated a nationwide cautioning system whereby offenders of less serious offenses such as shoplifting, vandalism, or theft were brought to the police station and formally cautioned. This approach enabled law enforcement to officially record that the offender had been caught but that no other corrective action was planned. Subsequently, a process of enhanced cautioning was instituted whereby the offender was referred to some community agency that might reduce the likelihood of reoffending by offering treatment, community service, or both.

The result of keeping these misdemeanor offenders out of the criminal justice system is significant cost savings. Unfortunately, there is no evidence on whether these programs work to reduce the number of crime victims or save taxpayers money in the future, although logically they are believed to do both.[43] No evidence does not mean they don't work—it only means that sadly, politicians have not focused on innovations that have the potential to save money while avoiding reoffending.

In the Netherlands, the HALT program is a diversion program for less serious offenders that began as a small one-off project in Rotterdam in 1981. It has since spread to become a national institution whereby juveniles involved in minor offenses such as vandalism are required by law enforcement or the prosecuting authorities to repair the damage and to participate in treatment programs. This approach has now been multiplied across sixty-five sites across the Netherlands, and a national agency provides coaching and assistance to local HALT projects. The reductions in reoffending are impressive at 70 percent. This is certainly a model for smart politicians and legislators to explore further.

Restorative Justice

A few victims who want heavy punishment tend to focus on ideology (i.e., offenders should be punished) rather than on restitution (i.e., offenders should try to make things right for victims). France has a court system where the victim has standing—yes, the victim is represented by a lawyer—to ask for restitution. Estimates are that 50 percent of cases in French criminal courts are settled when the offender demonstrates that restitution had been paid to the victim.[44]

Internationally, a movement for such "restorative justice" is growing. The concept is appealing. Its proponents talk about the need to help victims work through their feelings and reach a resolution with offenders. It is expected that this process helps to support victims through emotional processes and trauma following the victimization. One of the concept's tenets is that crime is a violation of not only the victim but also the community as a whole, and so it may also advance the restoration of the community.

There are several models for restorative justice. The basic elements include some type of meeting between the victim and the offender (if both agree), with a professional coordinator or mediator organizing the meeting. Some types of restoration are called "victim-offender reconciliation" because the main objective is to reach reconciliation between the victim and the offender. Other types are called "circle sentencing" because community members sit in a circle to listen to the victim, the offender, and other community members talk about what happened before deciding on a sentence for the offender.

The evidence supporting the satisfactory effects of restorative justice for victims is strong. Research shows that victims feel much less angry after going through this process than if they had gone through the standard court process.[45] In addition to satisfying the needs of victims, restorative justice also offers cost savings when compared with the traditional court process. One UK study found that for every British pound spent on delivering restorative justice, more than one pound was saved in direct criminal justice costs, and nine pounds were saved in fighting the cost of crime (including costs to victims and society).[46]

For evidence on how restorative justice has successfully reduced reoffending and revictimization, we can look to Heather Strang and Larry Sherman's review of the research on international restorative justice programs up to 2007. They stress that not only were victims more satisfied with restorative justice than they were with the traditional court system, but the evidence shows that it saved taxpayers money by avoiding the use of the courts and incarceration.[47] Their conclusions went on to include some evidence to show that reoffending rates for some of-

fenders who went through restorative justice were lower than the reoffending rates for offenders who were incarcerated. More specifically, a
2008 report for the British government confirmed that using restorative
justice with adult offenders who committed serious crimes such as assault, robbery, and burglary reduced the frequency of reconviction by
an average of 27 percent.[48] Unfortunately, there are no meta-analyses to
confirm these conclusions.

However, the most recent international review (this one commis-
sioned by the Australian government) is more cautious in its conclusions
about the ability of restorative justice to reduce rates of reoffending.
This review emphasizes that restorative justice as a concept "is not based
on any generally accepted theory about the determinants of offending,
and was never designed to reduce the risk factors known to be associated
with involvement in crime (e.g., drug and alcohol abuse, poor impulse
control, association with delinquent/criminal peers)."[49] For restorative
justice to become part of smarter crime control, therefore, its qualities
of satisfying the victim and saving taxpayers money must be combined
with innovations that are proven to reduce reoffending.[50]

Decriminalizing Marijuana Use

One of the most important examples of the positive impact of avoiding
the criminal court system is in the area of illegal drug use. On any given
day, more than 500,000 persons are incarcerated in the United States on
charges that specifically relate to drugs. They make up about 22 percent
of the jail population (167,000 inmates), 18 percent of the state prison
population (242,000 inmates), and another 45 percent of the federal
prison population (98,000 inmates).[51] Not all of these inmates were
sentenced for nonviolent offenses, however, and not all were sentenced
for only drug offenses. Still, in many cases, this equals a lot of taxpayers'
money for minimal (or no) protection for crime victims.[52]

The European Monitoring Centre on Drugs gathers detailed data on
drug use, public health policy, and crime policy for members of the European Union and some other countries such as Norway and the United
States. In its annual report for 2011, it used survey data to compare
marijuana use in several European countries. It showed that marijuana
use was increasing in some countries but decreasing in others. It found

no relationship between increased criminalization (i.e., increasingly severe penalties) and decreased use.[53]

In part thanks to good research like this, in 2012 the US states of Colorado and Washington voted to decriminalize the use of marijuana. Marijuana had already been legal for medicinal use in approximately twenty states.[54] Politicians in New York State such as the governor and the mayor of New York City want to change their laws around drug possession and use in that state but not to go as far as Colorado or Washington. But even though more than 50 percent of Americans across the country are in favor of some degree of legalization, federal legislation still considers marijuana a narcotic at the time of this writing.[55]

Though the Netherlands has never changed its laws to decriminalize or legalize the possession of marijuana for personal use, law enforcement and prosecutorial authorities in the city of Amsterdam have had a declared policy since 1976 of not using criminal powers or penalties against personal use—what amounts to de facto legalization—but this does not apply to big-time traffickers. This non-enforcement policy has resulted in a system of three hundred cannabis cafés that have evolved since the 1980s. These cafés, which are licensed by the city, provide a location for both buying and using marijuana. Despite the ease of purchase and public use, marijuana is generally used at lower levels in the Netherlands than in other European countries.[56] The Netherlands also has one of the lowest rates of heroin use in Europe, which challenges the belief that marijuana is a "gateway drug."

One particularly interesting piece of research has compared marijuana enforcement strategies in San Francisco (enforcement) and Amsterdam (non-enforcement).[57] The study compared surveys of experienced marijuana users in both cities and found little difference in use. The conclusion from that study was that the criminalization of marijuana does not impact the use of marijuana by experienced marijuana users in any major way. However, it *does* impact the use of incarceration, for so many of the young black men held behind bars in the United States were convicted of the felony of possessing marijuana, sometimes in public view because they were on the street when arrested.

It is estimated that the legalization of marijuana would save about $9 billion for taxpayers annually—mostly in reduced costs of incarceration—without any increase in harm to potential victims.[58] Further, if it were taxed in a similar way to tobacco or alcohol, states would likely be able to collectively collect another $9 billion in annual revenue. Any progress like this would need to go along with reinvestment in proven programs in schools that enable youths to decide not to use drugs, such as Life Skills Training, which is discussed in the next chapter. The 2013 national drug control strategy recognizes an eighteen-dollar benefit for each dollar invested in these programs in schools.[59]

AREAS THAT REQUIRE MORE KNOWLEDGE TO SUPPORT SMARTER SENTENCING AND COURTS

Courts Are Lagging Behind on Data and Research to Improve Their Effectiveness

It is striking and disappointing that so little has been done to research and develop solutions for the courts. They are lagging behind the advances in law enforcement, corrections, and prevention. An important start would be to routinely collect data on persons appearing in front of the courts. This should be a nationwide initiative and could be based in part on the UK's National Offender Management System (but with much more data on costs, whether restitution is paid, and whether reoffending occurs).

Furthermore, the courts would greatly benefit from a user-friendly website such as the likes of crimesolutions.gov that had a special focus on helping courts direct appropriate responses to offenders and victims within the court system. Having this kind of data available is the only way to truly enable inspiring innovations, such as San Francisco's sentence planner, to be effective. Such information would also inform various problem-specific courts, such as domestic violence courts, which focus on connecting victims to the best resources available.

Domestic Violence Courts Intimate partner violence cases take on a variety of complex, clustered issues, including divorce proceedings, alimony decisions, and criminal violence issues. To better tackle this myriad of interwoven issues, domestic violence courts have come into being. The number of these courts is growing, but too slowly. Today, there are two hundred to three hundred domestic violence courts in more than thirty states.

The typical domestic violence court has the same judge permanently assigned to all proceedings between the victim and his or her offender spouse. There is a concerted effort to fast-track proceedings and a concentrated focus on victim safety. There is also a key component that is missing in so many other criminal courts: a resource coordinator, whose job is to bring together necessary social services as well as support for the victim. Indeed, victim support is paramount, and the best domestic violence courts make sure that victims don't feel "used" by the courts to get convictions.[60] One evaluation from the U.K., where similar efforts have also led to the creation of this type of court, indicates 3 key benefits of domestic violence courts: (1) that the "clustering" and "fast-tracking" of aspects of domestic violence cases enhances the effectiveness of the court and of the support services for victims; (2) that these arrangements make advocacy and information-sharing easier to accomplish; and (3) that victim participation and satisfaction is improved, and thus public confidence in the criminal justice system is increased overall.

Although domestic violence courts have undergone a number of evaluations, what is not so clear in either the United States or the United Kingdom is the impact of domestic violence courts on reoffending rates and on repeat victimization. US reviews focus particularly on offender accountability and deterrence.[61] One recent evaluation of twenty-four domestic violence courts in New York State focused on their impact on reoffending rates but was able to identify only some very modest improvements.[62] However, the programs it was evaluating were not using the smartest approaches for reducing repeat domestic offending.[63] In fact, in practice, there is still little consensus in how to best achieve this goal. For example, some domestic violence courts use treatment programs for batterers as well as alcohol and drug abuse treatment programs and mental health treatment programs. The result is that these general approaches likely have room for more fine-tuning and evaluation of outcomes. One important evaluation of treatment strategies for domestic violence was cautious about the most common treatment model—the Duluth model—but optimistic about what could happen if effective treatments were used in its place.[64]

Although their impacts on offenders might not be cut and dried, domestic violence courts clearly offer a better process for victims, and thus they fall into the category of "smart" innovations. However, when it comes to achieving sizeable reductions in harm to victims, there must be a renewed focus to find out what works in terms of treatment for batterers.

Problem Analysis Courts While problem-solving courts have led to many effective ways to reduce costs and stop reoffending, they have not yet focused on tackling the roots of the general problems that lead to crime in the first place. However, there are existing models that the criminal court system can turn to in order to hone its focus on stopping future crime by concentrating more on the causes of problems. For instance, coroners' courts investigate deaths and make recommendations for actions that will avoid that same sort of death in the future. Similarly, there is a need for criminal courts to become dedicated to analyzing the causes of crime in order to spare future victims and avoid wasting taxes. For instance, courts could be required to include in their sentencing decisions recommendations for improvements to the existing crime-control strategies; these recommendations could mention issues such as increased funding for community treatment centers or smart enforcement of gun laws. This would amount to only a small addition to judges' workloads and would surely be a valuable use of their significant abilities.

Response to Victims Regrettably, the needs of crime victims are not a high priority in criminal courts. In my 2010 book *Rights for Victims of Crime*, I have proposed specific ways for courts to pay more attention to the need of victims to not be revictimized, to get restitution, and to feel that the justice process has respected them. This focus would necessarily impact costs but would importantly encourage justice even for victims.[65]

Decriminalization of Other Illicit Drugs An important analysis of the long-term trends in drug use and incarceration showed that even as incarceration skyrocketed in the 1980s and 1990s, the price of marijuana, cocaine, crack cocaine, and heroin dropped almost as rapidly, while the number of drug-related visits to emergency departments grew almost as fast as the incarceration rate.[66] This is a clear case of supply and demand: if supply shrinks, the price increases; if supply increases (as it apparently did in this case), then the price decreases. And if drug use increases, more people go to emergency departments with drug-related problems. This analysis provides clear evidence that the arrests and prison sentences made in the name of the very expensive war on drugs did little to help solve the drug problem and, in fact, may have made it *worse.*

In April 2013, an impressive list of superstars that included leaders from civil rights movements, the faith community, politics, business, academia, and entertainment signed a letter to President Obama calling on him to go further in pursuing alternatives to the "enforcement-only" war on drugs, referring to the isolationist way that I have shown law enforcement and courts to operate in this book. The letter also emphasized, like I have, that these are only *reactions* to drug problems from their isolationist standpoints. The signers of the letter criticize the iron fist being used.[67] The press release that accompanied this letter called for "new approaches to [the] failed drug war" and asked for a "move from criminal justice toward [a] public health approach" that favors evidence-based prevention and rehabilitation.[68] The letter cites drug treatment as being seven times more effective than incarceration and connects reexamining the war on drugs with a plea for changes to the system of mass incarceration. They had done their research, as I have, to help the president formulate smarter policies.

Simply detaining those convicted of drug offenses if they are nonviolent is not the best use of taxpayers' dollars. Indeed, in order to save money down the road, drug treatment needs to come into play as soon as possible—even before the court stage if possible. One study by the Washington State Institute for Public Policy (WSIPP) found that for each dollar spent on drug treatment in prison, six dollars is reaped in savings. Although this is clearly a good return on investment, it is not as good as if the user had received drug treatment *before* offending in the first place or if the user had not been incarcerated at all (at great cost to taxpayers). After all, as mentioned for marijuana, for every dollar spent on community-based (i.e., non-prison-related) drug treatment programs, over eighteen dollars is saved in public safety and monetary spending.[69]

The Global Commission on Drug Policy brought together leaders from across the world who had recently held top political appointments. This commission looked at the evidence on what was working—and what was not working—when it comes to drugs. Notably, it brought together good research on a number of significant changes in criminal courts to justify their proposal to make drug users *patients* rather than criminals.[70]

Portugal is an example of a country that has formally decriminalized the use of all drugs, including marijuana use, in 2001.[71] The Portuguese variation took all offenses regarding illicit drug possession for personal use out of the criminal courts and referred them to a civil tribunal designed to reduce use through referring users to treatment facilities. Though one study showed some marginal increase in marijuana use after decriminalization, the increase matched that occurring at the same time in nearby Spain and Italy (where marijuana laws were still enforced).[72] Another very important postlegalization trend that relates to crime victims is that the proportion of imprisoned offenders in Portugal who after release committed serious criminal offenses under the influence of drugs and/or to fund drug use dropped from 44 percent before decriminalization to 21 percent after.[73] While some of this drop can be attributed to a general reduction in intravenous drug use across various European countries, the drop remains an important consideration for politicians.

The other form of decriminalization that has received some evidence-based analysis is the medical prescription of heroin for heroin addicts. A study in Vancouver, Canada, showed this to be effective in reducing harm to crime victims and costs to taxpayers for health services.[74] The best-known example of this comes from Switzerland, where, following scientific evaluation that showed it to be effective, a proposition to legalize prescription heroin was approved through a public referendum.[75] To date, there have been no studies on how this change has affected criminal justice costs or revictimization rates.

Another example of averting drug-related offenses from criminal courts is the decriminalization of the injection of cocaine, heroin, or other illicit drugs at safe injection sites. These sites are not so much about stopping the use of illicit drugs as they are about reducing the harm that results from their use, including stopping the spread of HIV and hepatitis C as well as preventing overdoses. Switzerland is one country that set up such sites following a referendum that presented evidence on their harm-reduction qualities. Vancouver, too, has been home to an experimental safe injection site. In both cities, users still have to buy their drugs in an illicit market. The evaluations of the Vancouver safe injection site show no increase in the numbers of victims of property offenses associated with the experiment and importantly have shown no increases in the appeal of drug addictions in Vancouver—for the first law of drug addiction is that no one wants to be a drug addict. Based on these evaluations, the Canadian courts—yes, the courts—have ruled these sites to be acceptable, as they meet a health need for the users. As a result, other Canadian jurisdictions will be implementing similar projects in the future.

Clearly, any move to a Swiss, or Portuguese, or Vancouver model must be associated with careful research and must respect not only the needs of potential crime victims but also those of the communities where the drug use occurs.

CONCLUSIONS

Points to Note: Smarter Strategies for the Effective Use of Criminal Courts

US courts handle more than one million felony convictions every year. Most of these offenders come from prison and go back to prison—and leave a trail of victims in between. Clearly, something about the existing criminal justice system just isn't working to reduce reoffending, and it is costing victims and taxpayers dearly.

Pragmatic solutions have been demonstrated to improve on the current isolationist court systems, including problem-solving courts that focus on communities, drugs, and (to a lesser extent) alcohol and the mentally ill. Guiding the courts on what works is important, and more data are needed to enable this.

Sentencing commissions could also be improved to provide more effective reductions in reoffending rates and certainly greater budgetary control over incarceration. Avoiding the courts through diversion, restorative justice, and the decriminalization of marijuana would save billions of dollars for taxpayers without any increases in harm to potential victims. Developments in Canada and Portugal to decriminalize "hard" drugs also suggest this would save taxpayers money without increasing harm to victims.

More work is needed on domestic violence courts in terms of what treatments are effective. Innovations to analyze what courts can do to tackle the roots of crime problems and to better engage victims also need further work.

Actions for Politicians to Stop Crime and Reduce Costs by Avoiding Unwarranted Use of Criminal Courts

1. Legislators and courts must:
   a. Shift sentencing away from proportionality and consistency and toward embracing crime reduction (particularly the reduction of reoffending);
   b. Use a budget for "correctional measures" and hold judges accountable for controlling the overuse of incarceration and for inducing crime reduction;
   c. Be informed of effective ways to reduce reoffending, such as advisers to the San Francisco DA.
2. Legislators must invest in problem-solving courts while reinvesting adequately in community treatments, including:
   a. Drug courts for offenders engaging in violent and property crimes (see point 5 below for others);
   b. California's Proposition 36, which reduced violence and costs while avoiding prison construction;
   c. Community and mental health courts that focus on proven treatments, including evaluation of their impact on crime reduction and cost savings;
   d. Domestic violence courts because they protect victims, but we must find more effective ways to stop domestic violence offenders from reoffending.
3. Legislators must require police and prosecutors to divert:
   a. Less serious offenders (i.e., shoplifters or vandals) from the courts and adapt the UK cautioning system while investing in effective community treatment centers.
   b. Cases to restorative justice, where victims get more satisfaction while fostering greater use of proven ways of reducing reoffending.
4. Legislators should act to legalize marijuana, as doing so does not increase general use or other drug abuse but would save many billions of taxpayer dollars on isolationist law enforcement, courts, and corrections, while decreasing the criminogenic aspects of the drug war and felony convictions that have contributed to too many crime victims.

5. Legislators should carefully study the recommendations from the Global Commission to decriminalize certain illicit drugs and use public health strategies for other illicit drugs, for this has not led to increases in illicit drug abuse or common crime rates in other jurisdictions.

6. Legislators must invest in a national data system so that they and the courts can monitor and improve the actions of the courts in the interests of avoiding harm to victims and saving taxpayers' costs.

This chapter shows that although courts can play a limited role in reducing offending by becoming more invested in problem solving, the main ways to save taxpayers money are to divert and decriminalize behavior that does not cause harm to victims.

4

CORRECTING CORRECTIONS

Away from Mass Incarceration
and Toward Stopping Crime

INTRODUCTION

Interestingly, the idea that prisons and probation should *correct* is a relatively new one. Centuries ago, prisons were merely detention centers that held inmates until final action could be taken. For example, debtors were held until they paid; felons were held until the judge sentenced them to death or transportation.

Much has changed since the 1770s, when the famous British prison reformer John Howard promoted the reformatory treatment of prisoners and the abolition of capital punishment. Today, we consider barbaric prisons to be almost a novelty, to the point where the infamous federal prison at Alcatraz became a park and a movie set; Boston's Charles Street Jail became a luxury hotel; and the old jail in Ottawa, Canada, became a popular youth hostel. Slowly, however, many prisons in affluent democracies have again become institutions that are primarily designed to detain people, not correct them. Nowhere is this more true than in the United States.

This marks an unfortunate slide backward, because our correctional institutions used to be much more advanced. Following World War II, both California and the United Kingdom boasted the world's most advanced correctional programs based on the best research for effectiveness. Not only could the likelihood of reoffending be predicted from basic data in an inmate's files, but innovations had shown that these rates of reoffending could actually be *reduced*—at least in part. In particular, the California Youth Authority had developed a maturity scale, which it used to decide what types of treatment would most effectively work to correct specific types of young men. In the United Kingdom, so-called borstals were flourishing as a prison alternative, where young offenders lived in rural colonies and were reformed by model mentors who were also their guards.

So how have today's "correctional" institutions backtracked to become undereffective holding facilities that come with an extraordinarily hefty price tag for taxpayers—$80 billion a year, in fact—and employ close to eight hundred thousand persons, most of whom are guards? A system about which US Attorney General Eric Holder said, "Too many Americans go to too many prisons for far too long and for no good law enforcement reason"?[1]

This chapter looks at some of today's primary misconceptions about corrections—namely, that more is better, and that particularly punitive models are better—as a first step toward deconstructing where our legislators have let us down. It then proposes relatively easy, pragmatic reforms that our existing correctional facilities can adopt to reduce future reoffending and victimization—that is, to effectively *correct*. This chapter doesn't intend to offer a "miracle cure" for violence or government overspending; what it does offer, however, is smarter alternatives to the United States' seemingly insatiable appetite for incarceration as its primary form of crime control.

MORE IS *NOT* BETTER: HOW THE UNITED STATES' EXPENSIVE ADDICTION TO PRISONS IS NOT SMART AND IS FAILING ITS MARGINALIZED COMMUNITIES

Hyperincarceration

In the United States today, the incarceration industry holds 2.2 million offenders. Most of these inmates are men, and disproportionately they are young black men. Most of them are being held for typical felonies (i.e., murder, violent crimes, robbery, burglary) that do harm to victims, but as we have seen, many others are there for drug offenses.

Today we know the shocking prison statistics, but up until the 1960s, the United States did not keep detailed statistics on who was behind bars (unlike most other affluent democracies). In the 1960s, the President's Commission on Law Enforcement and Criminal Justice pumped unprecedented funds into getting data on crime, law enforcement, courts, and corrections.[2] For the first time, the United States got numbers on its jails (i.e., county-run facilities) to add to its data on prisons (i.e., state and federal facilities). The results confirmed that the United States—the global champion of human rights and freedom, hot on the heels of the radical reforms of the civil rights movement—was the free world's leading jailer. Per capita in the 1970s, the United States had at least double the number of people behind bars as Canada or the United Kingdom. Only undemocratic countries such as Russia and South Africa had higher numbers of inmates. Many were shocked.

Few would have predicted that the US use of incarceration would soon skyrocket from around 500,000 incarcerated in 1980 to 2.3 million in 2010 on an average day. Of these, approximately 1.3 million are being held in state prisons, another 207,000 are being held in federal prisons, and 749,000 are being held in local county jails. The speed with which this growth took place is shown in figure 4.1. Of those in local county jails, about 460,000 are not yet convicted and are being held awaiting trial.[3]

As we saw, this rate of incarceration means that more than 700 people out of every 100,000 are incarcerated—as compared to Canada and Europe, where around 100 people per 100,000 are incarcerated (see figure 1.3 in chapter 1).[4] Shockingly, the total represents 20 percent of all prisoners being held in the entire world.[5] The US rate of incarceration now exceeds that in Russia (at 490 per 100,000), which successfully reduced its incarceration rates by a wide margin.[6] So we are now left asking ourselves, "What has gone wrong?" Did this unique and expensive experiment help crime victims or use taxpayers' money well?

At just the state level and recalculating the rate for adults, one in every 107 adults is incarcerated. That's a spike of more than 700 percent since 1970.[7] Curiously, California is celebrating taking thirty thousand inmates out of its state-funded prisons while it realigns them into county

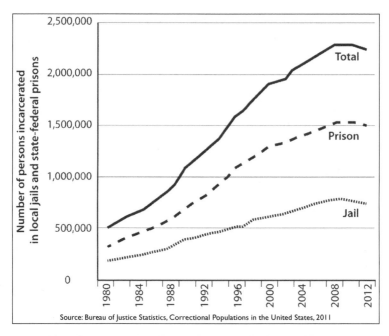

Figure 4.1 Mass Incarceration: Rates Quadrupled from 1980 to 2010

jails administered by local governments. This seems to be a smoke-and-mirrors operation for the taxpayers, who pay either way. The federal system, too, has seen a 790 percent increase during that time. The system has become known as "mass incarceration," but I prefer "hyper-incarceration." And all this in the land of the free and the home of small government. Whichever way you look at the statistics, the reality is that no other country on earth has invested so much money in keeping so many of its people behind bars or has allowed such a rapid increase in its number of prisoners. Indeed, no other democracy in the history of civilization has even come close.

Not surprisingly, all of this does not come cheap. The bill for mass incarceration is over $80 billion a year.[8] Of this, the local government—counties—pay $26 billion a year for jails, and the states pay close to $50 billion a year for their prisons, accounting for one out of every fourteen general-fund dollars. What's more, one in every eight state employees—whose salaries are paid for by taxpayer dollars—works for a corrections agency.[9] The number of employees at the federal, state, and local level grew from around 400,000 in 1980 to 785,000 in 2010, with another 25,000 working in private facilities.[10] If the United States as a whole (at the local, state, and federal government levels) were to reduce the rate of incarceration to its own immodest rate in 1970, when crime levels were similar to today, it would save $55 billion annually. If it were to reduce the number of prisoners behind bars to levels such as those in other affluent democracies in Europe or Canada, it would save $70 billion a year.

These alarming numbers also have a necessary flip side—growing numbers of ex-inmates being released from behind bars. More than 650,000 men leave state prisons each year. Between 40–60 percent of these men will be caught for reoffending (and labeled recidivists) and will be back behind bars within three years, leaving yet another victim (or many more) in their wake. Another nine million persons are being released each year from county jails, with equally dim results. This is not quite as bad as the court statistics of 75 percent returning, but it should make anyone seriously question whether any correcting is going on in these facilities. Arguably, in this system, incarceration makes crime worse more than it corrects the likelihood that offenders will victimize again.

So if it's not, in fact, *correcting*, what—if anything—is all that public money actually achieving? Is the average US taxpayer getting any value for money by paying for so many persons behind bars? And if not, when will citizens and smart politicians stand up for change?

No Chance to Thrive: Racial Minorities in the Correctional System

There are some apparent trends in incarceration. For instance, the peak ages for incarceration are twenty to twenty-nine, and the rates of incarceration for males dwarf those for women. What's particularly disturbing, however, is that incarceration appears to be racially biased. Indeed, the folly of the US mass incarceration policy is even more depressing when it is looked at along racial lines,[11] for the rate of incarceration for black men is six times as high as for white men. These trends are illustrated in figure 4.2.

Here's another shocking statistic. According to 1991 incarceration rates, the average American male had a 9 percent chance of being incar-

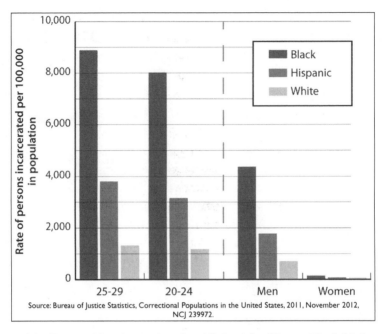

Figure 4.2   **Rates of Incarceration Are Highest for Young Black Males**

cerated in his lifetime. Clearly, this is extremely high. But now consider that the average Hispanic male had a 16 percent chance, and the average black male had an astounding 28.5 percent chance—yes, that's more than a one in four chance of spending part of his life behind bars,[12] and it often resulted in devastating collateral consequences.

The Collateral Consequences of Incarceration

There's another side to this story as well—one that affects entire families and communities. As the saying goes, if you do the crime, you do the time. But in reality, if a person does the time, that person will also experience a raft of negative effects (politely called "collateral consequences") on his or her life after release, including shortened life expectancy, difficulty reengaging in family life, and difficulty in finding and keeping employment—well-established risk factors for chronic offending.[13] While this is true for all prisoners no matter what their race, the sheer magnitude of black and Hispanic prisoners makes it of particular consequence to the "problem places" where they too often come from and go to.

Sadly, one out of every four black children born in the past thirty years has had a parent behind bars for at least part of their childhood.[14] This is one factor that contributes to the disturbing shortage of engaged fathers in disadvantaged neighborhoods. Furthermore, even after being released from incarceration, convicted felons lose their right to vote and so become disenfranchised. Of the total US population, nearly six million people (or 2.5 percent) have been disenfranchised; however, for the black population, more than two million (or 7.7 percent) have been denied the right to vote.[15] This represents a staggering loss of democratic voice among the black community. And when people are unable to vote, they are unable to influence the very services that might help them get jobs and reintegrate into family life—and avoid committing future violence against victims.

One way to alleviate the impact of this consequence is to take a critical look at the threshold for nonviolent felony offenses that do not cause serious harm to victims. For instance, changing the threshold for the least serious felony theft from $500 to $5,000 would keep many less serious offenders from being sentenced for felonies and would avoid their serving lengthy sentences behind bars. The Pew public opinion poll from 1960 saw public support for a shift from $500 to $1,500, but just the inflation increase of $500 in 1960 to 2013 would reach $4,000.

The American Bar Association has set up a website that shows the negative consequences after incarceration for each state.[16] They are also described in Michelle Alexander's seminal book *The New Jim Crow: Mass Incarceration in the Age of Colorblindness*, as well as in Bruce Western's *Punishment and Inequality in America*, which analyzes the fallout of being released from prison. These consequences are not new; I had already demonstrated these problems and their impact on reoffending in my own pioneering study of "Men Released from Prison" back in the 1970s, but the loss of the vote is only one irreversible and devastating consequence that makes the cost of being incarcerated a heavy burden for entire communities to bear.[17]

While all this might sound like misplaced sympathy, it is fundamental to public safety and to civil rights—including the right for all young citizens to grow up within families and communities that at least give them a shot at prospering in a crime-free life. The colossal size of this incarceration system, as well as its enormous costs and, in this case, unnecessary ineffectiveness, are critical to the right for potential victims not to become victims of crime and violence.

THE EFFECTIVENESS OF MASS INCARCERATION: A LOOK AT THE FACTS

Some will argue that prisoners deserve the negative life consequences resulting from their incarceration. Ideologues will argue that offenders have impacted a victim's life, so they deserve no better. Others will choose to overlook the negative impacts on prisoners if they believe the policy leads to fewer victims overall. But do these unprecedented levels of mass incarceration *actually* make a real difference to crime levels?

The evidence suggests not. In 1996, the National Commission on Criminal Justice found that levels of incarceration correlated positively with levels of violence—not the reverse. States such as Louisiana, with higher levels of incarceration, also tend to have higher levels of violent crimes such as murder. So more incarceration generally goes hand in hand with more violence—*not* less violence, as many ideologues might attempt to argue.[18] This has been true for many decades.[19]

Some ideologues might point to Florida as an example of a state that is seeing a rapid rise in incarceration (from 70,000 inmates in the early 2000s to more than 100,000 inmates today) and a simultaneous drop in crime.[20] However, some states such as Massachusetts and New York that have seen more modest prison growth (or none at all) have also experienced dropping levels of violence and property crime. Interestingly, New York's crime drop was slightly larger (29.2 percent) compared with Florida's (28.2 percent), even though New York's prison population has dropped (from 70,000 inmates in the early 2000s to 60,000 inmates today).[21] In fact, in the past couple of decades, New York City has seen an increase in misdemeanors and a decrease in felonies—which means that the offenders who *are* being locked up are getting shorter sentences and are spending less time amid prison culture. Yes, this is happening while crime is still going down.

The previous example confirms that the use of incarceration can be reduced while the crime rate is decreasing. As always, there are pundits who will read different trends into these statistics, but one strong interpretation is that less use of incarceration generally goes with less crime. Still, as with anything to do with incarceration, one should not be too quick to assume cause and effect. Let's look at the research to see what the evidence says.

The Evidence for the Relationship between Crime and Incarceration

A number of sophisticated studies have been performed on the impact of increased incarceration on crime rates in the United States. Importantly, they use statistical modeling to allow for a number of explanations for changes in crime rates other than incarceration alone.

After looking at the US findings, many influential pundits today agree that until around 2005, increased incarceration *did* have at least some effect on decreasing crime rates.[22] The studies suggest that incarceration may have accounted for about 25 percent of the drop in crime.

But the effectiveness of incarceration—even back then—was not explicit. One good estimate is that a 25 percent increase in the number of persons incarcerated might have achieved a 2 percent reduction in rates of crime.[23] So the 300 percent increase in the number of persons incarcerated leading up to 2005 might have achieved a 24 percent decrease in crime rates. Some may argue that a 24 percent decrease in crime is good no matter how you cut it—even if it did take an additional $50 billion increase in annual incarceration spending to accomplish.

But the question remains: Could this same reduction have been achieved more cost-effectively and with fewer outrageous collateral consequences—some of which are proven to actually increase crime? The answer to this is yes.

We know that because, if we look at index crime rates in other affluent democracies such as the United Kingdom and Canada, we can see that crime levels (at least for property crime) have actually dropped without any major changes (or expenditures) in incarceration.[24]

Another contentious issue revolves around the length of time that offenders should serve and the related expenses. From 1990 to 2009, the average length of prison time served in US state prisons grew by 36 percent to an average of thirty-six months. This growth translates into an additional $10 billion-a-year price tag paid for by state taxpayers.[25]

But does this additional $10 billion add any benefit for these taxpayers or make communities any safer? After all, many of these longer sentences were passed for victimless crimes related to drugs, including drug possession. The Pew Center on the States has looked into public opinion regarding reasons for releasing a greater number of nonviolent prisoners after serving only shorter sentences. Their findings show that 78 percent of the public accepts shortening prison time to reduce budget deficits, and 45 percent supports it strongly.[26] So why aren't politicians and legislators listening to this public pulse—especially when it is so much easier on the public purse strings?

A SMART LOOK AT REOFFENDING

If our corrections system is really meant to *correct*, then a reoffending rate of zero should be the end goal. However, among nearly 300,000 prisoners released in fifteen US states in 1994, 67.5 percent were rearrested within three years. A study of prisoners released eleven years previously estimated that 62.5 percent were rearrested.[27] In fact, across the United States, almost half of all released offenders (43 percent) will be thrown back in jail for either reoffending or violating their release conditions—and those are only the ones who are caught.[28]

Clearly, this prison system is failing in terms of "correcting"—and Americans are no longer satisfied with this shortfall. In the public poll conducted for the Pew Center on the States, 87 percent of respondents agreed, and 66 percent *strongly* agreed that "it does not matter whether a nonviolent offender is in prison for 18 or 24 or 30 months. What really matters is that the system does a better job of making sure that when an offender does get out, he is less likely to commit another crime."[29]

Dealing with Repeat Offenders

The ivory tower theory of incarceration favors the idea of imprisoning people to incapacitate them from further offending—that is, they can't commit another offense as long as they remain behind bars. The theory rests, in part, on the fact that a small percentage of offenders account for a large number of offenses. So (the theory goes) if you incarcerate these persistent offenders, you will reduce crime. Right? Well, not necessarily. As you'll see, the idea of putting persistent offenders behind bars might not be as satisfactory to the public as some would hope, and regardless, it is easier said than done.

It is well established that yes, a small number of offenders account for a majority of offenses; a good estimate is that 5–7 percent of offenders account for 55–70 percent of offenses.[30] It is also well established that each of these "chronic" criminals over his or her lifetime will cost victims and taxpayers on average $2 million, with much higher estimates when tighter definitions are used.[31] These offenders tend to come from those areas in cities that police researchers define as problem places. But chronic offenders tend to commit fewer violent crimes and more *property* offenses. So punishing repeat offenders with stricter incarceration would leave many property offenders serving harsher sentences than their violent offending counterparts.

Another issue is that persistent offenders tend to "age out." To give an example based on crime trends, a twenty-five-year-old offender may commit thirty offenses a month. However, by the time he reaches age thirty-five, he may have stopped offending altogether. So incarceration may not be providing any public benefit after such an offender reaches thirty-five—it would only be costing taxpayers money.

The last problem is catching the persistent offenders who actually pose a danger to the public. Whereas repeat drug offenders (i.e., frequent marijuana users) are easy to arrest en masse, property criminals tend to be harder to arrest, and property crime cases often remain unresolved.[32]

When it comes to repeat drug offenders, let's look at the issue of reasonable rate of return on investment. Does it actually make sense to lock up drug offenders to keep them from getting locked up again for another drug offense? Probably not. Researchers calculate that we are "past the point of diminishing returns, where each additional prison cell provides less and less public safety benefit."[33] One study found that the state of Washington initially received more than nine dollars of benefit for each dollar spent locking up a drug offender. However, there are so many people behind bars today that now the state receives just thirty-seven cents of benefit for each dollar spent—and these are not benefits to victims.[34] Contrast this against the costs and benefits of drug treatment programs, which actually *do* go a long way in rehabilitating drug users and reducing future offending—and reap much higher returns on investment without expensive periods of incarceration.

Predicting Who Will Reoffend without Intervention

Even though we have a lot of statistics on reoffending rates, it is difficult to identify which offenders will persist. The closest we can come is to calculate a group probability, meaning that an offender can be statistically placed in a group where maybe 60 percent of the group will probably be multiple offenders, as opposed to another group with only a 40 percent risk. This means that we cannot accurately identify whether a particular individual with a particular record or even a particular personality is going to be a persistent offender.

Still, we are getting better at identifying which offenders are clearly at *low* risk for reoffending. For instance, the Pew Center on the States has used analysis to identify which offenders would be at low risk of reoffending if released. The conclusion was that 14 percent or more of the state prison population is at very low risk of victimizing again and so could safely be released without further time behind bars or interventions. A very small number of these men are predicted to be rearrested for violent offenses, which would likely account for no more than 0.2 percent of violent offenses in a year. So releasing these low-risk offenders would save a lot of money on incarceration and pose very little risk to the public. The Pew's opinion poll shows that the public agrees that releasing these men would be a smart option.[35]

These estimates imply that the other offenders are at much higher risk of reoffending, and so that group is the main subject of the next major section of this chapter, which looks at which interventions have been proven to reduce reoffending and to what extent.

The Science behind the Predictions

Some of the most extensive studies on reoffending done by governments are actuarial—that is, they examine the statistical correlation between prisoner characteristics on admission and the probability of different future behaviors. Prisoner characteristics include basic inmate information such as their gender, age, IQ, conviction history, and so on—what the experts call "static risk factors" because they cannot be reversed. They also consider aspects of the inmate's life that may be amenable to changes via correctional programs, such as the inmate's educational level, work training, or cognitive thought processes. These are called "dynamic risk factors" because they can be "corrected" through programs during incarceration.

The conclusions from these studies are that reoffending rates can be partially predicted from known prisoner characteristics on their entry into prison. Inmates with more previous convictions, who were younger at the time of their first arrest, and who were convicted of property offenses (all static factors) are more likely to be reconvicted.[36] However, there is a chance of potentially "correcting" some of a prisoner's dynamic factors, including employment problems, associating with other offenders, being unmarried, or suffering from alcohol and drug abuse—all factors on the short list for increasing the risk of reoffending. Interestingly, these correlations have been known for nearly a hundred years.

One set of prediction scores using the above factors was updated recently for the California Department of Corrections and Rehabilitation. This actuarial prediction takes the race of the inmate into account as well as other static risk factors. It also predicts which inmates will be reconvicted for which offenses. It is a "moderate predictor," meaning that it is much better than chance but not perfect.[37]

Other countries are also using actuarial predictions. For instance, the British government has a sophisticated static risk assessment scale for predicting parole outcomes. The scores inform the parole board about the actuarial risk of a particular prisoner being reconvicted within two years of release. These scores show that paroling inmates with lower probabilities of reconviction does indeed result in lower rates of reconviction. When parole boards select these lower-risk inmates, they get lower reoffending rates. This is known as the "selection effect," meaning that selecting those for parole who have a lower risk of reconviction is the key to reducing reoffending (and not that the parole program is responsible for any sort of treatment effect).

In fact, the standard supervision of parole generally has very little "corrective" effect at all in either the United States or the United Kingdom—a shortfall that should be looked at. Because the United

Kingdom has better data in this area, it was possible to do a large-scale study. This study concluded that parole itself reduced reconviction rates from a predicted 42 percent down to only 40 percent for a sample of nine thousand average offenders (and from 16 percent to 14 percent for violent offenders).[38] Even if parole does nudge the numbers slightly in the right direction, these are not large differences—and are not reassuring to potential victims.

While research studies confirm that reoffending after release can be predicted by a combination of static and dynamic factors of offenders' lives before admission, events after their release can modify these predictions—particularly if the ex-inmate gets a job, maintains a relationship with a significant other, or stays away from criminal associates and avoids drunken fights.[39] So by focusing more correctional attention on these sorts of dynamic factors of an ex-inmate's life after release from prison, we can also reduce reoffending.[40]

HOW CORRECTIONS *CAN* ACTUALLY "CORRECT"

Experts emphasize the need to shift corrections practices away from what feels good to what is proven to work. Indeed, the logic for effective corrections—that is, for *effectively* reducing the likelihood of reoffending—is to understand what risk factors or unmet needs will lead to reinvolvement with crime and then to act using evidence-based approaches in order to change the presence of those risk factors or to meet those needs.

There are a variety of approaches to correcting offenders, ranging from drug treatment programs, to vocational training, to cognitive-behavioral therapy. The most effective of these can be readily applied to even existing corrections systems as relatively inexpensive pragmatic reforms that can take effect immediately.

Luckily, several hundred studies over the past two or three decades have worked to determine which of these strategies work best to reduce the likelihood of ex-inmates committing new victimizations. One of the most comprehensive and respected scientific reviews of this reoffending research was brought together by Doris MacKenzie in her 2006 book, *What Works in Corrections*.[41] If ever there was an evidence-based handbook on what works to reduce reoffending, this is it.[42] MacKenzie concludes that if the current corrections system results in a 50 percent reoffending rate, then adding the proven rehabilitative approaches that are based on skill-building, behavioral, and multimodal techniques could bring reoffending rates down as low as 30 percent.[43] She also points to approaches that the research has shown *not* to work, such as using deterrence—the fear of further punishment—on its own in correctional settings. Other popular innovations such as intensive supervision and electronic monitoring have likewise been proven not to work; the rates of reoffending with these approaches are the same as they are with the current system.

Another, more recent review that echoes MacKenzie's conclusions was published in 2010 by Mark Lipsey and colleagues, who looked at the effectiveness of a variety of popular approaches to reduce reoffending (e.g., cognitive-behavioral therapy, social-skills training, academic advancement, job training, etc.). Figure 4.3 shows that these programs can reduce reoffending from an average of 50 percent down to as low as 23 percent.[44]

Cognitive-Behavioral Therapy

Lipsey and his colleagues found cognitive-behavioral therapy, which aims to change the thinking patterns of individuals and their attitudes, to be the most successful of the correctional approaches he reviewed.[45] MacKenzie had earlier reviewed three types of correctional cognitive-behavioral programs, which are based on the theory that offenders get involved in offending because of the logic of their thought processes and so aim to change their thinking and attitudes to crime. She, too, found that their results are generally positive and noted that many cognitive-behavioral programs seem to be most effective with higher-risk offenders—especially when anger control and interpersonal problem solving are key elements. However, some studies show success with low-risk offenders as well. Further, it is relatively cheap to implement, costing less than $1,000 per offender. This investment is estimated to get a return of twenty-three dollars for each dollar spent.[46] So this is a smart program that should be widely implemented throughout correctional facilities.

Cognitive-behavioral therapy can also be successful with sex-offender

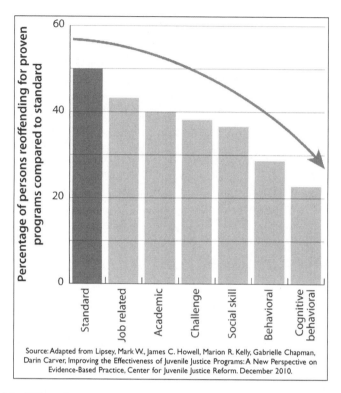

Source: Adapted from Lipsey, Mark W., James C. Howell, Marion R. Kelly, Gabrielle Chapman, Darin Carver, Improving the Effectiveness of Juvenile Justice Programs: A New Perspective on Evidence-Based Practice, Center for Juvenile Justice Reform. December 2010.

Figure 4.3   What Correctional Programs Actually Correct Reoffending?

treatment. MacKenzie looked at twenty-five independent studies undertaken since 1970. Her conclusions are clear that both targeted cognitive-behavioral therapy and medicinal drugs that reduce the sex drive—which are sometimes colloquially referenced as "chemical castration" drugs—are effective in reducing sex reoffending by an estimated 12–22 percent. It is important to note, however, that even a 1 percent reoffending rate means that there are new victims—possibly children—of sexual offenses, so even these reductions leave much room for improvement from the perspective of potential victims of crime.

Reducing the Likelihood That a Young Person Will Reoffend

An important trend in the United States in particular has been the steady reduction in the use of incarceration for youth[47]—a drop that goes hand in hand with a similar drop in youth crime. Not surprisingly, many of the research studies on reoffending have focused on how to effectively correct young offenders outside of the prison system. One 2012 meta-analysis reviewed 548 independent studies of approaches to juvenile reform.[48] As these studies reflect, reoffending programs generally take on one of two very different approaches to targeting young offenders.

The first approach features external control techniques for suppressing delinquency, such as instilling discipline (e.g., paramilitary boot camps); deterrence through fear of the consequences of bad behavior (e.g., prison visitation programs such as Scared Straight); and surveillance to detect bad behavior (e.g., intensive probation).

The second approach focuses on facilitating personal development through improved skills, relationships, and insight. These programs focus on restorative elements (e.g., restitution, victim-offender mediation); skill building (e.g., cognitive-behavioral techniques, social skills, academic and vocational skill building); counseling (e.g., individual, group, or family therapy; mentoring); and multimodal interventions designed to provide services tailored to the individual needs of juvenile offenders. The conclusions overwhelmingly point to this personal development approach as being the most effective way to stop young offenders from reoffending, although the surveillance element of the external control approach also has some limited positive impact.

On the flip side, programs that take the external discipline approach to correcting overwhelmingly do not work. Scared Straight is a popular deterrence program wherein young offenders are sent to visit a maximum security prison to scare them out of reoffending. However, the scientific evidence shows that this program makes no difference to reoffending rates—and in fact actually tends to *increase* the risk of reoffending.[49] So whatever is spent on this program using taxpayers' money is counterproductive.

In terms of discipline, boot camps on their own do not work to reduce reoffending, either.[50] In fact, boot camps have actually been shown to *lose* $19,011 per participant. However, there is promise that the inclusion of a therapeutic element and an aftercare component (i.e., drug treatment and employment programs) may make a key difference in their efficacy. These results are not surprising, for as you have seen in chapter 3, drug courts and programs such as HOPE, which combine control with treatment, *do* get positive results.

California's Chance to Implement What Really Works

It's also not surprising that many corrections officials and jurisdictions are resistant to reforming the corrections system. After all, corrections is a massive and expensive industry that employs nearly a million people across the United States, and an overhaul would be complex to say the least. However, California's counties are now facing a nearly unprecedented opportunity to implement strategies that *really* work to reduce reoffending. In 2011, the State of California enacted Assembly Bill (AB) 109—what some deem the most radical reform in American criminal justice history. In a bid to save the state (but not local counties) money, the bill diverts less-serious offenders (i.e., those with no history of violence, sex offenses, or serious crime) from state prisons by sending them to local county jails instead.[51]

A billion dollars and more has subsequently been diverted from the state system and allocated to California's fifty-eight counties. These counties have tremendous discretion in terms of how the funding is used, but hopefully they will spend the money in accordance with the bill's objectives: to implement effective programs that actually work to reduce reoffending and to prevent future victimization.[52] As we have seen in this chapter, we already have a strong idea of what works (and what doesn't). The evidence in this chapter confirms that these less-serious offenders could be safely released, particularly if supervised and supported to engage in proven treatment programs. Only time will tell whether the political will exists for California's counties to improve on the old, ineffective system and choose more innovative, effective corrections solutions to save taxpayers money without increasing the risks to public safety.

Important Steps toward Smarter Corrections

The Council of State Governments and the Pew Charitable Trusts are engaged in an impressive and exciting program to assist states with smarter corrections. They work with states that want to better husband taxpayers' money by reducing (at least on the margins) the use of mass incarceration by investing money in evidence-based, fiscally sound community programs that work to supervise and actually "correct" less-serious offenders for the benefit of public safety.[53] To date, no fewer than thirty-one states have engaged in this program to some degree. Several have innovated evidence-based programs in their communities, and a few have even adopted relatively comprehensive justice reinvestment legislation that shifts some less-serious offenders from behind bars to supervision and treatment in the community. A number of states have benefitted from this program in terms of being able to innovate and pass legislation that is rooted more firmly in the evidence.

Texas's recent correctional innovations provide a promising example. The innovations were inspired by 2007 projections that if the state kept going as it had been, it would need more than 17,000 new prison beds by 2012—at a cost of $2 billion to taxpayers. Leaders began looking for smarter ways to solve the problem and in 2007 began allocating a fraction of that amount to expand community-based options such as probation (diversion), problem-solving courts, and evidence-based drug treatment. All told, it invested more than $241 million in evidence-based strategies to reduce reoffending—and saved nearly $2 billion in return. Notably, the reform package included graduated sanctions, incentives to promote compliance with the terms of probation, and drug courts. It also cut the maximum probation terms of some property and drug offenders from ten down to five years. Since enactment of these reforms, the reoffending rate has dropped by 25 percent, and crime rates are at their lowest level since 1973.[54] In fact, Texas actually *closed* a prison in 2011 and is thinking of closing two more facilities.[55] While this is encouraging, we can't forget that crime has been dropping in many states, and so some reduction in Texas is to be expected. Still, the great strides that it achieved in little over half a decade show that smart crime-control strategies really do work better and are much more cost-effective.

These actions not only show political will to act, but also demonstrate that action is getting positive results, at least within the isolationist top-down corrections and court systems. But they are still small steps in shifting the use of corrections to actually "correcting" and protecting at an affordable price. This retooling has been helped not only by the concern to control state expenditures but also by drops in crime rates back to levels not seen since the 1960s and early 1970s, when incarceration was at a level approximately one-fifth of what it is today—and was, in today's budget terms, using $60 billion fewer dollars annually on corrections.[56]

However, much more must be done to foster the payment of restitution to victims, wherever this is reasonable. We know how to make this a reality but have not acted. Ultimately, it is smarter to avoid the costs to taxpayers of incarceration while enabling offenders to work in the community and repay restitution to victims.[57]

CONCLUSION

Points to Note: Smarter Strategies for the Effective Use of Corrections

In the past thirty years, US incarceration levels have skyrocketed from being exceptionally heavy mass incarceration by standards of other affluent democracies to being veritable hyperincarceration unknown anywhere else in the free world. And while keeping offenders behind bars does provide modest protection to potential victims, at these rates this benefit is far outweighed by the use of exorbitant amounts of taxpayers' money—and the public agrees. With crime rates dropping, both New York City and juvenile corrections have demonstrated that allowing incarceration to decrease by 50 percent or more does *not* necessarily threaten public safety.

Such heavy use of incarceration leads to consequences that increase reoffending. We know that offenders who get jobs, maintain strong interpersonal relationships, and stay away from alcohol and troubling associates are more likely to succeed in living a crime-free life after release. So correctional policy needs to reduce the many counterproductive consequences of felony convictions and incarceration to help the men released from incarceration get jobs, be family members, and avoid the situations that lead to further victimization—and its steep costs to taxpayers.

Nearly a century of experimentation in corrections provides some clear conclusions about what types of offenders will reoffend most and what works to actually "correct." These confirm a rate of return of over twenty dollars for every one dollar spent on changing attitudes through a proven technique that would reduce rates of reoffending from 50 percent to around 25 percent. This knowledge is being used by some pioneering states in a Justice Reinvestment program to reduce reoffending (and thereby spare victims) and to avoid prison construction costs. It stresses the importance of assessing the needs of offenders and targeting resources to those most in need.

Actions for Politicians to Correct Corrections Toward Stopping Crime

1. Legislators should ensure that nonviolent, nonserious, and non-sex-crime offenders serve their sentences in the community:
   a. By changing the law to shorten sentences to lengths similar to those in other affluent democracies;
   b. By investing in supervision and proven treatment in the community; and
   c. By enabling the payment of restitution to victims wherever possible.
2. Legislators must ensure that time behind bars includes engagement in proven programs by funding those programs and encouraging inmates to use them.
3. Legislators must reduce the consequences of a felony conviction and incarceration so that they do not interfere unnecessarily with the life chances of an offender after serving his or her sentence by focusing on:
   a. Access to jobs, staying in a family, and avoiding alcohol, drugs, and criminal associates;
   b. Reinstating voting so that politicians will focus on equitable services to problem places; and
   c. Changing the threshold for property offenses from $500 to $5,000.
4. Legislators must examine the reasons for the disproportionate use of incarceration for young black males and ensure that more black children grow up with a father, including setting up a presidential task force to recommend effective solutions.
5. Legislators must invest in comparable data on the characteristics of all offenders and reoffending rates in order to inform ways to improve "corrections."

This chapter has focused on what can be achieved within the existing corrections systems. The next chapters focus on other ways to prevent so many young men from becoming "problem people" concentrated in "problem places."

II

ACTIONS FOR
SMART PRE-CRIME PREVENTION

5

PREVENTING YOUTH FROM BECOMING REPEAT OFFENDERS

INTRODUCTION

From the perspective of sparing citizens from becoming victims of violence and crime, it's no secret that something is wrong with our criminal justice systems right now. Despite holding seven times as many men behind bars as other affluent democracies, the homicide rate for men of age twenty to twenty-four in the United States is seven times that of other affluent democracies.[1] This young age also coincides with the peak age for men to be arrested.[2] Furthermore, there is a revolving door in the courts, where more than three-quarters of felony defendants have a prior arrest history and 69 percent have multiple prior arrests.[3] The national rate of reoffending is not known but is estimated to be between 40 and 60 percent. Clearly, the reactive crime control industry of isolationist and top-down law enforcement, courts, and corrections is just not working, and many Americans, particularly young people, are paying the price with injuries and loss of life.

When traditional law enforcement groups use geographic information on "hot spots," they use the only tool they have when they work in isolation—enforcement after the fact. However, that same geographic information could—and should—be analyzed by others to justify different, *preventive* solutions that could save billions of dollars in harm to victims and billions more in criminal justice costs.

Unfortunately, in its efforts to put out the fire, traditional law enforcement translates geographic data into blunt, reactive instruments such as stop-and-frisk in an effort to suppress the problem. Smarter crime control strategies would translate that information for much more effective and cost effective ends. Smarter national and local politicians might say, "We know where the majority of crimes are happening. Now let's use that knowledge to not just *react* to them but to actually *stop* them from happening in the first place—and let's start by working better with young people before they have a chance to begin down the wrong path." This is the kind of smart thinking that potential victims need and that taxpayers want if it is going to save them harm and money—which it is.

Let's shift the terminology and consequently the way of thinking. The term "hot spots" might help focus enforcement efforts, but "problem places" focuses on *solutions* for those places,[4] which are concentrations of both victims of violence and costs to taxpayers. In this chapter, we look at solutions based in prevention rather than reaction. Importantly, the ideas in this chapter are not proposing prevention instead of cure, but rather prevention as a *central component* of cure.

America's Crisis of Problem People Growing Up in Problem Places

Sadly, when we look into the young faces in problem places in disadvantaged neighborhoods, we know that more than average numbers of children will grow up to become offenders.[5] This is not just sad for these children but unacceptable for their future victims and unnecessarily costly for taxpayers.

Each child who grows up to be a frequent, persistent, or prolific offender will rack up millions of dollars in costs to taxpayers—and much worse in terms of harm to victims. Two influential researchers actually calculated how much harm can be ascribed to the typical high-risk youth with more than six police contacts (this is the group that collectively commits about 50 percent of all crime). The answer: a staggering $4.2 million per offender.[6] So potential victims and taxpayers alike should rejoice if we can get legislators to invest in proven ways to prevent youth from becoming repeat offenders in the first place.

Many of these youth who are at risk of becoming prolific offenders are concentrated in a small number of problem places—all of which are in disadvantaged neighborhoods and most of which are populated disproportionately by racial minorities. These problem places collectively account for a large portion of people behind bars and, consequently, for the taxes expended to pay for them through the reactive systems of law enforcement, courts, and corrections. The Council of State Governments gives three important examples of how problem places are costing taxpayers dearly; I have added Milwaukee.

- In 2007, Michigan taxpayers spent more than $430 million to imprison people just from Wayne County (which includes Detroit). This was one-third of the state's overall corrections spending for that year, even though Wayne County is home to less than 20 percent of the state's population.
- In 2007, Arizona spent more than $70 million to incarcerate offenders from a single zip code; the incarceration rate for this neighborhood was a staggering 31.8 per 1,000 residents, compared with a statewide average of 2.2 per 1,000 residents.
- In Houston, Texas, just ten of the city's eighty-eight neighborhoods account for almost $100 million a year in prison expenditures.[7]
- In Milwaukee, two-thirds of the county's incarcerated African American men come from just six zip codes—all in the poorest neighborhoods.[8]

It seems clear that one smart way to reduce corrections costs is to minimize the number of children and youth from problem places who grow up to be offenders. But by making positive investments earlier in the lives of these children—in what's known as pre-crime prevention—can we actually *stop* the harm from violence to victims in the first place? And by so doing, can we also avoid paying the increasingly high costs for law enforcement, courts, and corrections? The answer is a resounding yes.

So resounding, in fact, that President Obama highlighted the opportunity in his State of the Union address in 2013: "Tonight, I propose working with states to make high-quality preschool available to every child in America. Every dollar we invest in high-quality early education can save more than seven dollars later on—by boosting graduation rates, reducing teen pregnancy, even reducing violent crime."[9] In actuality, reduced costs to victims of violent crime account for most of those seven dollars, since the studies show that the overwhelming outcome of investing in preschool for disadvantaged children is a reduction in offending and, therefore, fewer victims.[10]

As President Obama mentioned, we *can* stop violence by lifting up our children with education. And yes, preschool is part of the solution. But nurturing kids and investing in youth has to happen during *all* stages of a child's development and in *all* the most important spheres of his or her life. For example, in 2009, the World Health Organization concluded that nurturing relationships between children and their parent(s) is one key way to stop violence. Indeed, nurturing our kids needs to happen in the home, inside the classroom, and within the community. Obviously, this is no small feat. Luckily, we already have reams of evidence telling us exactly what works when it comes to turning our youth around—proven ways that are endorsed by respected authorities such as the US Department of Justice. But to actually stop crime, we must target these strategies to problem places and do it across the board.

PRE-CRIME PREVENTION: A PROVEN SOLUTION FOR STOPPING CRIME

Part I of this book looked at what *wasn't* working with reactive crime control (i.e., law enforcement, courts, and corrections operating in isolation) but also showed some potential for successes within these systems—but only *after* violent crimes have happened and created victims. Now, in part II, we'll focus on how to stop that violence before it happens at all. In this chapter, we look at violence prevention—what I and others refer to as "pre-crime prevention," which stops youths from accumulating the negative life experiences that are precursors for multiple offending. As you will see in this chapter, lots of strong research confirms that violence is stopped by programs that focus on the early years of a child's life as well as on his or her family, school, and community.

These programs are most effective when targeted in the problem places that are known to law enforcement for high rates of crime, and they are turnkey solutions just waiting to be implemented by smart politicians.

The proven programs are based on the results of longitudinal studies that tell us what negative life experiences—"risk factors"—predispose some youths to turn to crime. The research confirms what many already know: that poor parenting, alcohol and other drugs, lack of opportunities, and failure in school are on the list of risk factors. The best of these programs stop violence by focusing on these risk factors. Most of the research that proves the effectiveness of these programs—and in fact proves it beyond a reasonable doubt—was completed right in the United States, so there are few excuses for not implementing them more.

For politicians educated in law schools or outside of the behavioral sciences, the names of these projects might seem obscure, not yet familiar. But if the declining rates of violence are to continue, all decision makers must get to know at least the main programs. Luckily, we can turn to a number of respected authorities that have become household names because of their commitment to good science and their concern for better health and justice. These include the US Department of Justice, the Centers for Disease Control and Prevention, and the World Health Organization. All have done their due diligence to reject what does not work and to endorse what has been *proven* to reduce the numbers of victims of violence. For example, the Department of Justice recognizes only good, validated, evidence-based programs on its website crimesolutions.gov.[11]

Several organizations have done a lot of the detailed work to translate top ratings from the experts into recommended program lists. For instance, the Center for the Study and Prevention of Violence in Colorado has twenty years of experience with its "Blueprints," which are recommended programs identified from the evaluations of one thousand pre-crime prevention programs that target social risk factors. From these, they have accepted a dozen of the best projects as "models."[12] These models are generally recognized as the gold standard for programs that have been proven effective to stop crime and that can be replicated elsewhere.

The Washington State Institute for Public Policy (WSIPP), an agency of that state's legislature, has become the place to go for estimations of the costs and benefits of these programs, which WSIPP has rated in the way of "consumer reports." These reports were originally meant to inform decisions about where to make investments in Washington State but are increasingly consulted from around the world.[13] WSIPP provides many estimates of cost benefits, reductions in harm to victims, and avoidance of expenditures from taxes. These estimates have been used to avoid prison construction and to promote many smart actions consistent with the themes of this book. These seals of approval also make it easy for politicians to choose programs that are proven to work so that public money isn't wasted on well-intentioned programs that don't work (e.g., boot camps for young offenders or Scared Straight, as you saw in part I).

In table 5.1, I have selected some of the best of these programs and shown the age ranges on which they focus, the proven results, and the cost estimates taken from the work of the WSIPP, which are usually calculated on a per-child basis. I have also included some of the other respected authorities that have endorsed these programs as being effective in reducing violence or crime. For instance, all of the projects (except the Youth Inclusion Program) were identified as effective by the US Department of Justice on the crimesolutions.gov website. I have added the Youth Inclusion project from the United Kingdom to

Age ranges	Name of program	Cost	Net benefit	"Blueprints"	Crime solutions	Rating by key groups
	Early childhood					
0-2	Nurse family partnership	$9,600	$13,181	model	effective	6
0-4	Positive parenting program	$143	$722	promising	effective	5
3-4	Highscope preschool	$7,523	$14,934	promising	effective	5+
	Pre-teen school					
5-11	Stop now and plan	$4,200 (est)			effective	4
12-14	Life skills training	$34	$1,256	model	effective	5
5-18	Big Brothers and Big Sisters	$1,479	$5,728	model		5
	Family					
12-18	Functional family therapy	$3,262	$30,706	model	effective	3
12-18	Multi-dimensional treatment foster care	$7,922	$31,276	model	effective	6
13-18	Youth inclusion program	$5,000 (est)				
	School and peaceful conflict resolution					
5-11	Steps to respect	$34 (est)		promising	effective	3

Table 5.1 What Pre-crime Prevention Stops Youth from Becoming Chronic Offenders?

the list because these programs have an impressive record of success in more than seventy problem places and have now been expanded to sixty more sites and extended to younger age groups. The final column shows the total number of respected authorities that have rated the program—often these also include the Office of Juvenile Justice and Delinquency Prevention and the Substance Abuse and Mental Health Services Administration.

Before explaining each of these programs, I want to share another British best practice, which is the reason funding was shifted into the Youth Inclusion projects even while rates of youth incarceration were being reduced. It is an impressive model for states and cities that choose to shift from *reactive*, isolationist crime control to smart pre-crime prevention.

A Model Example: The United Kingdom's National Youth Justice Board

In 1996, the British Audit Commission published a report with the poignant title "Misspent Youth." The report was an analysis of the returns that British taxpayers got from paying for reactive and standard law enforcement, courts, and corrections as a way to respond to young people and crime. The report concluded that the resources spent catching, convicting, and "correcting" youth could be much better used—that is, that pre-crime prevention is much more effective and cost-effective than reactive cure. In sum, the report found that taxes were being misspent on youth—and that youths' lives were allowed to drift into crime and so were being misspent as a result. That's a powerful condemnation to be sure.

The report made a number of recommendations about how the money should be reallocated. These recommendations ranged from providing parents with parenting skills, to supporting teachers, to providing positive leisure opportunities for youth. As a result, just two years later, the newly installed government of Prime Minister Tony Blair acted to create a permanent Youth Justice Board (YJB), mandated to stop crime and reorganize the youth justice system by using *evidence* for effective practice. This agency draws on leaders in law enforcement, social services, education, and more. The result is that England and Wales have leapt ahead of other countries in providing good youth justice and in multiplying successful pre-crime prevention programs across problem places.

The United Kingdom's YJB is committed to tackling the risk factors for offending (i.e., poor parenting, violence, and abuse) that many young people in problem places face. That is, it is committed to pre-crime prevention. It also focuses on dealing with young offenders in effective ways to best reduce future repeat offending. To this end, it brings together a range of agencies in partnership to work on issues of schooling, housing, social services, and more. To date, the YJB has cut delays in juvenile courts in half and has started to see some reductions in young offenders' reoffending. It has also developed the important model of a Youth Inclusion program to stop youth from drifting into offending.

One unique lesson of the United Kingdom's YJB is that it sets out specific goals relating to the reduction of youth offending, and it holds its funding recipients accountable for helping to meet those goals. It also invests a portion of its funds toward quality evaluation of its efforts to stop crime. The United States could certainly turn to the United Kingdom's innovative Youth Justice Board for a prefab example of how it could begin to effectively deal with at-risk youth and young offenders on a nationwide basis, particularly when it comes to pre-crime prevention to stop violence against victims before it happens.

WHY IT'S SMART TO INVEST IN EARLY CHILDHOOD DEVELOPMENT

As early as 1961, inner-city violence had been recognized as a way of life that some youths are simply "born into"; just look at the Broadway musical *West Side Story* about rival gangs in the Bronx. Even though it was written over half a century ago, the musical's insights still remain surprisingly relevant.

In fact, *West Side Story*'s song "Gee, Officer Krupke" continues to epitomize the debate about youth offending. The song wonders aloud whether a teen's delinquency comes from his being evil, or being unwanted at birth, or being brought up by drunk and dissolute parents, or simply being at a difficult stage. It debates solutions that include social work, psychiatry, and employment—even a year in prison.

But while the song ends in frustration, rejecting all those fixes for delinquency, the research since 1961 has helped us identify several realistic solutions. It's also enabled us to better understand why a year (or even a whole young adulthood) in prison is generally not a good solution and also why some children face greater odds of being violent than others.

In fact, the compelling research on what types of negative life experiences predispose boys to get—and stay—involved in crime highlights "inconsistent and uncaring parenting" as a key reason.[14] This parenting shortfall may be because in many problem places, a parent is in jail, or is suffering with addictions, or is working around the clock in minimum wage jobs; it may also simply be that the parents were never on the receiving end of good parenting skills themselves when they were growing up. Regardless of the reason, children who are brought up under these conditions have difficulty in thriving.

Taking a Stand against Violence against Children

When it comes to violence within the home, children are just as often the victims as spouses. In addition to being easy targets for violence, children are often victims of neglect as well. Every year in the United States, close to 3.3 million reports are referred to child protection agencies due to signs of negligence and abuse.[15] Sadly, 600,000 children will be confirmed as victims of maltreatment—meaning that they have clearly been victims of physical, sexual, or emotional abuse or were not provided with basic care such as food, housing, and medical treatment.[16] The consequences of these confirmed cases alone are estimated at $124 billion a year.

These staggering numbers call for greater attention, not only for the child's sake but also for the sake of long-term public safety, where the list of links between child abuse and crime are both multiple and very disturbing. For instance, we know that children who are victims (or even witnesses) of violence at home are more likely to be violent when they grow up than other adults.[17] In fact, child maltreatment approximately *doubles* the likelihood that an individual will engage in crime; the outcomes are even more exacerbated in cases of sexual abuse.[18] According to one expert group, children who experience abuse and neglect are 59 percent more likely to be arrested as a juvenile, 28 percent more likely to be arrested as an adult, and 30 percent more likely to commit violent crime.[19] We also know that children of low socioeconomic status are more likely to be mistreated at home, and these underprivileged victims suffer even more damaging effects.

Even though the main recourse for dealing with child abuse is usually a child protection agency instead of law enforcement, most child abuse would meet the criteria of a crime. I am not proposing that we lock up all those parents, however. What I *am* proposing is that we focus our honed skills and our resources on helping those parents become positive parents, because that is what the science has proven will reduce future violence. After all, we know that if we prevent violence within the home, the next generation will be less likely to become offenders and to victimize others. And although it's trickier to influence what happens within the four walls of a home than it is within a school or community center, we know it can be done.

A Model Example: Nurse-Family Partnerships   One proven way to stop violence against children is to identify at-risk mothers and direct prevention at them by investing in more public health nurses. Indeed, in 1977, David Olds led an impressive scientific study—The Nurse Home Visiting Program—that demonstrated how public health nurses were more effective in stopping crime than standard (reactive) law enforcement or corrections measures. His subjects were four hundred predominantly white first-time mothers who were identified as being at-risk (i.e., mothers who were teenagers, had low income, and/or were struggling with addictions). He sent public health nurses every two weeks to visit half the women and help them better understand fetal and childhood development and parenting practices. The visits took place from pregnancy until the child turned two. The other two hundred women did not receive any visitations and were left to cope for themselves with help from the standard community services of their choice.

The long-term outcomes were impressive to say the least. Of the children who did *not* receive visits, 50 percent were abused or neglected, compared with 25 percent of the children who did receive visits—a reduction by half. The results were equally as impressive for preventing violent offending during the children's teenage years. Of the children who did *not* receive visits, 37 percent were arrested by the age of nineteen, compared with 21 percent of those who did receive visits—again, cutting the numbers nearly in half.[20] These differences are just as large as the outcomes from the most successful reactive crime control measures associated with isolationist and top-down law enforcement, courts, and corrections, as discussed in part I. The results are even more impressive when you consider that these numbers don't reflect all of the victims that were spared; after all, many of the young men who would otherwise have gone down the road to prolific offending were turned back before they harmed a single victim.

These impressive results were replicated in many good research studies, including one in an African American community in Memphis, Tennessee, and another in a Mexican American community in Denver, Colorado. The State of Hawaii took this promising data to heart and created its "Healthy Start" program, which focused on a much larger group (1,353 families) and demonstrated that the program can be implemented statewide with evidence of many cost benefits.

The original Nurse Home Visiting Program was estimated to cost $7,733 per family, with net benefits of $15,916 (without counting the savings to victims). The WSIPP sees two dollars in benefits for each dollar invested, but its method decreases the value of the long-term benefits because one must wait for them.[21] In Hawaii, given the economies of scale, the cost per family was significantly less at only $3,200. To put this into perspective, the average annual cost of a law enforcement officer today is more than $120,000 (or $160,000 if you assign the costs of civilian personnel and equipment). For the equivalent of the salary of just *one* officer, thirty families in at-risk "problem areas" could be receiving the benefit of the program—and cutting the number of would-be offenders in half for the rest of their lives.

It is results like this that have Nurse-Family Partnership programs certified as effective in stopping violence by groups such as the new but influential Coalition for Evidence-Based Policy, where the program placed in its elite group of top-tier social programs that work.[22] This coalition of respected experts has already influenced federal politicians on other issues. Nurse-Family Partnership programs were also certified as one of the first Blueprints for violence prevention[23] and have been labeled an effective program by crimesolutions.gov.[24] Further, they have received endorsements from Child Trends, the US Department of Justice's Office of Juvenile Justice and Delinquency Prevention, and the Substance Abuse and Mental Health Services Administration of the US Department of Health.

Programs such as this provide a community-based, turnkey solution to reducing violence. We *know* it works, and it is available to all of us *right now*. It is a recurring theme of this book that successes such as this provide a rich arsenal for programs that politicians could—and should—implement in order to achieve large, cost-effective reductions in violence. But too often, when success stories like this one are reported to local, state, and national politicians, they are ignored when it comes time to actually implement new policies or approve the next budget.

So why not challenge our elected officials and community politicians by asking, Why not invest in preventing violence against children? Why not help give at-risk kids a chance at better parenting? And why not invest in our own safety at the same time?

A Model Example: The Positive Parenting Program—The "Triple P" Program   One of the most effective and affordable programs to improve consistency and care in parenting is called Triple P—for the Positive Parenting Program. Triple P provides parents with simple and practical strategies to help them parent more effectively, prevent their children from developing problems, and build strong, healthy relationships. By so doing, it decreases child abuse—and thereby breaks the cycle of violence by stopping the children from growing up to become offenders. Originally developed in Australia, Triple P is currently used in twenty-five countries; thirty years of good research shows that the program works across different cultures, socioeconomic groups, and family structures—all while being surprisingly affordable.[25]

One strong evaluation for Triple P's effectiveness was funded by the Centers for Disease Control and Prevention. In it, nine out of eighteen South Carolina counties were randomly chosen to receive the Triple P program. Over two years, the counties that received the program had a 44 percent reduction in foster home placements, a 35 percent reduction in hospitalizations and emergency room visits for child injuries (e.g., child abuse, harm caused by poor supervision, etc.), and a 28 percent reduction in substantiated cases of abuse.[26] The results are even more impressive when you consider the minimal cost of the program: approximately ten thousand families received some level of Triple P programming, at a cost of only twenty-three dollars per family, or a total of $230,000.

Indeed, Triple P is a ready-made program that can be implemented affordably in any community. Positive scientific reviews have been pouring in for this program from influential and respected authorities. For instance, the Department of Justice has identified Triple P as an effective violence prevention program,[27] the Coalition for Evidence-Based Policy rates it as nearly top tier,[28] and the Blueprints process heralds it as promising.[29] These certifications apply to its impact in reducing violence against children, but as we've seen, a reduction in violence *against* children will also reduce violence *by* those children as they grow older.

Model Example: Using Preschool to Give Children a Boost   As President Obama mentioned in his State of the Union address, investing in preschool for young children prevents crime down the road by enabling them to thrive. There is also good monetary reason to invest in this kind of enriched experience for children. In fact, as you will see shortly, the returns on investment are at least seven dollars for each dollar invested—numbers that no smart legislator could possibly ignore.

Enriched preschool experiences work to offset the risk factor of inconsistent and uncaring parenting. For instance, in the 1980s, the Perry Preschool Program emerged as a successful initiative that prevented crime through targeting children's social development. On one level, the program provided self-initiated learning activities that encouraged sound intellectual and social development for children ages three and four. But more than that, the program delivered consistent, enriched child care to at-risk kids so that they had a chance to thrive, unfettered by the disadvantages of inconsistent and uncaring parenting. The care was delivered for at least two and a half hours every day by qualified child-care workers, who each worked with no more than eight children at once. They also provided some guidance to parents on childhood development.

Good scientific evidence shows that children who went through the program were more likely to stay crime-free later in life. The study included 123 low-income African American children who were identified as being at high risk of school failure later on (and, as we've seen, school failure is one of the primary risk factors that predispose young people to crime). Half of the children were randomly assigned to the program, and the other half were left to the guidance of their parents as usual. The study then compared how those individuals who had been enrolled in the Perry Preschool Program fared in life, up to the age of forty, compared with those who had not been enrolled in the program.[30] The comparison found that the program resulted in an impressive reduction in arrests by the age of forty, from 55 percent for the non-Perry Preschool group down to 36 percent for the Perry Preschool group. Once again, we can see how stopping crime at this age through social intervention (i.e., through pre-crime prevention) is many multiples more effective at stopping harm to victims, because it successfully intervenes *before* the youth becomes the prolific offender on which the reactive and isolationist systems focus.

The original study also showed that a cost of $15,000 for enriched preschool for each child led to benefits that averaged $195,000 for each. Of these, $170,000 was combined reductions in cost to taxpayers and harm to victims; these costs might be divided as $60,000 in savings to taxpayers and $110,000 in savings to victims if the ratio is similar to the statistics used in chapter 1.[31] This is a return of eleven dollars for each dollar invested. Where else can you get such a good return?[32] But let's be more cautious, like the president. In the mid 2000s, Nobel Prize–winning economist James Heckman "rediscovered" the Perry Preschool and reanalyzed the cost benefits. He estimated the annual rate of return of the Perry program to be 5–7 percent above the average rate of return for smart investments.[33] Given his analysis, he has become an ardent advocate for the increased use of this program—and likely inspired President Obama's 2013 State of the Union speech and the figure of a seven dollar return for each dollar invested.

Today, these impressive results have been recognized by Blueprints as a promising program, by crimesolutions.gov as an effective program, and by three other prestigious agencies.[34] However, just imagine what the results could have been had the number of these preschool programs been multiplied throughout problem places and neighborhoods decades ago. Importantly, think about how much costly grief to victims would have been avoided, and think what would have been saved in costs of reactive crime control. Further, many would-be offenders would have been living productive lives instead of aggravating their disadvantages behind bars. Fortunately, nothing is stopping politicians from implementing programs such as this now, in communities across the United States and, indeed, around the world.

INVESTING IN HELPING PRETEENS SUCCEED IN SCHOOL AND IN LIFE

Children and adolescents spend much of their time in a classroom, and there are many ways that parents can support their children to do well in school. At the top of the list is taking a real interest in their child, so that he or she is more likely to complete school. As we saw above, parents can get assistance right from their children's earliest years to learn how to provide consistent and caring parenting and to present enriched learning opportunities to their young children through pre-school programs. Both of these strategies help children to thrive later in school and life.

Children can also avoid a cycle of delinquency if they learn to make good life decisions, and this sort of learning can happen in schools (although it doesn't happen often enough). Schools tend to focus on reading, writing, and arithmetic as the core objectives that will help children "succeed" in life. Failure in these academic areas may contribute to youth dropping out of school and getting involved in delinquency that is beyond the norm for teenagers. What's more, it is now clear that other "core" topics are equally as important as the traditional three Rs to a young person's success. For instance, issues of self-control, dealing with emotions, and interpersonal problem-solving skills are important to reduce longer-term involvement in crime and violence.

Programs that focus on building these core personal skills can be integrated into school curricula and therefore do not normally require large investments in adding salaried personnel. However, they *do* require the school systems to give priority to including such programs, which does not happen as much as it should—particularly in schools in problem places, where these types of learning opportunities are needed most. We'll look at some of the best and most effective examples of these programs next.

Stop Now and Plan (SNAP)

Stop Now and Plan, or SNAP, is an award-winning program developed by the Child Development Institute over thirty years ago. It targets at-risk families to reduce aggressive and antisocial behaviors by promoting greater skills in dealing with emotions in social situations. SNAP is designed for families with children ages six to twelve and uses a combination of family intervention, cognitive-behavioral strategy, and problem-solving skills to augment the teaching of certain life skills that might be missing from the family. In particular, it helps children and parents effectively deal with anger by teaching them how to stop and think before they act. With practice, parents and children learn to stop, calm down, and generate positive solutions at the "snap" of their fingers.[35]

Preliminary evidence suggests that SNAP has been proven to cut delinquency scores in half, and there is a reported reduction of conviction by age eighteen, from 57 percent for nonparticipants down to 31 percent for participants.[36] The program lasts for six months for low-risk families and eighteen months for high-risk families, costing $1,400 and $7,000, respectively (in table 5.1 I have used $4,200 as an average). For this price, there are proven cost benefits. Some evaluations of these cost benefits suggest that for every dollar invested, four dollars is saved in law enforcement, courts, and corrections costs alone. What's more, seventeen dollars may be gained for each dollar invested if we expand the scope of savings beyond criminal justice to areas such as reduced harm to victims and reduced lost productivity due to incarceration.[37]

SNAP has not yet been included in the Blueprints data set, although it is identified as effective by crimesolutions.gov.[38] SNAP is also endorsed by some Canadian agencies, but other programs in the table have received wider endorsement by agencies in the United States. The bottom line for the moment is that this project has a good logic model, intervenes before a lot of damage is done to victims, and is probably cost-effective. Hopefully there will be more replications of this program in the future, leading to greater knowledge and confidence in its effectiveness. Notably, a number of further studies on SNAP are expected to be published in 2013.

A Model Example: Life Skills Training

The Life Skills Training program is a Blueprints Model Program that focuses on children ages twelve to fourteen to prevent violence as well as abuse of alcohol and other drugs. It has components that teach self-management skills, social skills, and information and resistance skills in relation to alcohol and other drugs. It is typically taught in the classroom by teachers and so does not require a large infusion of funds. In fact, the Washington State Institute for Public Policy estimates the costs at thirty-four dollars per individual, with a whopping payoff in crime reduction worth $251 in reduced reactive crime control (that's more than seven dollars in savings for each dollar invested) and an even larger $785 in reduction of other costs, mostly reduction in harm to victims (that's twenty-three dollars in savings for each dollar).

Life Skills Training has received an extensive set of evaluations. One review in an influential text referred to fifty-five studies involving eighty-nine separate randomized experimental-control group tests.[39] This program has also caught the eye of the White House for its emphasis on prevention over incarceration for, as the 2013 national drug control strategy states, "Preventing drug use before it begins—particularly among young people—is the most cost-effective way to reduce drug use and its consequences. In fact, recent research has concluded that every dollar invested in school-based substance use prevention programs has the potential to save up to $18 in costs related to substance use disorders."[40] Life Skills Training is one such program that is effective at bringing about these positive results.

A Model Example: Big Brothers, Big Sisters

Why not provide our at-risk youth with positive role models and mentors? As we've seen, early intervention is a major factor in reducing the likelihood that at-risk children will commit violence and crime later on in life. A major component of this is supplementing the child's family experience if necessary in order to provide consistent, caring parenting or adult involvement, which is a known "protective" factor against crime. Like young children, teens also require a consistent and caring adult presence in their life, and receiving this is proven to reduce offending down the road.

Initiating a mentoring program is something that can easily happen in any community. In fact, this is something that the National Association of Attorneys General (NAAG) in the United States called for over a decade ago, when it appealed to people to participate as mentors, coaches, and volunteers in their communities in order to provide support for children as a way to prevent tragic violence.[41] And this call for action was not directed solely at adults; it also encouraged youth to positively influence their peers and their juniors against violence by being mentors themselves. Unfortunately, since NAAG made this appeal, many thousands of young people have died, and thousands more have been locked up—likely as a result of not having a positive role model in their life. Will today's politicians have the vision that yesterday's politicians lacked?

If parental figures have a hard time serving as positive role models, the most affordable strategy for providing this positive adult presence is to connect at-risk youth with adult mentors. The best-known mentoring program is the Big Brothers, Big Sisters program. The program is simple: it connects adult mentors with youth from single-parent families who are between the ages of six and eighteen. Through meeting about three times a month for four hours each time, youths are provided with a caring relationship and a role model.

Big Brothers, Big Sisters has been awarded Blueprint approval as a model program. Research on the effectiveness of this program shows that 46 percent of the youth who participate are less likely to start using drugs, and 32 percent are less likely to hit someone. While more solid research needs to be done, there is every reason to believe that Big Brothers, Big Sisters is irrefutably effective at keeping large numbers of at-risk youth crime-free. As such, the program has spawned a number of spinoffs—in part due to the large cost savings associated with mentoring. In fact, the Washington State Institute for Public Policy calculated that the widespread use of mentoring is far more beneficial and cost-effective than incarceration. For instance, for every dollar spent for mentoring, the institute could identify more than four dollars in net benefits. It estimates the cost of the program at $1,479 per youth, which brings a reduction in reactive crime-control costs of $495, a savings in reduction in harm to victims of $1,759, and nearly $3,500 in other benefits.

INVESTING IN HELPING TEENS IN DIFFICULTY

A recent *Wall Street Journal* editorial drew attention to the disproportionate numbers of young black males who are killed and who are killers.[42] In fact, while overall homicides have been dropping since the mid-1970s, the number of black victims and murderers has remained stubbornly high and has actually *increased* since 2000.[43] We've discussed these shocking and sad numbers in the first chapter. What's most interesting about the article, however, is that it likens those statistics with the large number of black children who grow up without a father in their lives.[44] A lot of this lack is no doubt due to mass incarceration. It's no stretch to assume that repairing this parenting gap would lead to better results for our kids—and, ultimately, less crime (and fewer victims) in our communities for a more affordable cost. There are three proven ways to help a teenager get back on the rails, all of which are discussed in the following sections.

A Model Example: Functional Family Therapy

Among the recognized programs for strengthening the relationship between a teenager and his family is functional family therapy. This is identified by the US Department of Justice as an effective solution for stopping crime[45] and by Blueprints as a model program.[46]

Functional family therapy was the innovation of James Alexander, a psychology professor, and Bruce Parsons, a social work professor. Thirty years ago they observed that it was not sufficient to work solely with the youth at risk if they wanted to succeed in reducing offending and other problem behaviors. Rather, they realized that this objective required work within the entire family. In the intervening years, a systematic approach has been developed that includes the training of therapists and assessment of the results they obtain. Today, functional family therapy usually takes place in twelve sessions over a three- to four-month period. At its core is a focus on fostering the protective factors—and mitigating the risk factors—that impact a youth's development.[47]

The results of the research are impressive. In terms of the number of youth who are arrested, graduates of functional family therapy programs are at least 25 percent less likely to be arrested than their counterparts whose families did not complete the program. Each youth requires ten to twenty hours of direct service from therapists, costing between $1,000 and $4,000 per family. Contrast that with the $10,000 or so price tag that must be added to $50,000 or so for incarceration to deliver the comparable therapy later. In fact, the Washington State Institute for Public Policy showed that functional family therapy garnered a return of twenty dollars in reduced offender and victim costs for each dollar invested.[48] Clearly, this is an excellent use of each dollar in light of the high number of offenses that are prevented (and the high number of victims that are spared)—all while creating strong familial patterns that will be passed down through the generations.

A Model Example: Multidimensional Treatment Foster Care (MTFC)

Sometimes, in order to provide youth with the caring and consistent home environment they need in order to thrive, they must be removed from their family homes if authorities have determined the parenting influence to be inconsistent and uncaring. Multidimensional Treatment Foster Care (MTFC) programs focus on placing youth that have chronic antisocial behavior, emotional disturbance, and delinquency into new family homes within the community that are able to provide a consistent, caring family environment. These foster families are recruited, trained, and closely supervised to ensure that they can provide MTFC-placed adolescents with clear and consistent limits and follow through on the consequences. The families are also trained to provide positive reinforcement for appropriate behavior, a caring relationship with a mentoring adult, and separation from delinquent peers.[49] Individual and group therapy is also provided to support the youths, help them learn interpersonal skills, and enable them to take part in sports activities.

MTFC is shown to get impressive results in the first two years following enrollment, such as a reduction in violence from 38 percent for the nonparticipant control group down to 21 percent for MTFC participants. It also reduces the number of self-reported offenses. It costs $7,922 per youth and garners savings of $6,628 in reactive crime control and hospital costs, plus $24,261 in reduced harm to victims.

A Model Example: The Youth Inclusion Program

We discussed the United Kingdom's success with its Youth Justice Board (YJB) earlier. One prime example of the YJB's knowledge-driven approach to programming is its Youth Inclusion Program, which is soundly based on the pre-crime prevention approach. This national program is geared to at-risk youth ages thirteen to sixteen who live in seventy of the most problematic places in the United Kingdom. The concept of the program is simple: youth are provided with mentoring, homework help, and skill-building activities (e.g., sports, IT training) for ten hours a week. Truly, the aim is to make these at-risk youth feel like valuable, *included* members of their community. The program also offers assistance in terms of dealing with violence, drugs, gangs, and personal health.

A preliminary evaluation of the Youth Inclusion Program reports a 65 percent reduction in youth arrests, a 27 percent reduction in youth removed from schools, and a 16 percent reduction in overall crime in the targeted neighborhoods. The program costs only about $5,000 per place per year. Coincidentally, this is the cost of taking a young offender through the youth justice system in the United Kingdom for a single offense—without including the costs of incarceration. The results of the evaluation provided support for the YJB to expand this program to more than one hundred neighborhoods and to start an equivalent program with younger youth ages eight to thirteen; similar positive results are expected for both the preteens and their communities. Unfortunately, it is not possible to convert these data into comparable statistics that can be contrasted against the US programs, but the program would likely have similar benefits to the other two US programs described above.

INVESTING IN HELPING TEENS SUCCEED IN SCHOOL, COLLEGE, AND LIFE

As youth become independent, there is even more that parents and communities can do to help promote their children's success (especially for children in problem places). For example, they can advocate for local schools and school boards to integrate proven violence-reduction strategies into their school curriculums. They can also encourage school administrations to implement proven strategies that help children and teenagers complete school, as well as collaborate with their children and the schools to tackle bullying and violence within the school environment.

Stopping Bullying as a Way to End Present and Future Violence

Caring parental involvement has been recognized, once again, as playing a key role in the reduction of bullying at school. As you read in chapter 1, one in fourteen children is bullied at school. Bullying is just another word for assault, and so anything that reduces bullying reduces violence by definition. Moreover, by reducing the prevalence of bullying, it seems likely that at-risk youths (both the would-be bullies and the would-be victims) have a better chance of staying away from violence as adults. Indeed, there is likely a link between bullying in school and teenage (and later adult) violence outside the school, but the strength of this link remains to be determined. Also, with bullying under control, youth are more likely to engage in their studies—and are therefore also less prone to becoming offenders.

This lesson has not come easily. Following the 1999 shooting at Columbine High School in Denver, Colorado, where two bullied students took the lives of many of their fellow students, discussions on school safety and youth violence reached unprecedented levels. After listening to the experts, NAAG (see above) emphasized the need for preventive actions by *parents*, not by law enforcement and lawmakers[50]— which is definitely a step in the right direction, as you saw in part I. Although they did fall short of limiting their appeals to strategies that have been proven to work, a large part of what NAAG advocated was for parents to remain caring, consistent caregivers by listening to their children, by paying attention to their interests, by spending time with them, by setting boundaries for them, and by instilling values, including respect for others.

Model Examples: Steps to Respect and Similar Programs   The Steps to Respect program illustrates what can be achieved through efforts to promote peaceful conflict resolution and to stop bullying in schools. It combines teaching socially responsible beliefs and social-emotional skills to youth with increasing staff awareness and responsiveness. This program is meant to be integrated into the curriculum in school in grades 3 through 6 over a three-month period. While the results are not as clear as in other projects, they are definitely in a positive direction. Steps to Respect is recognized by crimesolutions.gov as an effective pre-crime prevention program and gets a promising rating from Blueprints. The cost to implement this program in schools is small.

One celebrated bullying prevention program that shares this focus on parents and family is Olweus, Norway's national antibullying program. The program is unique in that it works with the bully, the victim, *and* the parents to bring an end to the abuse. It is based on a 1-2-3 model: the first time a bullying incident is reported, it generates a discussion and a warning to the offender; the second time, there is an attempt to find the cause of the bullying by working with the parent, thereby encouraging family responsibility; at the third instance, the victim and/or the bully (and sometimes their families) are referred to a professional social worker to try to remediate deeper issues.

Olweus's approach is scientifically proven to be effective at stopping bullying. Research has shown that this simple program has resulted in a 50 percent reduction in bullying in Norway.[51] As such, it had received Blueprint Model Program status for many years, but it has now dropped back to promising status because not all replications in the United States have been as successful as the original program in Norway.

Youth Teaching Other Youth about Peaceful Conflict Resolution to Stop Violence

When children are born and raised in problem places, they likely witness more instances of problematic "problem solving" than other children. Recognizing that good problem solving is a skill that is *learned* (hopefully from parents, but not always), the World Health Organization calls for educating our youth in positive problem solving so that they know how to avoid instigating violence. Schools and youth centers seem to be the obvious choices for where best to advocate for healthy conflict resolution. For instance, school curricula could innovate to include programs that teach students how to resolve conflicts peacefully, or youth could go into schools to teach other youth, as you will see in an example below.

In fact, the youth-teaching-others model has proven very effective in many public health initiatives. For instance, in the 1960s, much of the emerging awareness about the dangers of smoking was communicated through school programs. Interestingly, children brought this message home to their parents and became teachers and advisers themselves. Similarly, it is possible that if children advocate against violence at home, then gradually more parents will seek other nonviolent ways to resolve conflict in their own lives.

Unfortunately, to date there is little good scientific research about which available programs best go about teaching youth the benefits of positive conflict resolution. Nevertheless, teaching our youth how to resolve disputes without resorting to violence makes good sense, and we do have some promising examples of what others are trying in this vein.

One organization that has taken to heart the idea of training youth in conflict resolution is the Canadian youth organization Youth Organizing to Understand Conflict and Advocate Non-Violence (YOUCAN). Its mission is to equip and inspire youth to peacefully resolve conflicts and develop healthy relationships in their communities. By sending peer mentors into schools, this for-youth-by-youth organization has trained more than 16,000 children and youth in ways to resolve conflicts without resorting to violence. YOUCAN has developed eight core training modules that focus on active listening, peer mediation, de-escalating violence, dispute resolution, peace circles, and cross-cultural conflict resolution.

Like many effective pre-crime prevention strategies, the YOUCAN modules are modeled after public health programs—in this case, public awareness programs that reduce drowning fatalities. After noticing that many countries had succeeded in reducing drowning by teaching people how to swim and how to perform lifesaving, YOUCAN decided to apply the same approach to conflict resolution; it focused on teaching others how to resolve their own conflicts to avoid violence as well as how to intervene in others' conflicts to potentially save lives. Notably, it also provides training to young persons so that they can train others to do the same. The YOUCAN program needs scientific validation, but it seems promising that the program could lead not only to less violence between young people but also to less violence in other settings, such as the home.

ENCOURAGING OUR ELECTED OFFICIALS TO TAKE ACTION ON PRE-CRIME PREVENTION

The programs mentioned above are inspiring. Reading about them even makes some people want to take action to implement them (or something like them) for the sake of the young people whose futures can be improved. Unfortunately, when it comes to budget time, all too often the wind falls out of the sails, and the same old strategies are reinstituted for another year. Innovative solutions are left to "somebody else" to figure out, often against the backdrop of apologies because "we just don't have the money."

I suppose it's just "easier" to keep on doing what's always been done instead of rocking the boat and risking electoral defeat. Sadly, people are often all too willing to do what's always been done *even if it doesn't work*, or if it works only after many community members have been victimized, or if it costs a lot to taxpayers, as we saw in part I.

But one thing that *can* move people to action is tax dollars and budget sense. For this reason, the Rand Corporation calculated what it would cost taxpayers to achieve a 10 percent reduction in crime in California.[52] This calculation has been used by the International Centre for Prevention of Crime, which is affiliated with the United Nations, as well as in my book *Less Law, More Order* in an attempt to get governments to think about investing in pre-crime prevention instead of reactive crime cleanup.[53] In sum, it shows that the average tax-paying family that wants to reduce victimizations by 10 percent can either (1) spend $220 a year for incarceration, or (2) spend $45 a year (less than a quarter as much) on a positive parenting program (discussed above). That is, it costs *five times as much* in taxes to use traditional reactive crime-control measures to match the effectiveness of proven pre-crime prevention strategies—and that's considering only expenditures in incarceration costs, without the greater costs of things such as harm to victims.

Pre-crime Prevention Programs Make Budgetary Sense

In figure 5.1, I present comparisons of the costs of pre-crime prevention from this chapter with the costs of reactive and isolationist strategies such as those in part I of this book. The Washington State Institute for Public Policy has calculated the cost for most of the programs discussed in this chapter, and I have added some estimates for SNAP and the Youth Inclusion Program. WSIPP has calculated savings in terms of reactive crime control and then, separately, in reductions in harm to victims. Unfortunately, to date it has not made these calculations over the decade or so that is needed for the early childhood programs to show similar benefits, although Heckman and others have filled in this gap for the Perry Preschool. Others have shown the staggering costs of changing nothing in the present reactive system or only tinkering on the margins with incarceration.[54]

The monetary investments needed for the programs discussed in this chapter and their promise of a prevention dividend are extraordinarily

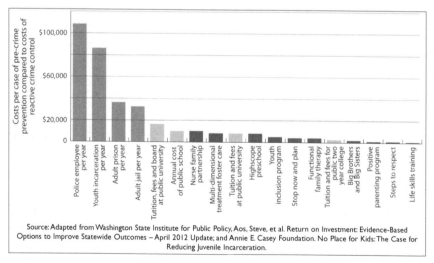

Source: Adapted from Washington State Institute for Public Policy, Aos, Steve, et al. Return on Investment: Evidence-Based Options to Improve Statewide Outcomes – April 2012 Update; and Annie E. Casey Foundation. No Place for Kids: The Case for Reducing Juvenile Incarceration.

Figure 5.1   Reactive Crime Control: Much More Expensive Than Effective Pre-crime Prevention

small when compared to the expenditures on reactive crime control being made today. Those programs that focus on individual teenagers at risk in problem places are the most expensive, at $5,000 to $10,000 per individual, but their potential for savings with youth in problem places are huge—and importantly do no harm. Those that focus on much broader populations (i.e., in schools) cost much less but will need to be matched with more intensive versions working with more at-risk youth in problem places.

It is reasonable to figure that the cumulative impact of investing in the programs listed here might achieve a 50 percent reduction in reactive crime costs and harm to victims. Though individually these programs lead to about 20 percent reductions in numbers of offenders, keep in mind that most offenders in problem places are involved in multiple offending—so one less offender means multiple fewer crimes. Smart politicians will recognize that there is an opportunity to seize today; with crime rates going down across the United States (except, importantly, for inner-city violence that often involves young people), they have a real opportunity to reduce the gross expenditures on traditional *reactive* crime control—primarily incarceration—and invest that extra money in pre-crime prevention in problem places.

This *is* possible to do, and we can look across the Atlantic to see how. Indeed, the United Kingdom is taking advantage of its decreasing crime rates to make nationwide cuts to law enforcement, courts, and corrections at a level of 20 percent—and this is being done without the benefit of the United States' hugely excessive experiment in mass incarceration, since the United Kingdom did not let its expenditures skyrocket over the past twenty to thirty years like the United States did. So if it is possible for the United Kingdom to make a 20 percent cut to its leaner crime-control budget, then the same must be true for the United States. So a smart (and achievable) public safety reinvestment would be to shift 20 percent from incarceration to pre-crime prevention over a five-year period.

The benefits from investments in early childhood will reduce child abuse within a few years, but it will take a generation for common crime rates to come down because of it. But if the investment is sustained, the common crime rates will continue to come down for all as they enter their years with a high risk of offending. However, unless these

efforts are started now, they will not be successful even within a generation—which is a sad state of affairs to leave our children with. Some
ancient Native American philosophies espouse the prominent idea of
"seven generations"—that is, that people need to work toward ensuring
not only that they'll be taken care of today, but that their communities will be taken care of *seven generations* from now. This is exactly
the sort of long-term vision we need our politicians to exhibit when it
comes to stopping crime, but starting with one generation. Putting a
young offender in jail today at great cost to society does not benefit this
generation and does harm to the next. Investing in children and youth
in problem places, however, will benefit not only this generation but
generations to come.

It does not seem like a hard choice, especially since the aforemen-
tioned investments also help these youth to flourish in other ways.
Unfortunately, all too many politicians chose to allow explosive growth
in incarceration rather than to invest in what is fair, cost-effective, and
effective at stopping harm to victims. With both violent and property
crime rates coming down from their all-time highs, there is a special opportunity today to save money by cutting expenditures and reinvesting
some of those dollars in what works to keep us safe and to reduce the
calls from (and costs of) problem places.

CONCLUSION

Points to Note: Smarter Strategies for Effective "Pre-crime" Prevention for Stopping Crime

The US Department of Justice's crimesolutions.gov identifies 72 out
of more than 240 programs that are endorsed as "effective." Of these,
no less than forty-four have to do with investing in children and youth.
Among these forty-four programs, I selected five that were also endorsed by Blueprints as model programs and three that were endorsed
by Blueprints as being promising. I also looked at the Perry Preschool
Program, as President Obama has promoted this program following its
endorsement by a Nobel Prize–winning economist. I added the Positive
Parenting Program as well because of its low cost and high estimated
returns, and also the Steps to Respect program because it is an antibul-

lying program that embraces peaceful conflict resolution—a focus that likely stops violence on the streets and in homes beyond the school years. All of these programs have also been endorsed by other respected authorities on the subject. Finally, I included the United Kingdom's Youth Inclusion Program because it features many of the proven characteristics of the Blueprints programs.

These projects individually have been proven to lower crime rates—sometimes by as much as 50 percent. Their cost advantages over the standard reactive systems of law enforcement, courts, and (particularly) corrections vary in intensity, but there is no doubt that real investments in these programs at different points in the cycle would be more effective at stopping crime than continuing to pay for today's expensive reactive measures. Importantly, these programs prove that a 50 percent reduction in crime rates within a five-year period is not only possible but would be of great advantage (and cost savings) to taxpayers.

The majority of the programs mentioned in this chapter are focused on persons in problem places and are not general programs meant for everyone. It is in this capacity that they must be multiplied. Instead of reacting with billions of dollars in an ineffective way after many people have already become victims, an investment in these problem places would give a chance to these children to grow up without a high risk of becoming a violent criminal and (mis)spending their years behind bars.

Actions for Politicians to Prevent Youth from Becoming Repeat Offenders

1. Legislators must match efforts to use law enforcement to decrease crime in problem places with pre-crime prevention. At a minimum, every additional dollar for reactive crime control such as law enforcement should be matched by an additional dollar targeted to provide better futures for youth in those problem places.
2. Legislators must fund the investment initially while deliberately decreasing the use of incarceration, as discussed in chapter 3 and to be discussed further in chapter 10. A reinvestment of 20 percent from incarceration to effective pre-crime prevention would be a reasonable initial target.

3. Legislators should identify areas known to have correctional costs above the US average (such as Milwaukee) so that they can invest in:
   a. Positive parenting programming for all, with an additional investment in public health nurses for mothers most at risk;
   b. Preschool for all, with enriched programming to help children attend and succeed in preschool, as demonstrated by Perry Preschool; and
   c. Life Skills Training and SNAP in schools.
4. Legislators should identify areas where smart law enforcement is planning to engage in hot-spots tactics and ensure that investments are also being made to offer:
   a. Proven family-based therapies, such as Functional Family Therapy;
   b. Youth Inclusion programs and mentoring; and,
   c. Where necessary, programs such as Multidimensional Treatment Foster Care.
5. Legislators should establish promising programs to promote peaceful conflict resolution and reduce bullying in all schools.
6. Legislators should establish permanent crime-reduction boards, similar to the Youth Justice Board in the United Kingdom, to lead, implement, and evaluate these proposals.

This chapter has shown that smarter crime control must focus on investing in social pre-crime prevention strategies, including early childhood development, preteen programs, and services in problem places. The costs of these effective programs are much cheaper and more cost-effective than reactive crime control. In sum, reductions in numbers of victims can be achieved through much less punitive and less costly methods than standard reactive crime control.

6

SMARTER PREVENTION OF GUN VIOLENCE

Targeting Outreach and Control

The rate of gun homicides per capita in the United States is twenty times higher than for other affluent democracies—and forty-three times higher for those ages fifteen to twenty-four.[1] Three out of four homicides are committed with a handgun, not an assault rifle or shotgun.[2] Chillingly, the number of annual handgun homicides in the United States (6,009 in 2010)[3] equals the *total* number of American casualties in the Afghanistan and Iraq wars over a seven-year period.[4] Yes, a new war has come to the streets of the United States—and the only way we can effectively fight back is to get a better handle on prevention.

Whichever way you view the statistics, the United States has a gun homicide problem. Indeed, handgun homicides in problem places must be viewed through the lens of a public health crisis, and urgently. The all-reactive, isolationist, and top-down criminal justice approach discussed in part I is simply not working. This failed war on gun violence is the chilling reality that *should* be getting the headlines—not just the exceptional and sensational mass shootings that make up only a tiny fraction of all gun violence but that receive a majority of the press coverage. Perhaps the reason for the lack of public attention is that most of these homicides happen in urban and particularly disadvantaged problem places.

So far, the United States' main response to the gun violence crisis has been to react with law enforcement to identify, seek to arrest, and then incarcerate an offender for a long time—which does fill prisons but does little to reduce the violence. Another enforcement-focused response has been focused deterrence and stop-and-frisk—either smartly or not—to stop young men from carrying guns. Although these tactics have had some success, as you saw in chapter 2, they have not stopped the rise in the numbers of victims of gun homicide, and taxpayers are still paying the bills for incarceration. And while smart law enforcement does contribute a little to a solution, reactive crime control is just not working well enough when it is isolationist, and certainly not in inner-city areas. Indeed, the national gun homicide statistics are just as depressing today as they were ten, twenty, and even fifty years ago, and gun homicides have been excluded from the great crime decline in the United States.

Whenever a mass shooting occurs (which is all too often), an international debate about US gun laws is sparked—although inner-city handgun violence is usually the elephant in the room of these disputes. And while pundits and politicians debate background checks, magazine size, mental illness, and more, law enforcement is left to deal with a perpetrator who has either killed himself or who needs to be processed through the system, likely to face the death penalty. Again, reactive crime control is occupied with picking up the pieces, not finding sustainable solutions.

In the previous chapter, we looked at proven pre-crime prevention as the way to stop violence smartly by improving early life experiences for children and adolescents, particularly in problem places and neighborhoods. In this chapter, we turn to some of the promising ways to tackle inner-city gun violence as well as actions that might reduce high-profile mass shootings. We will start by looking at how targeted social outreach strategies work to reduce gun violence at the grassroots, particularly in combination with targeted or focused deterrence strategies—that is, law enforcement that is working cooperatively with other agencies and not in isolation. Then we'll turn to whether there are smarter gun laws that might reduce the gun homicide gap between the United States and other affluent countries. Table 6.1 provides smarter ways to deal with today's gun crisis, as will be discussed in this chapter.

Reduce Gun Violence (partnered prevention and control)		
	Effective prevention	Smart reactive crime control
1	Mobilise cities to develop and implement an "office" and violence prevention plan, including diagnosis of problems building on mapping data from health emergency, police and social services, target actions to "problem places and persons", invest in community mental health services	
4	Outreach social, mentoring and sports services	Target likely offenders - focused deterrence (eg call-ins)
5	Invest in services from hospital emergency departments	Stop and frisk to remove handguns
6	Victim services and "Cure Violence" mediation	Use proven recidivism reduction to reduce reoffending
7	Invest in preventing child abuse and other domestic violence	
	Youth PROMISE Act to fund evidence-based violence prevention & intervention practices and empower local control and community oversight	
8	Legislation to (1)curb firearm trafficking; (2) restrict some gun purchases based on strengthened background checks; (3) ensure child safety; (4) ban military-style assault weapons; and (5) restrict guns in public places.	
9	Invest in surveys, data, research, development, proven practice on web, and evaluation of reduction of violence and costs	

Table 6.1   What Stops Gun Violence?

PREVENTING GUN VIOLENCE BY COMBINING PRE-CRIME PREVENTION, CONFLICT RESOLUTION, AND FOCUSED ENFORCEMENT

Among males age fifteen to twenty-four, homicide is the leading cause of death for blacks and the second leading cause of death for Hispanics. Nine out of ten of these deaths are from gunfire. For every youth murdered with a gun, there are about four additional youths treated in hospitals for nonfatal gunshot wounds resulting from criminal assaults. Exposure to gun violence has harmful effects on mental health and stops innocent citizens from taking part in healthy activities.[5] So gun violence in problem places is a national public health epidemic.

As mentioned in part I, in 2012, Anthony Braga and David Weisburd completed a review of crime "hot spots" to see how problem-oriented policing strategies such as targeted patrols in these areas can effectively stop crime by tackling key risk factors.[6] Their general conclusion was that focused deterrence strategies (e.g., police warnings to let known gang members know that they are being watched) *do* reduce gun violence, at least to some extent, which is good news. However, they were also aware that some of the success of these focused deterrence actions may have been associated with social outreach to the young men involved in a lifestyle that too often leads to serious injury and death.

The extent to which law enforcement is responsible for successfully stopping gun violence as compared to the social outreach component is of interest since law enforcement officers are generally securely employed at competitive wages. Those who perform outreach to gangs, however, rarely get a competitive wage—at least not when compared to that of a police officer. Furthermore, they are usually not permanently funded, and as the experiences in several cities show, these services tend to be expanded when gang shootings increase only to be abandoned later on when the problem is temporarily cured, leaving many outreach workers in limbo.

The outreach services that these workers provide include job training, employment, substance abuse treatment, and housing assistance—all of which directly address key risk factors for offending. As we will see, many of these initiatives focus on young men (the most common perpetrators of gun violence) who live in problem places (the most common backdrops of gun violence). All in all, it seems clear that social components *must* play a key role in reducing gun violence. So if we want large reductions in gun-related homicides, we must fund these services better and make them permanent components of any smart public safety strategy.

Lessons to Share: Boston

Boston achieved a large reduction in gun-related homicides through deliberate policy. Two efforts to combat gun violence were working separately: on one hand, the police department was working in isolation and looking at its data in terms of how enforcement might crack down on the main offenders; on the other hand, the School of Public Health at Harvard University was diagnosing the social and other risk factors that lead to violence. When these two efforts came together, they produced a synergy that resulted in positive policy to stop violence. In line with the conclusions from police data analysis and the public health diagnosis, Boston launched a full spectrum of policing and social initiatives in 1996, which successfully stemmed a rising wave of gang violence involving young men in problem places.

The law enforcement portion of this initiative was termed Operation Ceasefire. It focused police efforts on a range of enforcement procedures to seize guns and threaten to put persons persistently carrying guns behind bars. The objective was to make at-risk youth believe that they would experience heavy and predictable punitive consequences for carrying handguns and for engaging in violence. To this end, the police used whatever laws they could to intervene—including aggressive enforcement of liquor, traffic, and probation violations—but without any change in laws to register or control firearms directly. Many of these interventions were guided by David Kennedy.[7] Notably, these interventions specifically targeted men known to police—they weren't just stop-and-frisks based on a gut feeling about furtive behavior, as in New York.

The social component, guided by the public health analysis, included prevention programs such as social workers who outreached to youth in street gangs to help them and their families access much-needed social services.[8] Boston increased its services for runaways and established programs to mentor and reduce school dropout rates. Importantly, Boston also increased job training and mobilized local firms to create jobs for at-risk youth. For instance, the John Hancock Mutual Life Insurance Company invested in a summer program that gave Boston's inner-city youth a greater chance of completing high school and going on to college.

There was a third component, which was that the policing and public health efforts operated in partnership but with a clear division of labor. For instance, the police gave out leaflets telling the young men where they could get help and support. So the combination of police using focused deterrence while outreach services were offered—a sort of stick and carrot—encouraged young people to take up the offers of service. A fourth component was the mothers of the young men, who pressured political leaders to focus action on solving the problem and who encouraged their sons to abandon violent lifestyles that put them at risk of death and injury from street violence and police enforcement. They did this both privately and in street demonstrations.

Evidence for the effectiveness of Boston's combination of smart policing and targeted social outreach is strong. Homicide in the city fell from an average of forty-four persons per year murdered in the period of 1991 to 1995 down to fifteen in 1998, none of which involved youth gun violence. While some of this drop might have happened because national trends were bringing violence down across the United States, and while the numbers are small because Boston is not an enormous city, the size and speed of the drop of 63 percent is remarkable.[9] The police component was clearly an active ingredient in this quick drop, but importantly, the success cannot be reduced to the police operation on its own—the social component was of vital importance. However, while the budget for the police was not reduced when homicides decreased, funding was cut for many of the community services that likely contributed as much as policing to the elimination of youth violence. Unfortunately, gun violence in Boston then started creeping up again.[10]

There are two lessons from Boston's original success followed by the recurrence of the violence. First, to prevent gun violence you need both smarter policing *and* social outreach services. Second, you need a leadership center in the city—and not one based in the isolationist police department—so that the partnership continues and funding is sustained for the targeted social development programs as much as for policing. Perhaps if Boston had created a small but permanent crime reduction planning group similar to the Youth Justice Board discussed in the previous chapter, Boston would not have been faced with a recurrence in gun homicide tragedies.

Lessons to Share: Chicago

Similarly, some districts of Chicago that had high rates of shootings and gun fatalities benefitted from a public health strategy that focused on mediating gang disputes and tackling the social causes of violence. This strategy, now code-named Cure Violence, reduced the shootings and fatalities by as much as 34 percent.[11] It was based on a public health analysis of the distribution of homicides and shootings in the city. This geographic epidemiological analysis showed that the shootings were grouped in problem places. Worryingly, the shootings seemed to spread from one problem place to another. Explicitly described as a public health approach, it was managed by Gary Slutkin, a highly reputed public health expert from the School of Public Health at the University of Illinois.[12]

Unlike Boston, Cure Violence did not involve widespread law enforcement tactics. Rather, it was successful because it targeted a recognized pocket of persons most likely to be shot or to become shooters.

It recruited street-level workers who outreached to the target group to mentor them and help them consider and access education and jobs. These street workers—known as "interrupters"—also engaged in cooling off victims of violence so that the victims did not retaliate. They intervened in disputes that might have turned violent and mediated to resolve the conflicts peacefully. As in Boston, it also worked with mothers as well as residents in these problem places to exert public pressure on the young men to reduce violence and activities that lead to violence.

Cure Violence was evaluated by one of the best-known researchers in the United States, Dr. Wesley Skogan. He found that shootings declined by 17 to 34 percent in the targeted neighborhoods and that there was an overall reduction in victimizations. His team also interviewed three hundred high-risk individuals targeted by the program. These interviews showed that 76 percent of those individuals had been unemployed before the program and that 87 percent of them got help finding a job from their outreach worker. He also found that 37 percent had wanted to continue their education, and 85 percent of those got help doing so. Employment and education opportunities likely played a pivotal role in reducing gun violence in these neighborhoods by offering gang members the opportunity to pursue a new lifestyle. In fact, 34 percent had wanted to disengage from their gangs, and every one of them received help to do so.[13]

Interestingly, Chicago was also the site of a replication of a spinoff project of a law enforcement strategy discussed in chapter 2, known as Project Safe Neighborhoods (PSN). While many PSN projects failed because they relied too heavily on isolationist policing tactics, Chicago's version of PSN achieved a 37 percent reduction in homicide rates during the observation period due largely to its particularly creative problem-oriented policing innovations, including a call-in system to warn offenders that they were on the police's radar and efforts to change the attitudes of offenders in regard to the police.[14] Unfortunately, Chicago does not seem to have been able to organize any sustained partnership between this success and Cure Violence, and perhaps because of this, Chicago's problem places continue to have problems with gang- and gun-related homicides.

But even on its own, Cure Violence has some important lessons to share. For instance, it has become the subject of a riveting documentary and is being replicated in other cities and countries.[15] One of these replications took place in problem places in Baltimore, with encouraging results that show a reduction in shootings.[16] This evaluation clearly pointed to the importance of mediation between rival street gangs as the active ingredient in reducing violence. There were large reductions in homicides and nonfatal shootings by 35 to 45 percent in the areas where the project was best implemented.

Lessons to Share: Glasgow, Scotland

Glasgow, Scotland, provides a great model for best practice that explicitly shows how enforcement *together with* prevention can greatly reduce urban and gang violence. Its action on prevention is much more comprehensive than Cure Violence or Boston's social outreach alone, as it also includes some of the proven pre-crime prevention actions highlighted in the previous chapter, as well as strategies that focus on reducing violence against women and limiting abuse of alcohol (discussed in later chapters).

In 2007, the police service serving Glasgow instituted a public health strategy to diagnose ways to reduce knife and gang violence among young men. (Keep in mind that Scotland has had a tradition of having few handguns around, which was reinforced following the Dunblane mass shooting to be discussed below). This strategy was committed to coordinating smart policing strategies with evidence-based investments to tackle those negative life experiences that are proven to lead to violence. Specifically, it included programs to help parents provide consistent and caring parenting and education, efforts to persuade victims of urban violence to change their lifestyles to avoid revictimization, enforcement targeted at persistent offenders, and measures to prevent young men from carrying knives in the first place.

Importantly, Glasgow also established a permanent violence reduction unit to take the lead on crime reduction. It is funded through the police department, so the comprehensive initiative is able to continue in a sustained way.[17] Preliminary analysis suggests that this initiative has cut violence in the targeted neighborhoods by 50 percent over only three years—a success rate as impressive as Boston's.[18] This evidence is encouraging, and the program has become part of a government-wide strategy. But Scotland is not satisfied with preliminary evidence alone; it has set up an evaluation by a local university to monitor the program's impact so that lessons can be learned for the future.[19] This is very different from the one-off programs that have succeeded in the United States, where positive results from an evaluator arrive after the project has completed, without any permanent leadership center to keep the momentum going.

Lessons to Share: Minneapolis

Minneapolis is another exciting success story. The city's politicians were concerned not only about high rates of serious injuries and deaths to its young people but also about the related costs to taxpayers. The city council declared youth violence a public health issue, used mapping to identify the problem places, and developed its Blueprint in Action program as a response. Blueprint in Action is a comprehensive strategy based on the public health model and is soundly based on a plan to prevent violence. The plan had four objectives. One was to connect at-risk youth to a trusted adult, which is consistent with the proven preventive powers of mentoring (although their implementation used school resource officers, which are unproven). The second was to intervene at the first signs of risk, which is likely consistent with the other proven pre-crime prevention measures from chapter 5. The third was to focus on reintegrating the youth released from the youth justice system into the community, which is a strategy consistent with the gaps discussed in chapter 4. The fourth was changing the culture of violence, which is also consistent with proven pre-crime prevention but goes beyond what has been discussed so far.

Blueprint in Action is achieving large reductions in violence—a 62 percent decrease in youth suspects in violent crime—but is importantly sustaining these decreases over time because its strategy is led by a permanent office under the leadership of the city's mayor.[20] The success in Minneapolis has led to the state legislature passing the Youth Violence Prevention Act, which also defined youth violence as a public health issue. Minneapolis is also one of four cities involved in the National Forum on Youth Violence Prevention, a nationwide initiative that attempts to braid the efforts of various agencies that otherwise work in isolation and therefore achieve only limited results in terms of stopping crime.[21]

Lessons to Share: Los Angeles

Los Angeles is another example of a city where political leadership decided it needed to broaden its focus beyond just law enforcement to reduce the numbers of victims of gun and gang-related violence. Indeed, after spending $25 billion on a thirty-year war on gangs, Los Angeles County had six times as many gangs and higher levels of gang violence. Clearly, reactive crime control measures were simply not working.[22] As the Los Angeles chief of police William Bratton said, "We cannot arrest our way out of the gang crisis."[23] Therefore, the city (with the full support of police leaders) began investing modestly in social services and outreach to tackle the social causes of this trend.

The mayor established the Office of Gang Reduction and Youth Development to implement comprehensive actions in problem places. These actions were guided by a call for action that included targeted investments embracing prevention of child abuse, smart probation and policing, youth outreach, and activities to make city parks safe. Indicators for success went as high as a 57 percent reduction in homicides in the targeted problem places.[24] Importantly, this initiative was coordinated by a permanent office within the city hall, and it engaged in a comprehensive list of crime prevention and smart policing tactics.

Sustaining Effective Gun and Gang Violence Prevention Strategies

While the smart policing strategies (i.e., focused deterrence) discussed in chapter 2 are frequently a helpful component of the gun and gang violence reduction strategies discussed above, three important factors must also be present in order to sustain any gains made in increased public safety: (1) the creation of an action plan based on a city-specific diagnosis; (2) a sustained investment in social prevention, as we have seen; and (3) a permanent and independent office to coordinate the partnered efforts between community agencies and law enforcement. For instance, Los Angeles, Glasgow, and Minneapolis all created an action plan based on a diagnosis that was administered through a dedicated office to ensure sustained funding of all components.

Unfortunately, smart programs like these have not gotten the public attention or funds that they need to reduce harm to victims and stop wasting resources on ineffective *reactive* crime control.[25] Regrettably, cities are still often relying solely on police enforcement when clearly a partnership with social agencies is needed in order to bring about lasting change. However, if smart prevention projects such as those mentioned above (even when underfunded) can reduce shootings and fatalities by around 30 percent when given the chance, just think how much gun violence would be avoided in problem places by funding these strategies adequately and *on a permanent basis*. For instance, why not reallocate 10 percent of what is being wasted on overused incarceration to these proven and promising strategies?

While there is some research to test how effective such programs are at reducing the numbers of homicides and serious injuries to victims, the size of this problem nationally deserves much better data and cost-savings analysis. With today's national violence problem, data from emergency departments in hospitals could provide even more useful data than the police, and good cost-benefit analysis will surely help secure sustained initiatives over time. Meanwhile, the above examples show how politicians *can* implement smart gun and gang violence reduction strategies in any community across the United States.

FINDING NEW MODELS THAT WORK TO STOP GUN AND GANG VIOLENCE

Clearly, there are initiatives out there that *do* stop gun violence in problem places. One of the main challenges now is to make these solutions accessible for politicians and the communities they represent. For instance, the Prevention Institute, based in California, has promoted a crime reduction initiative called Urban Networks to Increase Thriving Youth (UNITY). UNITY is a network of city officials representing their mayors who collaborate to exchange information on best practices. Its aim is to promote effective, sustainable efforts to stop violence and spread those efforts nationwide. It highlights examples of strategies across the United States that *are* working to prevent violence and gun-related crimes and shares them so that communities can inform their own strategies. It highlights successful reductions in violence such as those achieved in Minneapolis.

Notably, its efforts are based around highlighting knowledge of risk factors for crime as well as using proven strategies for prevention. It exemplifies effective ways of mobilizing different sectors (e.g., schools, housing, youth services, policing) in order to support prevention strategies.[26] It uses the four-step process that is now well recognized in public health and problem-oriented policing circles and that was common to the successful examples above: (1) diagnosing the problems; (2) planning a strategy; (3) implementing the strategy; and (4) evaluating the implementation. UNITY has a particular emphasis on assisting with the transformation from reactive to preventive approaches, and it has prepared a number of briefings and fact sheets about how to do so; these can be easily accessed by legislators across the United States. But it has not yet received the significant investment that it needs to reduce the number of victims injured and killed or to see funding shifted from blunt and ineffective law enforcement to laser-sharp smart policing partnered with targeted social investments in problem places.

The National League of Cities is also taking a practical approach to sustainable gun crime prevention by encouraging the US Department of Justice[27] to braid its funding with other federal agencies responsible for education, housing, and health—that is, the agencies directly responsible for the risk factors that lead youth toward crime.[28] By so doing, the league intends to help local communities secure sustained and adequate funding for their crime prevention initiatives. By ensuring constant funding to targeted programs within these agencies, the National League of Cities hopes to promote policies that change lives on the street for the better and thereby reduce the allure of crime for vulnerable youth. Notably, the National League of Cities also recommends that mayors and chiefs of police jointly lead enforcement and prevention/intervention services and that communities sustain a nerve center to guide and track progress across varying city departments and neighborhoods. Currently, the National League of Cities is supporting a partnership with thirteen major cities in California to combat gun and gang violence by focusing on successful practices that weave together prevention, intervention, enforcement, and a community's "moral voice."[29]

The successes of the original Boston initiative are at the base of a new Center for Crime Prevention and Control at the John Jay University in New York. The center's director, David Kennedy, has brought together a network of cities engaged in replicating and testing these approaches.[30] It has an impressive number of members in pursuit of its exciting mission to advance proven strategies to combat violent crime, reduce incarceration, and rebuild relations between law enforcement and distressed communities. Unfortunately, this mission does not seem to embrace proven preventive strategies as much as these best practices would suggest.

Model Legislation: PROMISE Act

One interesting way to advance what works in preventing youth gun violence is the Youth PROMISE Act. As proposed in the House and Senate, it is a piece of forward-thinking legislation that will implement and fund evidence-based practices related to youth offending. Its intention is to interrupt the "cradle-to-prison pipeline" that is far too prevalent in problem places by supporting proven prevention and intervention strategies. Under the Youth PROMISE (Prison Reduction through Opportunities, Mentoring, Intervention, Support, and Education) Act, communities facing the greatest youth gang and crime challenges will be able to save money and develop a comprehensive response to youth violence through a coordinated prevention and intervention response. The act will require local leadership and oversight of these programs through community-based committees.[31] While the act has not yet passed into law at the time of this writing, such an initiative is urgently required to turn the United States' one-off crime stopping successes into the nationwide sustainable reduction of violence in problem places.

Lessons to Share: Preventing Repeat Admissions to Hospital Emergency Departments

We often forget that the most reliable data on violence comes not from the police, but from hospital emergency room data.[32] For instance, every year in the United States, there are one million emergency room admissions for *intentional* injuries, including both interpersonal violence (e.g., fistfights and shootings) and self-inflicted injuries.[33] Indeed, emergency rooms are untapped resources for loads of valuable information about crimes that cause injury, including violence and traffic-related accidents, as well as the risk factors (e.g., alcohol) that trigger them. This includes violence against women or assaults between people who already know each other, where the victims may seek out an emergency room or confide in a doctor much quicker than they would approach and talk to police. These valuable data are ready and waiting to help inform policy makers about strategies to stop violence, including violence involving alcohol.

Hospitals also provide unparalleled opportunities to connect at-risk individuals with effective prevention, treatment, and social services. For at-risk youths who access emergency room services for injuries from violence, "first responder" hospital workers can give referrals to outreach services such as mentoring, counseling, individual and family therapy, and other targeted interventions that can reduce future involvement in violence.

In this vein, the Cardiff strategy is a well-known best practice among violence prevention specialists. It collects data about the circumstances in which injuries took place that led to persons being admitted to hospital emergency rooms in a city in Wales. From these data, it is possible to identify hot spots for alcohol-related violence—that is, locations where injuries occur much more frequently than others. These data enable smart policing and by-law enforcement to focus on managing the source of the excessive alcohol (the risk factor) and thereby reduce the violence. The results of the Cardiff strategy are impressive: it is shown to bring about reductions in violence of more than 40 percent in the problem places in question.[34] This strategy has been used successfully in Milwaukee. Amsterdam has also recently decided to tackle the alcohol-related roots of its violence using this strategy. It is an obvious quick win for cities, with huge savings in costs to hospitals and to police in calls for service, not to mention reductions in the number of victims of violent and sexual assaults. YouTube offers an excellent TEDx presentation on the model.[35]

The Violence Intervention Program at the Trauma Center of the University of Maryland was built around the realization that 30–60 percent of violent trauma patients return with new violent injuries, often more serious.[36] The program mobilizes hospital, social, and psychological services to work with an individual immediately following a life-threatening or life-changing event. Individuals are not only experiencing a medical crisis at this time, but also social, emotional, psychological, and spiritual crises. The program achieved a whopping 75 percent reduction in violent crime for those coming to the hospital trauma unit.

There are other programs. For example, one program targeted ten- to fifteen-year-old youths who arrived at emergency departments in the Washington, DC, and Baltimore areas with assault injuries. Hospital workers provided mentoring along with parent and home visits. This strategy was found to have benefits in terms of reducing aggression and delinquency.[37] Another study focused on a program in Flint, Michigan, that delivered a brief intervention among identified at-risk youths attending emergency departments. The results found that intervention effectively reduced peer violence and alcohol consumption.[38]

In a way, hospital emergency rooms are catchment areas for many of a community's most at-risk individuals who are engaging in risky activities. These risk factors and risky behaviors, which are manifesting in emergency room visits, make these individuals more likely to be involved in violence again, and so targeting prevention at them may stop further violence. Furthermore, data on these individuals may help to identify the problem places that lead to the violence and may indicate where more action is needed. Therefore, emergency rooms can complement the prevention programs that are going out into the communities by having the most at-risk members of a community coming right to them.

GETTING SERIOUS ABOUT STOPPING GUN VIOLENCE THROUGH GUN LEGISLATION?

Roughly one-third of US households have one or more guns (e.g., rifles, shotguns, handguns, automatic weapons, etc.). According to a US national survey, the proportion of households with guns has gradually decreased to 32 percent, though the number of guns owned has increased to around 70 million—meaning that a smaller number of people own a large number of guns.[39] When these guns fall into the wrong hands, they can lead to violence.[40] In fact, the National League of Cities has forwarded specific proposals to reduce intentional injuries from guns as part of a broader statement about prevention of gun violence.[41] All in all, it's time to look at regulation to keep some types of guns out of the hands of violent offenders.

Why Not Regulate Handguns More Effectively?

There is significant research on the role that handguns play in facilitating murders, robberies, and other crimes that devastate and destroy the lives of victims. After analyzing data collected in eleven countries for the International Crime Victim Survey, experts have confirmed a simple, irrefutable correlation: *more handguns in households mean higher homicide rates.* For that reason, a vast number of experts—though not US legislators—agree that the European and Canadian policies restricting handgun ownership are much better than the laissez-faire, extremist handgun policies and traditions in the United States.[42]

For example, the risk of becoming a victim of gun violence is six times greater in the United States than in Canada, a country that shares a great many similarities. A closer look at the gun trends on both sides of the border sheds light on why this is. In the United States, most gun owners (67 percent) have guns to protect themselves against other people, according to a Gallup poll.[43] In contrast, as Michael Moore's Oscar-winning documentary *Bowling for Columbine* highlights, people in Canada own long guns to hunt animals. The statistics back up this difference. About 14 percent of US households have a long gun, while 28 percent have handguns. In Canada, about 22 percent of households have a long gun, while only 4 percent have handguns.[44] Interestingly, when you take guns out of the equation, homicide rates are roughly the same in the two countries.

One interesting study by John Sloan and his colleagues compared the homicide rates of Seattle, Washington, with those of nearby Vancouver, Canada—two cities that are generally comparable in terms of demographics.[45] Seattle, however, had a homicide rate that was 50 percent higher. Why? The researchers pointed to the greater availability of handguns there. In fact, in the United States, over 60 percent of homicides and 40 percent of robberies are firearm related—most involving handguns rather than rifles and shotguns.[46] In Canada (which has *four times* fewer homicides per capita to begin with), only about 30 percent of the homicides and a quarter of the robberies involve guns.

But if we already know that handguns are used in such a great number of crimes in the United States, why are they so much more readily available in the United States than in Canada and other affluent democracies? A recent study by the DC-based Institute of Medicine showed this "health gap" and asked the same question.[47] It determined that the gap is, in part, the result of deliberate policy initiatives that have taken place in Canada, of which the most significant is the 1977 Firearm Control Policy.[48] Essentially, this program banned automatic weapons for civilian use, stopped persons from carrying handguns for self-protection, and required all guns other than long guns to be registered. Further, it required hunters to have a certificate to acquire a firearm, which ensures that the person does not have a criminal record and is not mentally ill; the process for obtaining a certificate is similar to the one for obtaining a passport in that potential owners had to get a respected member of the community to certify that they were not a risk. The program also encouraged long-gun owners to keep ammunition separate from their weapons and required them to take a course in the safe handling and storage of long guns. The contribution of all this to fewer homicides was evaluated scientifically and found to have been effective.

There are also many fewer handgun owners (and ergo many fewer homicides) per capita in Canada compared with the United States, where all other factors are roughly the same, in part because Canadians do not feel the need to own a handgun to protect themselves. This feeling is consistent with the realities that homicide and robbery rates with guns are much lower in Canada and indicates that strong implementation of the proposals in the first part of this chapter in the United States would reduce gun-related homicides and, consequently, might even make more Americans feel at ease without the burden of feeling responsible for their own self-defense.

Figure 6.1 compares the rates of availability of handguns and other guns in the late 1990s (the most recent comparative data available) with current murder rates. These show Canada and the United States with similar rates of non-gun-related murders, but with higher rates of hand-

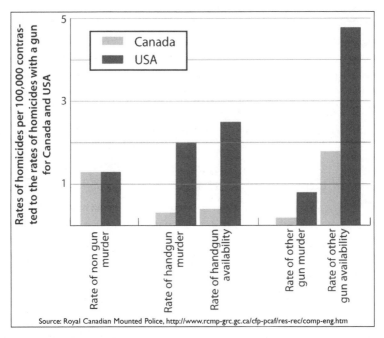

Figure 6.1   The Availability of Guns versus the Number of Homicides: Contrasting Canada and the United States

gun murders (seven times higher) and other gun murders (four times higher) for the United States than for Canada.

The Evidence for Smartening Up Firearm Legislation

Some states in the United States have come further than others in enacting smarter gun laws. By looking at the effects of various gun laws as they've been enacted, we can begin to see trends in which strategies are more effective. The Brady Center to Prevent Gun Violence is a nongovernmental group that has assessed the scientific research on state gun laws in order to propose widespread, evidence-based ways to reduce further injuries and fatalities from gun violence.[49] In this vein, the Brady Center analyzed sections of state firearm legislations and divided them into five categories, which coincide with the Brady Center's assessment of what is likely to reduce fatalities. The categories were: (1) to curb firearm trafficking; (2) to restrict some gun purchases based on strengthened background checks; (3) to ensure child safety; (4) to ban military-style assault weapons; and (5) to restrict guns in public places.

A group of researchers then compared the rates of gun-related homicides and suicides by state with a scale built around the Brady Center's classification of types of gun legislation. In sum, the researchers found that the more the states had adopted gun legislation meant to address one or more of these five concerns, the fewer homicides (and fewer suicides) occurred per capita.[50] This study shows that states *can* pass legislation that is consistent with the evidence, and it also suggests that states adopting these initiatives will likely have fewer homicides. Though this type of research cannot prove cause and effect like a random control trial might, it is encouraging for potential victims to know that violence can be reduced through smarter legislation.

Another important hub of knowledge is the Law Center to Prevent Gun Violence, which brings together legal professionals to study the data and make proposals to reduce gun homicides and violence. The center's main objective is to provide information on what states might do to enact smart gun laws that save lives.[51] To achieve this, the center tracks gun-related statistics and maintains a database on the various state laws and their interpretations of critical topics such as the use of background checks, the availability of assault weapons and machine guns, regulations on who can carry guns and where they can be carried, restrictions due to domestic violence concerns, and mental health reporting. When a separate group of researchers used this information to look at the relationship between the various state legislations, they also came to the conclusion that there are more homicides (and suicides) in those states with weaker legislation related to the critical topics listed above.[52] This study also shows that states can adopt smart legislation and supports the argument that if states pass certain key pieces of legislation, they will be able to reduce the number of deaths involving guns.

Why Not Enact Smart Gun Legislation to Help Prevent Mass Shootings before They Happen?

According to the US attorney general, Eric Holder, since April 1999—when the mass shootings took place at Columbine High School in Colorado—the United States has witnessed no fewer than forty-seven mass shootings involving over 640 victims, more than half of whom were killed.[53] These estimates are below those used by the homicide statistician James Fox, who uses the FBI definition of a "mass shooting" as being an incident that kills at least four victims. With this definition, he estimates that on average, there are twenty-five perpetrators killing one hundred victims each year.[54] Either way, the number of victims killed is approximately one hundred in a year. In the majority of these incidents, the perpetrators used high-capacity magazines[55]—which is a main contributor to the high death tolls.

Perhaps unsurprisingly, these events elicit heavy and sensationalized media coverage. For this reason, the average American might be surprised to learn that the number of mass shootings has *not* been rising in recent years, although it may seem that way because of the media coverage given to any one event.[56] But while an individual incident may involve many victims, the relative number of persons killed in mass killings is very small in relation to the total number of persons killed by guns in a given year: in recent years, it works out to be an average of one hundred victims out of the eight thousand-plus lives claimed by gun violence every year. But it has remained a steady blot on the public conscience, as the numbers have not decreased in the same way that the overall homicide rate has.

Indeed, the United States has sadly become quite familiar with mass shootings over the past three decades (and maybe more, if the data were available). The fact that the rates have remained steady suggests that this form of violence has somehow not been affected by the laws passed in particular states, as discussed above, or by federal actions (although these actions tend to be relatively weak and leave many wide gaps). By the time this book goes to print, there will surely be other incidents that will jar our consciences, but most of us have not forgotten Columbine, and few will forget the child victims of the mass shooting at a Newtown, Connecticut, elementary school in 2012.

A Model Example: Gun Laws and Gun Amnesties in the United Kingdom and Australia

In other countries, mass shootings that involved small children or large numbers of victims have precipitated gun-law reforms that have had positive and important preventive effects.

For example, in 1996, Dunblane, Scotland, experienced the mass shooting of sixteen primary school children that involved a handgun. In less than two years, handguns—regardless of the near-sacred place they occupied in a small minority of the British sporting culture—were prohibited across the United Kingdom. The ban was accompanied by a nationwide amnesty to get owners to give up their handguns, and in this way the number of handguns in circulation was greatly reduced. Since that time, gun-related homicides have declined in the United Kingdom, though there has been some resurgence in gang-related handgun use in large urban centers such as London. Still, gun-related violence in the United Kingdom is infinitesimal when compared with any city in the United States.

Shortly after the Dunblane mass shooting, Port Arthur, Australia, experienced a horrific tragedy that claimed the lives of thirty-five adults. In this case, the killer used automatic weapons—including an AR15 that was similar to the weapon used over a decade later in Newtown, Connecticut. The Port Arthur shooting resulted in the Australian government enacting a comprehensive set of gun restrictions, including a restriction on guns that load automatically. Like in the United Kingdom, there was a national amnesty for owners to turn in their newly prohibited guns, and this effort led to the recovery of close to 700,000 guns. Since then, Australia has experienced a 40 percent reduction in gun-related homicides, and so far there have been no more mass killings in the country; there have also been fewer suicides.[57]

Some US police researchers have argued that voluntary amnesties do not reduce violence in the United States. But before we dismiss gun amnesties, let's remember that the gun amnesties considered in the police research were *not* the same gun amnesties as those in the United Kingdom and Australia.[58] Rather, the gun amnesties in the United Kingdom and Australia were nationwide and focused strategies, while those in the United States targeted much smaller areas, were marred by disparate messaging, and were voluntary.

It is unlikely that anything similar to Australia or the United Kingdom's gun amnesties could happen widely in the United States at this point. Although the evidence points to the effectiveness of using laws to restrict guns and to prevent violence, it's possible that the United States is still a long way from enacting smart nationwide legislation to keep guns out of the hands of dangerous offenders, as shown by the US Senate's April 2013 vote against implementing stricter background checks and banning assault weapons.

Taking Guns Away from Abusive Partners to Save Women's Lives

Every year in the United States, approximately 1,600 women are murdered by their intimate partners—that's 40 percent of all homicides involving female victims, some of whom are estranged or separated from their male partners, and some of whom are pregnant. In contrast, only 750 (or 5 percent) of the homicides involving male victims every year are committed by an intimate partner.

What's more relevant to this chapter, however, is that guns and intimate partner homicide go hand in hand. For example, of *all* the females killed with a gun, almost two-thirds are killed by their intimate partners; usually these homicides are committed with a handgun. In fact, access to firearms increases the risk of intimate partner homicide by more than *five times* compared to instances where no weapons are available. In addition, abusers who possess guns tend to inflict the most severe abuse on their partners.[59]

Evidence clearly shows that removing guns from the equation reduces the risk of fatal attacks on female partners by 10 percent.[60] Unfortunately, it is not yet known to what extent the states with stricter gun legislation and enforcement have decreased their numbers of intimate partner deaths. Hopefully research will become available in the near future to better inform how gun laws can prevent violence against women. It may be difficult for studies to gauge this correlation, because the number of intimate partner homicides has been dropping steadily over recent decades for a number of reasons, such as increased opportunities for women to leave men who are violent and increased availability of shelters for battered women. These reasons will be discussed in more detail in the next chapter.

CONCLUSION

Points to Note: Smarter Prevention of Gun Homicides

A depressing accumulation of statistics shows that the United States loses more young (mostly black) men to handgun violence each year than in seven years of war in Iraq and Afghanistan combined. Fortunately, this gun violence is preventable in the short term by combining smart policing (i.e., focused deterrence) and targeted social outreach and mediation. To sustain the reductions, however, investments must be made in proven pre-crime prevention that is spearheaded by small leadership centers established in cities. As in Minneapolis, the savings in reactive crime control and hospital emergency care will be significant.

Emergency room data are proven to be an effective complement to police data in terms of focusing on solutions to violence. Emergency rooms can also be utilized to initiate and refer at-risk youth to programs that reduce their offending and risky behaviors.

But law enforcement and its dedicated researchers must shift out of their isolationist mindsets, for as some are already acknowledging, we cannot arrest our way out of these challenges, and we need to be smarter with reduced police resources. Indeed, it is self-evident that the extraordinary expenditures on reactive crime control—particularly the incarceration of young black males who are also most at risk of killing and getting killed—are not an adequate solution.

Solving the problem of gun violence requires a two-pronged approach: investing now with outreach and pre-crime prevention in problem places to reduce the allure and accessibility of gun-related lifestyles in the first place, and enacting proven legislation. While lagging states should follow what leading states have already achieved, it may help to win the first battle in order to win the second, particularly at the federal level.

Actions for Politicians for Smarter Prevention of Gun Violence

1. Legislators must invest now in the social agencies that are able to assist young men in problem places to choose a lifestyle free from handguns, including support legislation such as PROMISE, and encourage interventions following emergency department admissions.[61]
2. Legislators must encourage cities to take a leadership role in "public health" strategies that reduce inner-city violence.
3. Legislators must act to encourage law enforcement to use smart, proven policing tactics but in sustained combination with the social agencies that can be targeted to problem places and neighborhoods.

4. Legislators should support the work of networks, such as the National League of Cities and UNITY, to share and implement best practices for comprehensive, evidence-based gun violence prevention.

5. The Department of Justice should add a section on its crimesolutions.gov website on gun violence that includes examples such as Minneapolis and Glasgow (which can never be random control trials but that logically are saving large numbers of lives).

6. Advocacy groups should extend their criticism of mass incarceration and the war on drugs as being racially biased to include criticism of the lack of prevention to save the lives of young black men getting shot.

7. State legislators should enact legislation in the five areas proposed by the Brady Center, which has been adopted by other states and is shown to correlate with fewer gun deaths.

8. Legislators should look for ways of reducing the numbers of guns, particularly handguns.

This chapter shows that smarter crime control must focus on investing in social preventive strategies, including early childhood development, services outreach into problem places, mobilizing interveners, and mediation and mentoring. It must also focus on smarter law enforcement through focused deterrence, taking guns from offenders, and enforcing gun regulations. In sum, reductions in the numbers of victims of gun violence can be achieved through much less punitive and costly methods than the standard reactive crime control.

7

PREVENTING VIOLENCE
AGAINST WOMEN

INTRODUCTION

This chapter is about smarter ways to prevent violence against women, particularly intimate partner violence and sexual violence—two topics that have been very much overlooked until the past few decades in the United States as well as in other affluent democracies.

The numbers are shocking: every year in the United States, a million women are raped, and more than a million experience serious physical violence by an intimate partner.[1] These statistics seriously question whether government actions up to now have been focused on the right issues. Much of this physical and sexual violence occurs behind closed doors. Some occurs on the street and at places of employment. It is predominantly committed by men (particularly, young men). Men are also *victims* of intimate partner violence and sexual violence but at lower rates; disturbingly, a quarter of the sexual violence against men occurs in childhood. At whatever age, sexual and intimate partner violence and the related offense of stalking can do immense damage to victims, with repercussions that may persist over a lifetime. Intimate partner violence can also be part of a vicious cycle, where children who witness it in their homes grow up to use that same violence in their own adult lives.

In terms of smart crime control, and unlike every other chapter in this book, the United States is smarter than most other affluent democracies when it comes to violence against women. Indeed, it has gone out of its way to be better informed and has also legislated its national Violence against Women Act (VAWA). This act established a national office and aims to reduce violence against women, but for the moment it is largely focused on reaction, including funding reactive systems to assist victims and improve enforcement and prosecutions rather than funding pre-crime prevention. On the bright side, publications on the latest surveys have concluded with suggested actions related to pragmatic reforms and evidence-informed suggestions for prevention, not just reactive crime control and mass incarceration. Nevertheless, there is still a tre-mendous lack of information on this crisis. For this reason, unlike every other chapter in this book, I can't point to a significant accumulation of knowledge from scientific experiments or citywide initiatives, and there is no list of tested programs that are scientifically proven to work. This lack of available information worldwide is something that must change.

Nevertheless, there is no reason to wait while better knowledge is developed, as there are some proven and many promising strategies for reducing violence against women from these disturbing levels, includ-ing investing in pre-crime prevention that will also contribute to less violence against women. In this chapter, we focus on some preventive actions specific to violence against women. We know that one important answer to solving the problem of sexual violence and intimate partner violence involves changing attitudes of men. We know that much can be achieved in this vein with men in their teens, and we have had some success in doing just that. We also know that men (and women) can be mobilized to become interveners who will stop violence before it starts by taking simple actions.

We also need to look at how to make the reactive system of crime control smarter. If women had more confidence in the police and the courts, not only might they report more, but they also might use the threat of that system as boosting their confidence to say no to violence. If women had more access to refuges and domestic violence courts, maybe this would also encourage them to stand up to perpetrators. And if women could be sure that perpetrators would not come back at them with a gun, then their lives would be at less risk.

So there are many actions that are promising to significantly reduce the number of women harmed by violence. In table 7.1, I have listed several of these actions based on those that are pre-crime prevention and those that can be applied to existing police and court systems to make reactive crime control smarter. I have also mentioned the need to continue to collect good data and to invest in assessing which innovative interventions are indeed reducing harm to victims and saving money for taxpayers. These actions are all discussed below.

SHINING A SPOTLIGHT ON THE ISSUE OF SEXUAL VIOLENCE AND INTIMATE PARTNER VIOLENCE

The impact of violence against women is immense. This victimization often brings longstanding emotional pain, including persistent fear and anxiety. But that pain is just the tip of the iceberg. Other impacts include physical harm, sexually transmitted diseases, unwanted pregnancy, and even harm to an unborn child during pregnancy. The measurable impact of sexual violence on adult women exceeds the combined impacts of homicide and deaths from drunk driving. This impact is estimated by looking at what civil courts would pay to victims for loss of quality of life. The main costs are the difficulties that a rape victim has in enjoying life, having confidence in her safety, and much more.

Its impacts, devastating as they may be to victims, also come with a cost to taxpayers. Ironically, the immediate tangible costs of sexual as-

Priorities for National Office to Combine to Reduce Violence Against Women	
Effective Prevention	**Smart Reactive Crime Control**
Invest in early childhood	Gender police response
Outreach to disadvantaged women in problem places	Invest in rape crisis, SANE and victim options so that victims seek help
Focus on responsible use of alcohol	Develop rights for rape victims in court
Change male attitudes to sexual violence, while in school	Increase access to refuges
Multiply campus strategies to reduce sexual assault	Control access to guns
Foster intervening to stop actions such as drinking that increase risk	Use domestic violence courts
Encourage men to speak out against violence against women	Use proven recidivism reduction to reduce reoffending
Invest in surveys, data, research, development, proven practice on web	

Table 7.1   What Stops Violence against Women?

sault can be relatively low in terms of emergency care, though if the victim has to pay for a forensic rape exam or additional care it may be significant in light of her income. However, rape often results in victims persistently using health-care services as well as having difficulties at work and significant lost productivity.

The Shocking Rates of Sexual and Domestic Violence

The numbers alone should be enough to make anyone sit up and take notice. In 2010, the United States undertook the largest and most sophisticated survey ever conducted on sexual violence and intimate partner violence in an affluent democracy. The survey is called the National Intimate Partner and Sexual Violence Survey.[2] It was organized by the Centers for Disease Control and Prevention, among others. Its conclusions are based on interviews with 9,086 women and 7,421 men.

This survey confirms that nearly one in four women and one in seven men have experienced severe physical violence by an intimate partner in their lifetimes.[3] Nearly one in five women and one in seventy men have been raped in intimate situations at some time in their lives, including alcohol- or drug-facilitated penetration.

For women, rape often occurs when they are teenagers or college age: two in five rape victims experienced their first rape before the age of eighteen, and four in five before age twenty-five, as shown in figure 7.1. These statistics reinforce a need to focus on what can be done in schools, which we discuss below. They also confirm the results of other specialized surveys on sexual assault on college campuses, which show that up to 25 percent of women experience rape or attempted rape during college[4]—that's over five times the rate for the general population.[5] Worse, drug-facilitated rape and incapacitated rape are almost *nine times* more common on college campuses. These findings counter the continual assertion by most colleges that sexual assault does not happen to their students. These statistics are shocking and undeniable, and they should have produced action by every college leader—but unfortunately, they have not yet. But it's not too late for college leaders (and leaders at all school levels) to organize annual conferences to discuss what can be done.

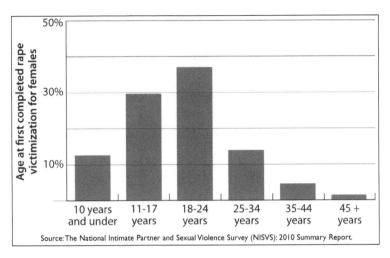

Figure 7.1   Rape for Females: More Likely to Happen before the Age of 25

As high as these victimization rates may be, it seems that rates of sexual violence are staying steady, though the science is not perfect. Experts using these sophisticated surveys do not believe that there have been decreases in the numbers of rapes and sexual assaults over the past few decades.[6] But even the national crime victimization survey is limited, as its questions on sexual assault are part of an omnibus survey of serious crimes.

What's even more significant is the number of rape victims who do not report their assault to police. The estimates from the 2006 survey shows that *84 percent* of rape victims do not call the police; this percentage is even higher on college campuses.[7] Whether or not police action can deter rape is another matter that is discussed below. Still, relatively few rapes coming to the attention of the police certainly limits the capacity of law enforcement to stop individual offenders from reoffending and to hold offenders accountable.

While rates of rape may not be decreasing, there are some encouraging downward trends in terms of intimate partner (domestic) violence. For instance, the number of women murdered by intimate partners dropped steadily every year from 1970 to 2000; this trend follows the general decline in murders.[8] In addition, researchers used regression analysis to conclude that these particular declines benefitted from changes in laws allowing for divorce and separation, increased eco-

nomic opportunities for women, and more spaces available in transition houses—all of which have enabled more women to leave violent
partners.[9] The declines also correlate with the increased use of arrest
for perpetrators by police when intimate partner violence is reported
(in cases where the perpetrators have something to lose from arrest), as
well as independent legal advocacy for women. Although these trends
are encouraging, they are not the result of any targeted *preventive* action meant to stop the abuse from happening in the first place. At best,
police intervention is meant to ensure the victim's immediate safety and
then reduce *re*offending and *re*victimization; it has also helped victims
get to refuges for battered women and access other victim services.[10]

While the United States may not be behind other affluent democracies when it comes to violence against women, it is not ahead of what
governments across the world agree to be the actions needed. In 2013,
the UN Commission on the Status of Women focused on sexual violence
and intimate partner violence in addition to issues such as human trafficking. The Commission drew attention to the huge amount of harm
caused to victims as well as the lost productivity and significant costs
that taxpayers pay annually in health care. They called for action in
three areas: (1) stopping the violence before it happens (prevention);
(2) improving the response to victims of sexual and intimate partner violence, and holding offenders accountable (both reactive crime control
measures); and (3) increased national plans and leadership. We'll look
at each of these below.

THE NEED TO SWITCH THE FOCUS TO *PREVENTING* VIOLENCE AGAINST WOMEN

Any action to prevent violence against women must focus on tackling
the recognized risk factors associated with sexual violence and intimate
partner violence.

Preventing Men from Being Violent, Including against Women

First, some of the violence against women occurs more frequently in
problem places, like other sorts of violence do, and so some of the typi-

cal sexual and domestic violence offenders do not differ all that much from other violent offenders. Therefore, it's evident that we need to take the same sort of actions that are discussed in chapter 5 to reverse the risk factors that lead offenders to become violent in the first place. Here, we can turn to the WHO to inform us of the different types of risk factors that are known to contribute to higher levels of intimate partner violence.[11] For males, individual factors include drinking heavily, being of low socioeconomic status, and witnessing violence. As mentioned above, the seeds for sexual violence and intimate partner violence are often sown when offenders are just children. They have often witnessed their fathers abusing their mothers, or they have been victims of sexual assault themselves. Both males and females in domestic-violence relationships often have a history of sexual violence in their own childhoods.[12] For women who are victims, many of the same risk factors come into play, though depression and mental illness are also part of the picture. We will discuss the role of alcohol in the next chapter.

Second, there are relationship factors, which include exhibiting male dominance and poor family functioning, as well as societal and community factors, which include male patriarchy norms that support violence as well as weak community sanctions against it. More experimentation is needed to get proof as to whether or not existing programs actually work to tackle these risk factors to reduce violence against women.

Preventing Men from Offending Before They Victimize Women in the First Place

This section looks at other ways that are promising to turn at-risk youth away from perpetrating acts of sexual and intimate partner violence. Following the widespread National Intimate Partner and Sexual Violence Survey, the Centers for Disease Control and Prevention confirmed that many assaults occurred during the dating years (i.e., high school and college). Therefore, in order to reduce rape and intimate partner violence, preventive strategies need to focus on fostering healthy relationships with peers and dating partners during the precollege and college period.[13]

Two strategies stand out. The first is to change the attitudes of young people in high school and college in regard to alcohol and drug abuse, violence, and sexual assault against women; in this way, many of the young men with potential to become offenders will be influenced to avoid violence. I will explain the model examples that have proven that this approach works.[14] The second strategy is to focus on bystanders as a way to change social norms and to promote bystander intervention (i.e., when a person not involved in a potential rape or sexual assault intervenes to divert the predator from continuing or to help the victim escape from the situation). I will also explain these model examples.

Model Examples: Changing Young Attitudes with Safe Dates and Fourth R   According to the WHO, at present there is only *one* strategy that has widespread evidence supporting its effectiveness, and this relates only to intimate partner violence (Safe Dates, or Fourth R, which uses school-based programs to prevent violence within dating relationships, as discussed below).

Safe Dates is a program to change attitudes of boys regarding sexual violence. It was developed and tested in North Carolina, and the website crimesolutions.gov has endorsed it as effective.[15] Safe Dates is a school-based prevention program aimed at elementary and high school students; it is designed to prevent dating violence, including the psychological, physical, and sexual abuse that may occur between youths involved in a dating relationship. The program's goals include changing adolescent norms about dating violence and gender roles, improving conflict resolution skills for dating relationships, encouraging victims and perpetrators to seek help for dating violence, and developing peer help-giving skills. The evaluation of this program used a quasi-experimental design that showed some changes in attitudes and, importantly, some reductions in rape and sexual violence.

Another impressive program meant to stop violence in dating relationships grew out of the work of the family court clinic in London, Ontario, Canada. For more than thirty years, this team has worked toward better ways to react to violence against women in the hope of stopping the violence. It pioneered police and social worker teams that responded to domestic violence cases, developed more victim-friendly ways for victims of intimate partner violence to appear in court, teamed up police and prosecutors with community agencies, and developed a battered wife advocacy clinic.

Recognizing the limits of these reactive approaches, it added a well-thought-out prevention program known as Fourth R. It is a high school–based curriculum meant to prevent sexual and dating violence by boys—and hopefully to change their attitudes as adults. It was called "Fourth R" as it adds "relationships" to the traditional three Rs of school programming: Reading, wRiting, aRithmetic, and so *Relationships*. The interactive curriculum integrates dating violence prevention with lessons on healthy relationships, sexual health, and substance use. It is delivered to grade 9 health classes by teachers with additional training in the dynamics of dating violence and healthy relationships. The costs for the program (both teacher training and materials) average sixteen dollars per student.[16]

The program was put to a rigorous empirical test that spanned twenty schools and 1,700 students, where the researchers first measured levels of sexual assault, dating violence, and bullying from the perspective of both boys and girls. Then, half the schools implemented the Fourth R curriculum, while the other half was encouraged to foster nonviolent dating relationships through the standard curriculum. The students were then assessed a year later in terms of how much personal dating violence was perpetrated by boys and how many girls were victims of this violence. The study concluded that there was a 25 percent reduction of boys' reported use of dating violence. Even though this program was tested using a random control trial, crimesolutions.gov has rated it only as promising.[17] Hopefully it will be upgraded soon.

The World Health Organization has looked for additional effective programs to reduce violence against women in vain. Still, it decided that these two programs, even on their own, justified a proven effectiveness rating for preventing present and future violence against women programming.[18] Therefore, organizations need to implement—and researchers to evaluate—more of these programs; after all, the risks are small, and the potential benefits are huge. They will almost certainly do at least some good (and probably *a lot* of good), which is more than can be said for much of the reactive crime control efforts that endeavor to pick up the pieces that occasionally come to their attention after violence against women has occurred.[19]

Model Examples: Encouraging Bystander Intervention with Green Dot and Don't Be That Guy   As you saw earlier, college students experience rape or attempted rape at a rate five times higher than that for the general population.[20] Bonnie Fisher, one of the leading researchers on this issue, is a strong advocate for getting federal legislation to force universities to take action.[21] She has been active in evaluating various preventive actions that can be taken. The Green Dot program is an example of one such action.

Like Fourth R, Green Dot focuses on changing attitudes toward rape and sexual violence, this time at the college level.[22] Developed on the campus of the University of Kentucky, the Green Dot program is an outstanding example of a way to encourage bystander intervention.[23] It does this through an inspiring lecture that invites new students to learn more about what needs to be done to reduce rape and sexual assault on campus. It also provides students with simple ways to intervene to stop a series of events that may end up in a sexual assault. Similarly, the Don't Be That Guy campaign, a program that originated in Edmonton, Alberta, Canada, encourages young people to talk about what consent means and to intervene when necessary.

The evaluations of Green Dot show that it is able to significantly influence bystander interventions.[24] As yet, however, the evaluations do not show exactly what direct impact these interventions have on the rates of sexual assault. Still, Green Dot is a promising example that colleges can implement today, even without waiting for the extensive evaluations that are slow in coming. Indeed, this program will invariably do more good than waiting until the violence has occurred and expecting an expensive, blunt reaction from crime control that is limited in effectiveness.

Model Examples: White Ribbon and Advocacy by Sports Teams   Other programs have a similar aim to that of Green Dot, and some of them focus particularly on mobilizing males to advocate to other males for an end to violence against women. The Canadian White Ribbon campaign encourages men to show that they are against violence against women by wearing a white ribbon. The slogan is that White Ribbon is men working to end violence by men against women. White Ribbon promotes its campaign in schools, with the general public, and with politicians. Although there are no evaluations for this program, there is a logic to this action, for we saw above that male attitudes toward violence against women is one of the contributing factors to its prevalence.[25]

Sports role models also provide an opportunity to change male attitudes when it comes to sexual violence and intervening. Endemic to sports headlines are football stars of all ages raping or sexually assaulting women and girls. For instance, the town of Steubenville, Ohio, made national headlines when two high school football stars raped a sixteen-year-old who had consumed so much alcohol that she could not consent. There are many more examples.[26] However, the prominence of the offenders brings additional challenges. For instance, social media is now being used to share not only differing views on the victims' responsibility, but also actual photos of the victims and even their names. On the other hand, the notoriety of these cases undoubtedly brings harm to the future sports careers of these one-time heroes.

One small step is for male sports teams and their coaches to become active in raising awareness about what is responsible behavior with respect to women. This would include a component in their training that is similar to the Fourth R. It could also include the role of the football team in talking up the issues. For instance, after a series of alleged sexual assaults by team members, the BC Lions Football team in Vancouver, Canada, became a leader in working with groups striving to eliminate rape. A key component of their work is to encourage men to be "more than a bystander"—similar to the Green Dot campaign.[27] The BC Lions' work focuses on men working as role models to change the attitudes of other men, and this initiative could easily be carried over to other sports organizations if there was the will to do so. This is an approach that deserves much more investment—and yes, more research—because it makes sense, especially since we know that the seeds of sexual and domestic violence are often planted when young boys witness their fathers acting as poor role models in terms of their treatment toward women.

IMPROVING THE REACTIVE CRIME CONTROL SYSTEM TO PUT VICTIMS' NEEDS FIRST

Why not have policing respond better to violence against women? There is a vast disconnection between the traditional, isolated policing mechanisms we looked at in part I and the needs of victims of sexual and intimate partner violence. As mentioned earlier, the nonreporting rates of rape and sexual assault are a staggering 84 percent—that means only one in seven victims goes to the police. The nonreporting rates are even higher on college campuses. While the reasons for nonreporting are complex, the reaction of traditional policing and courts is surely part of the equation. Perhaps part of this is the attitudes of predominantly male agencies such as law enforcement, where approximately four out of five sworn police officers are men. For the victims who *do* go to the police, many have to endure a police investigation that too often does not focus on the victims' needs. The criminal courts bring them mixed experiences, and they are often left with lasting trauma, not just from the victimization but also from the court process. Frequently, victims also have to endure the loss of friends in their communities, and many move away to start a new life. Perhaps it's no wonder that the reporting rates are so low. These statistics should set off alarm bells about how police respond to victims of rape and intimate partner crime,[28] but unfortunately, these bells are not sounding loud enough.

Indeed, the traditional isolationist approach to policing tends to emphasize only catching the offender instead of also focusing on victims and their needs, as the following Jane Doe story illustrates. In 1986 in Toronto, Canada, a serial rapist was on the loose. Police knew that he had targeted four white women with dark hair who lived alone and that his modus operandi was entering over the balcony. Still, the police did not warn women in the area, even though the likelihood of further victimizations seemed imminent. Why? Because their focus was solely on catching the criminal. So when the rapist attacked a fifth victim and she survived, she sued the police for not warning her—and she won.[29] To an ordinary citizen, it is obvious that the police should warn potential victims. Unfortunately, as we saw in part I, the dominant role of the police is to enforce the law (i.e., to catch the offender) *after* the crime happens instead of preventing the offense and helping the victim.

Above, we've seen some promising examples of how to stop violence against women before it happens. Below, we'll look at some ways that our existing systems can respond better to victim's needs after the crime has unfortunately happened.

A Model Example: All-Female Police Units in Brazil

Some police forces have been able to break the shocking nonreporting trend, and policing across the United States can learn from these. In particular, Brazil has nurtured one of the most interesting initiatives in terms of effective policing for victims of sexual and domestic violence. All-female police stations have been established in some of the main problem places. As a result, ordinary women who are victims of sexual and domestic violence feel more comfortable reporting, and they have more confidence that they will be treated with respect when they report abuse to the police.

In practice, what makes this approach effective is partly the inter-weaving of social services with policing, as these police stations also have doctors and psychologists available so that victims can get help while recovering from the violence and sorting out their lives after being victimized. The other important component is that the existence of these police stations is believed to empower women, as they can say no to both sexual and physical violence while having more confidence that their perpetrator will listen. If he does not, he knows there is a greater chance that the police will come down on him, so it is a kind of focused deterrence. Unfortunately, police services in the United States have resisted this type of initiative. Also unfortunately, the police researchers have not focused on making a case for why they should.

A Model Example: SANE Nurses and Rape Kits

One small piece of good news is that sexual assault victims are a step closer to having their financial needs met in terms of paying the bills incurred by their victimization. One of the recent programs promoted by the Violence against Women Act would see victims' sexual assault examinations paid for by the government, primarily through the Sexual Assault Nurse Examiners (SANE) program. SANE programs now exist in every state, with about five hundred programs in the United States. All SANE programs treat adults and adolescents, and about half of them treat children as well. SANE programs also typically handle sexual assault victims of both sexes.

Importantly, there is good evidence that shows that SANE programs are effective at responding to victims of sexual assault. In a recent review, one researcher has found positive evidence that sexual assault nurse examiners are effective at assisting victims with their psychological recovery because they minimize trauma, preserve dignity, allow victims to make self-determining decisions, and assist in providing medical care. In fact, 75 percent of sexual assault victims described their contact with SANE nurses as "healing" in and of itself. SANEs also contribute to enhanced interagency collaboration to improve overall community responses to rape, as well as improve the potential for a successful prosecution because they collect evidence in the correct manner.[30] But although the evidence is collected properly, there has been a backlog of rape evidence kits that have been stored without being analyzed. Fortunately, in response to public outcry, Congress amended the Violence against Women Act in 2013 to include a section known as the Safer Act that will help reduce this backlog.

A Model Example: Shelters for Battered Women

When we think of responding to intimate partner violence, the first thing that comes to mind is women's shelters. Today, there are more than 2,000 community-based projects in the United States that provide emergency shelter to 300,000 women and children annually. The victims who can secure shelter at these safe havens stay for a period of a few days to several months. They come seeking protection and a range of counseling, safety planning, and legal assistance services. Those who do receive these services are overwhelmingly satisfied.[31] Importantly, they are likely also playing a role in stopping violence. Regression analysis suggests that increased access to these shelters from 1970 to 2000 may have contributed to less violence against women. It is usually thought that this success is because the women are safe. But many men do not want to lose their partner, and so the existence of these refuges may also provide an incentive for them to control their violence. More research is needed to discover the exact impact that women's shelters have on violence.

Sadly, a large proportion of women and children who do seek out shelters and safe havens are turned away. An annual one-day census on victims of domestic violence looks at how many women and children are in shelters and how many are turned away on a given day. On average, there

are approximately ten thousand women and ten thousand children residing at shelters across the country every day. Unfortunately, nine thousand
victims are refused services daily because the programs are overburdened
and simply do not have the resources.[32] This is a serious gap that cannot
continue, and politicians need to turn their attention to it.

Women's shelters, sexual assault crisis centers, and SANE programs
are all good responses to victimizations after they happen. And, for the
most part, they are effective at providing the multisectorial services that
the UN's Commission on the Status of Women calls for, including health
care, psychological support, counseling, and social support.[33] But these
programs need ample and sustained funding to truly respond to all the
victims who need them. However, support for victims of sexual and domestic violence *after the fact* is not the same as effective programs that
prevent rape. The smart solution would be to nourish both approaches
simultaneously.

Refocusing Court Responses toward Preventing Reoffending

When it comes to the perpetrators of rape and intimate partner violence, most of the public and political discourse is focused on punishment in court. Some advocates for abused women have argued that
since we punish street violence with incarceration, we should likewise
punish domestic violence with incarceration. While principled, this argument overlooks the fact that punishing street violence with incarceration alone has only a limited impact and has resulted in exorbitant costs
and unexpected additional consequences, as was shown in part I.

Still, states passed laws that required police officers to arrest a suspect
if they were called to an incident involving violence within a family.
These laws, while well intentioned, ignored prevention and rehabilitation altogether and focused only on reactive measures. Proponents of
the laws pointed to one experiment conducted in Minneapolis in 1984,
which showed a 50 percent reduction in (reported) repeat violence by
men who had been arrested for assaulting their partner, compared with
men who had been only temporarily separated from their spouses and
cautioned not to assault them again. In other cities, however, these results failed to be scientifically replicated, which is the litmus test of all
scientific verification.

Scientific conclusions flipped back and forth between mandatory arrests making no difference at all on reported repeat violence and mandatory arrests making some difference. Eventually, it was concluded that mandatory arrest procedures had only minimal impact on men with little left to lose—which is typical of offenders of all ilks. However, mandatory arrests did have some positive impact on the reoffending rates of men who *did* have something to lose (typified by middle-class offenders).

What *was* clear was that the length of the penalty had no impact on reoffending rates and that reducing access to harmful alcohol had some impact. But even these experiments failed to look at whether mandatory arrests and prison time were better than a requirement for an offender to take part in a specialized treatment group if his participation would enable him to avoid prison time. In fact, until only recently, focus on the prevention of domestic violence and the rehabilitation of batterers has been very weak in the scientific literature.

In 2013, the respected Washington State Institute for Public Policy (WSIPP) published a review entitled "What Works with Domestic Violence Offenders," which looked at strategies to prevent domestic violence reoffending. The review concluded that the "Duluth strategy" (i.e., group therapy for batterers that is intended to change their controlling attitudes toward women) did not show any evidence of preventing domestic violence, even though it is mandated for all convicted batterers in Washington State. On a positive note, the report concluded that the innovative and proven reoffending prevention strategies (i.e., those discussed in part I, such as cognitive-behavioral therapy) probably can reduce reoffending by domestic violence offenders.[34] Another research study that looked into the effectiveness of batterer counseling programs is a longitudinal four-year evaluation that took place across four cities. It found that the vast majority of men who participated in batterer counseling (i.e., cognitive-behavioral programs) appeared to have stopped their assaultive behavior.[35]

So the evidence for the effectiveness of batterer programs is not conclusive. It seems clear that more research is needed in this field if politicians are to have the scientific evidence they need to make the smartest laws possible—and to ensure the *best* possible outcomes for women and family units. But in the meantime, we need to invest in efforts to stop young people from becoming offenders in the first place, such as the education and intervention campaign listed above.

IT'S TIME FOR A NATIONAL PLAN TO REDUCE VIOLENCE AGAINST WOMEN

Fortunately, the United States already has a strong legislative vehicle (the Violence against Women Act, or VAWA) for improving responses to victims of violence against women. VAWA was introduced in 1994 and reauthorized in 2000, 2005, and 2013. In theory, the Violence against Women Act has the dual purpose of serving the needs of victims of violence against women better, and of preventing violence against women. In practice, VAWA is good at tailoring its programs to issues of gender, at protecting victims from their accused offenders, and at generally *reacting* to crimes against women after they happen. However, to date, it is not so good at promoting programs that prevent violence *before* it happens. For instance, much of its funding goes to various local actions that are *reactions* to victimization, although in 2013 it did receive an injection of initial funding to use promising programs on university campuses. What's more, no significant monitoring or evaluation has been undertaken to assess whether or not violence against women is actually decreasing because of this act.[36]

One of the most important vehicles in the act that could promote prevention is the Office for Violence against Women (OVW), which is part of the US Department of Justice. Its mandate is to focus on domestic violence, sexual assault, stalking, and human trafficking. It focuses on women in particular because these crimes affect women most severely and generally have worse consequences for female as opposed to male victims. It also has programs that deal with specific vulnerabilities, such as female victims with disabilities and female victims residing on Indian reservations, for these groups are at particularly high risk. The OVW is a well-established and respected office, and as such it is in a strong position to coordinate the implementation of a series of proven preventive reforms.

While it seems clear that the smartest way to deal with abuse of this nature is to *prevent* it from happening in the first place, there is an unfortunate gap in the research in terms of how to effectively go about doing this. For instance, both the World Health Organization (WHO) and the US National Research Council comment on the lack of research about how to effectively prevent violence against women.[37] Indeed, there are more "promising strategies" than well-proven programs simply because the research has not been done. It is unfortunate to think of what biases are reflected in this lack of attention, and I would urge the research field to remedy this. Unfortunately, the research that *has* been done tends to focus on traditional policing and criminal justice approaches—that is, on solutions for *after* the violence has already occurred, rather than on stopping the problem before it starts. But as this book has strived to show, an ounce of prevention is worth a pound of cure.

CONCLUSION

Points to Note: Smarter Strategies for Reducing Sexual Violence and Intimate Partner Violence against Women

Rates of sexual violence are shocking, especially among young people, and don't appear to be declining. The pervasiveness of intimate partner violence against women is also shocking, though rates of fatal violence are trending slowly down, possibly as women gain more freedom to leave violent relationships through social and economic opportunities, liberalized divorce and family laws, and transition houses.

School programs that focus on changing boys' and young men's attitudes to sexual violence are effective. Efforts to get adults to intervene also hold considerable promise, and male leadership to change societal attitudes seems hopeful. Issues of access to guns were discussed in the previous chapter, and the common risk factor of alcohol is discussed in the next chapter. Investment in pre-crime prevention in problem places will also reduce violence against women.

If women have more confidence in reporting violence to the police, this alone may help them resist physical and sexual violence. So the high nonreporting rate of sexual violence needs attention. Likely, non-reporting of domestic violence is also high. By gendering the police response, ensuring access to SANE nurses and processing rape kits, and making refuges for women more available, women may become more empowered. Experts cannot agree on solutions for stopping domestic violence offenders from reoffending, although proven reoffending reduction measures may be helpful.

The Violence against Women Act is primarily investing in improving the reaction to these crimes, although in 2013 some initial funding has been added to use promising programs on university campuses and to get rape kits processed; this funding must be sustained and reinforced to make a real impact. The act also provides an important vehicle for sustaining research and development for more effective programs in the future. This research must include a critical look at the costs and benefits of the innovations.

Actions for Politicians for Smarter Ways to Stop Violence against Women

1. Legislators must reform the Violence against Women Act to require it to develop a plan that balances effective prevention with smart reactive crime control to reduce physical and sexual violence against women.
2. Legislators must fund a regular survey of sexual and physical violence in schools and on college campuses to build on earlier successful surveys,[38] and they must organize annual forums for school and college leaders to improve their responses to reducing such violence.
3. Legislators must fund an annual meeting of the leading sports organizations to discuss how sports might contribute to reducing violence against women.
4. Legislators must reform acts that guide law enforcement so that they put female victims at the zenith of their work.[39]
5. Legislators must increase funding for women's shelters, sexual assault crisis centers, and Sexual Assault Nurse Examiners (SANE) programs so that more victims seek help.
6. Legislators must fund a research and development agenda to increase the knowledge about what is effective and cost-effective in reducing violence against women.
7. Legislators must implement recommendations made in other chapters on investing in early childhood development, problem

places, prohibiting violent offenders from possessing guns, and efforts to limit abuse of alcohol.

This chapter has shown that smarter crime control must focus on investing in social preventive strategies, including mobilizing interveners and changing attitudes in schools and universities, in addition to the early childhood development and targeted social programs discussed in chapter 5. It must also focus on smarter enforcement by enabling women to have more confidence in the police and court response, by investing in more refuges, and by getting courts to supervise persistent offenders' participation in proven prevention. In sum, reductions in numbers of victims can be achieved through much less punitive and costly methods than the standard reactive crime control.

8

PREVENTING VIOLENCE ON THE ROAD AND ALCOHOL-RELATED VIOLENCE

INTRODUCTION

When it comes to stopping violence, we have to turn a part of our focus to alcohol. It is common knowledge among experts that the easier it is to access alcohol, the more violence there will be—on the roads, on the streets, and behind closed doors. This chapter looks at the role of alcohol, among other risk factors, in relation to traffic fatalities. It also looks at the science on ways to reduce those fatalities, including what we know about repeat offenders. It then turns to ways to reduce the problematic use of alcohol, especially among youth. Last, it will suggest ways to turn emergency rooms—first-response centers to violence, including violence that is alcohol related—into social services referral epicenters that can help stop violence.

So what can the United States do to bring its rates of alcohol-related injuries and deaths to levels closer to other affluent democracies? The solutions shown in table 8.1 are discussed below.

| Priorities for National Office to Reduce Fatalities on the Road and Alcohol Related Violence ||
Effective Prevention	Smart Reactive Crime Control
Continue culture shift	Legislate MADD agenda
Defensive driver training	Enforce speed limits and fixed speed cameras
Design safer cars and roads	Enforce seat belts, child protection, smartphone use
Intervenors (eg SADD)	Random breathalyser (MADD) and raise BAC to .05
Ignition interlock in every car (MADD)	Ignition interlocks for drunk drivers
Models – Life skills and Alcohol Screening	Enforce laws on selling and serving alcohol
Target problem places producing violence	
Invest in pre-crime prevention	Use proven recidivism reduction to reduce reoffending
Invest in surveys, data, research, development, proven practice on web	

Table 8.1   What Stops Traffic Fatalities and Alcohol-Related Violence?

MAKING THE PREVENTION OF ROAD CRIMES A NATIONAL PRIORITY

In chapter 1, we saw that the United States has the highest rate of traffic fatalities among affluent democracies (see figure 1.2). Its per capita rate of deaths involving a drunk driver is *eight times* that of the United Kingdom. Approximately 32,000 persons lose their lives in traffic crashes each year, and many more are disabled or injured.[1] Approximately 10,000 (or one in three) of these deaths, and an estimated 350,000 of these injuries, involved a crash with a driver who was known to have more than the legal limit of alcohol in his or her blood—over 0.08 percent alcohol in the bloodstream.[2] This amounts to one death every fifty-three minutes.[3] By 2010, the annual costs from known drunk driving were more than $130 billion—that's close to 1 percent of the GDP.[4]

Automobile crashes involving drinking and driving, dangerous driving, and negligent driving affect victims and taxpayers in many severe ways. The costs for health care, victim services, and lost productivity are important, but once again it is the loss of quality of life that skyrockets the total harm to over $130 billion annually. But as we will see, the World Health Organization, Centers for Disease Control and Prevention, and other respected authorities have considerable science that tells us what could reduce the number of victims and the harm—so there is hope.

And there is more good news. Alcohol-impaired driving fatalities have declined by 27 percent over the past ten years, from 13,472 deaths in

2002 to 9,878 deaths in 2011.[5] Just from 2006 to 2010, an annual self-report survey shows that drinking and driving episodes have dropped by 30 percent.[6] So it's likely that some of this reduction in deaths is a result of fewer drivers who are impaired. Another part of the reductions is likely because of smart policing, as traditional law enforcement has already worked to develop some effective ways to change unsafe behaviors on the road (i.e., slowing down, buckling up, not drinking alcohol, etc.). Importantly, these effective measures do not rely on the exorbitant use of mass incarceration for their effectiveness. Rather, they are smart policing strategies that use focused deterrence.

But, as shown in figure 8.1, there is still a long way to go. The US rates remain higher than other affluent democracies that have focused more effective strategies on the problem of drinking and driving and other traffic crashes. For instance, the United States has a rate of general traffic fatalities three times that of the United Kingdom, and its rate of drunk-driving fatalities is a whopping six times greater.[7]

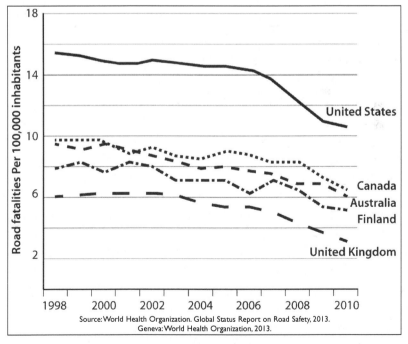

Source: World Health Organization. Global Status Report on Road Safety, 2013. Geneva: World Health Organization, 2013.

Figure 8.1   The Downward Trend in US Traffic Fatalities: Still a Need to Catch Other Affluent Democracies

Why Not Install a Nationwide Agency to Take the Lead on Reducing Road Crimes?

Although the risk factors associated with dangerous driving are widely recognized, the United States is lacking a lead agency to spearhead (beyond just sharing data) any widespread efforts to effectively address the known risk factors that make the roads hazardous for all citizens. The United States is also lacking significant targets in terms of reductions of road crime. This is unfortunate, for the World Health Organization has recently reported that an adequately funded lead agency, as well as a national plan or strategy with measurable targets, are crucial components of reducing traffic injuries and fatalities.[8] These are shortcomings that the United States should address immediately.

Targets are necessary because they give stakeholders a goal to collectively work toward. I would suggest that a realistic target for the United States to adopt would be a reduction by 50 percent in traffic fatalities by 2020. As you will see below, this target is highly achievable with some smart investments. Meeting that goal will also require the implementation of some evidence-based enforcement strategies geared at changing dangerous behaviors in order to achieve the much greater protection of potential victims. However, there may be trade-offs between the rights of citizens not to be killed on the roads and the rights of citizens to drive cars as unrestrictedly as they may be used to.

TAKING ACTION TO PREVENT ROAD CRIMES *BEFORE* PEOPLE GET HURT

We know that traffic injuries and fatalities caused by road crimes can be prevented and that optimized prevention will include a multipronged approach. For their part, car manufacturers have been working to reduce road fatalities and serious injuries through design innovation. The Insurance Institute for Highway Safety has played a leading role in informing consumers of the extent to which new designs reduce the risk of deaths and injury.[9] It has published estimates of reductions in fatalities and injuries due to different innovations over the years, including seat belts, child restraints, and antilock brakes. It reports that air bags alone can reduce fatal frontal collisions by 29 percent,[10] and seat belts reduce serious injuries and deaths by about 50 percent. There have also been innovations to reduce risk to pedestrians and to make cell phone access in cars smarter. So important are these safety features to public safety that the use of cars equipped with these features should be encouraged by legislators. In the European Union, for instance, minimum safety feature requirements for older vehicles must be met in order to keep the older car on the road.[11]

But car design alone cannot bring about the reductions in road fatalities and injuries that the United States should be targeting. Indeed, the World Health Organization reported on several effective interventions, including effective speed management by police through the use of traffic-calming measures; enforcing laws requiring the use of seat belts and child restraints; and setting and enforcing blood alcohol limits for drivers.[12] The WHO also noted that public awareness campaigns play an important role in supporting enforcement and legislative measures by increasing awareness of the risks and penalties associated with breaking road laws.[13]

The European Union has found that speeding is a key factor in around 30 percent of all fatal road accidents. The second-biggest contributing factor in fatal accidents is the failure to wear a seat belt, by the driver but also, unfortunately, by passengers, including young children. The EU reported that driving under the influence of alcohol or drugs is a third factor involved in around 25 percent of all deadly crashes;[14] unfortunately, we know this rate is even higher in the United States. Fatalities caused by negligence on the part of distracted drivers—particularly when using "smart" phones—are increasing, but better data is needed on this issue.[15] There are no good estimates on the numbers of victims killed by reckless drivers who were not drunk, but it is suspected to be a sizeable number. In the United States, much of the basic data on risk factors is brought together by the National Highway Traffic Safety Administration. Important analyses have used this data to better understand—and so to further encourage—a reduction in traffic fatalities.[16] The Centers for Disease Control and Prevention have defined a reduction in traffic fatalities as a winnable battle through addressing a variety of risk factors, including driver behavior.[17]

The Promotion of Effective Speed Management and Distracted Driving Interventions

We know that when law enforcement chooses to focus its resources on speed management, it can effectively reduce fatalities and injuries on the road. Still, only a small number of officers in traditional police forces are specially dedicated to traffic policing. [18] But you saw above how speeding plays a key role in one-third of fatal road accidents (about three thousand deaths annually in the United States). Stricter enforcement of speed limits by officers is a proven way to reduce fatalities. For instance, we can learn from the Netherlands, which has reduced road fatalities to one of the lowest levels in Europe by providing much stricter enforcement of speed limits—in this case, more than 450 drivers go through a speed trap each year per 1,000 habitants. [19] Speed limits can also be lowered by municipalities to great effect. For example, one UK study found that dropping speed limits in residential zones to twenty miles per hour cut vehicle crashes with child pedestrians and cyclists by 67 percent.

Investments in speed management technologies such as cameras can also be used very cost-effectively, as European examples again show. The European Traffic Safety Council noted that speed-camera technology was a very effective way to reduce road fatalities by an average of 19 percent. The reductions in urban areas were particularly impressive at 28 percent. What's more, cost-benefit analysis found that a one dollar investment in speed-camera technology generated twenty-five dollars after five years. [20] Importantly, the report also responded to arguments that the cameras are reminiscent of "Big Brother" by noting that public response tends to be favorable: "The brother that is watching you seems to be preferred to the brother that may be killing you." [21]

So why don't we extend more enforcement resources in this area, where we know they save lives? This could be as easy as a simple reallocation of resources—especially if officers' focus was shifted from *reacting* to minor offenders, such as those in possession of small quantities of marijuana.

Experts are also aware that an increasing number of road fatalities and injuries are due to persons who are distracted by "smart" phones and devices. Some researchers have used cell phone records to confirm an increased risk of injury or fatality, but technology is changing so rapidly that it is hard to publish conclusions that inform the usage risks of *today*'s technology.[22] Legislation is spreading rapidly to make certain types of device usage while driving an offense, but such legislation is difficult to enforce by policing. Likely, a more effective approach is to raise awareness within the schools to help young drivers avoid this risk, but more work must be done to develop effective youth programming as well as to tackle the issue of distracted adult drivers.

Promoting Effective Drinking and Driving Deterrence Strategies

Perhaps no organization embodies the will to promote effective strategies to prevent drinking and driving as much as Mothers Against Drunk Driving (MADD). MADD has fought hard to get action to reduce the number of injuries and fatalities caused by drunk driving. Its mission is to stop drunk driving and to support the victims of this violent crime. It also aims to prevent underage drinking because of the high number of young persons killed and killing on the roads.

In 1982, MADD got the US president to establish a Presidential Commission on Drunk Driving to look at the contemporary evidence and recommend a series of evidence-based and commonsense measures. The commission's proposals were smart (as opposed to the blunt overuse of incarceration-based instruments), and they were designed to target risk factors and change general driver behavior. For example, they brought about tougher penalties for drivers with a blood alcohol level over 0.10, and they raised the age at which someone could legally buy alcohol. Other recommendations were strategically meant to keep people from driving if they had drunk too much alcohol; for instance, they required servers in bars and restaurants to be trained not to serve more alcohol to persons who were drunk. These changes are all smart examples of how targeted, evidence-based strategies can work to target risk factors in order to stop crime (in this case, road crime).

Since the 1980s, MADD has remained a strong advocate for reforms and a key player in forcing legislators to face the reality of road crimes involving alcohol. Every few years, it does an assessment of the progress made by the federal government and states in terms of taking action to reduce drunk-driving fatalities. In 2000, MADD rated each state on thirty-two measures that are important to reducing drunk driving. Of these measures, a handful were given particular attention, including: (1) administrative license revocation; (2) a 0.08 blood alcohol concentration limit for adults; (3) graduated driver licensing systems for youths; (4) mandatory blood alcohol testing for killed drivers as well as surviving drivers; (5) vehicle impoundment for repeat DUI offenders; (6) alcohol ignition interlocks for convicted offenders; and (7) mandatory alcohol treatment for DUI offenders.

A group of researchers decided to evaluate how much impact these measures actually had on traffic safety. They rated states from grade A (those that had adopted many of the measures) to grade D (those that had adopted few of the measures). They found that states with a grade of D had 60 percent more reported cases of drinking and driving than states that had a grade of A. [23] Clearly, then, these legislative measures *do* work to keep people from drinking and driving—and they do save lives.

MADD has recently put forward a new "wish list" for road reform. Unfortunately, it includes several *reactive* proposals, including severely increasing (at a significant cost to taxpayers) the punishment for drunk drivers who kill another person or who have a child in the vehicle. While this might intuitively seem like a "fair" consequence for the offender at first glance, the evidence shows that severe punishments such as these are unlikely to lead to fewer fatalities, as you saw in part I.

In terms of *preventive* strategies—which actually have a greater likelihood of reducing deaths on the road—MADD's wish list focuses on two main evidence-based actions: ignition interlocks and sobriety checkpoints (discussed below). [24] Notably, the US Department of Justice, through its prevention-focused website crimesolutions.gov, also promotes an ignition interlock program and sobriety checkpoints among its proven "effective" programs to keep drunk-driving offenders from reoffending. [25] Still, while these proposals are important and may seem quite proactive through an American lens, they are much less strict than the best practices recommended by the World Health Organization, which has a worldwide perspective. Moving to meet such global standards would save a significant number of American lives, avoid countless serious injuries, and avoid related costs to taxpayers.

Ignition Interlocks   Ignition interlock systems are devices that are hardwired into a car's dashboard. They keep a person who is drunk from starting the car by disallowing the engine to engage unless the device registers a blood alcohol level of zero. MADD recommends statutes that allow for a judge or administrative agency to stipulate the installation of these devices in the cars of convicted drunk drivers for a period of time following their conviction. In this way, the offender would not be allowed to drive his or her car drunk—at least for a period of time.

Maryland's Ignition Interlock Program is an example of this program working to stop drunk driving.[26] In this state, a portion of convicted drunk drivers were ordered to install the device for a specified period. During the first twelve months of the project, only 2.4 percent of the interlock users had another alcohol-related traffic violation, compared with 6.7 percent of those who did not have the mandated ignition interlock. That means that the ignition interlock program reduced the number of repeat offenders by a factor of three. Another study that was followed up by the Centers for Disease Control and Prevention confirms this finding.[27]

However, ignition interlocks are more of an incapacitation measure rather than a long-term solution, as they have an impact only while the interlock is on the car. In fact, studies show that once the interlock is removed, the rates of impaired driving may rebound to what they are among the rest of the population of convicted drunk drivers.[28] (It is important to note that the impact is measured based on reconvictions alone and therefore underestimates the other journeys where the offender may have been impaired but never caught.) There is still a need for more research looking at the comparative effectiveness of ignition interlock programs relative to other measures, such as driver suspensions and court-enforced treatment, as well as how these programs impact the rate of alcohol-related crashes. Nevertheless, this sort of legislation is promising, and programs such as this will still form an integral part of preventing drunk driving—provided that they are instituted *in conjunction* with other measures proven to prevent reoffending, such as court-ordered treatment for alcohol abuse; we looked at some of these measures in chapters 3 and 4.

Interestingly, MADD has recently been promoting another proposal along these same lines. It is suggesting that *every* vehicle on the road in the United States be outfitted with a device that tests the blood alcohol level of the driver before the car will start. Research to develop such a universal interlock for cars seems promising, and may be only marginally more inconvenient than a key. This proposal would likely reduce alcohol-related road fatalities significantly, although implementing this strategy with a legal blood alcohol level of the international standard of 0.05 (instead of the current US 0.08) would reduce fatalities even more, as discussed below.

Administrative license revocation (ALR), which MADD also advocates, takes car restrictions one step beyond mandatory ignition interlocks. It is the removal of an offender's or suspected offender's driver's license at the time of arrest on the failure or refusal of a Breathalyzer test. However, evaluations of ignition interlock programs show that some persons continue driving even without a license. Therefore, this approach could be more effective if it were combined with making an immediate family member responsible for the car. Until there is better data, however, the effectiveness of any license revocation effort is unclear.

Sobriety Checkpoints The second main strategy that MADD is currently promoting is random stops by law enforcement (also known as sobriety checkpoints). These stops constitute an enforcement program that allows police officers to stop vehicles to check for the sobriety of the drivers. The idea is that these checkpoints increase the *perception* of greater certainty of getting caught and so being penalized with whatever sanctions are in place, and they accomplish this in two ways: first, a checkpoint program tests a high number of persons and is deployed in a widespread manner; and second, its application is unpredictable in terms of time and place, making it difficult for drivers to avoid.[29]

This strategy is proven to reduce the number of drunk drivers on the road and is identified as "effective" by crimesolutions.gov.[30] The Checkpoint Tennessee program is frequently held up as a proven example of its effectiveness. This program, which involved an intensive use of sobriety checkpoints, resulted in an estimated 20 percent reduction in alcohol-related crashes. Crucially, these reductions continued for almost two years after the program stopped.[31] Australia, an early adopter of random stops, has conducted extensive research on this strategy, and those results are also favorable. As a result, many places in Europe now use random stops; for instance, the Swedish and Finnish police perform three hundred and four hundred stops and therefore tests per one thousand inhabitants every year, respectively. But while such measures are effective in reducing crashes, citizens don't tend to like them.[32]

Mobilizing Youth to Save the Lives of Young People on the Road

Car crashes are the leading cause of death for American teens. Lack of use of seat belts, speeding, and drunk driving are as important for teens as for the general public.[33] As such, there is a real opportunity to reduce impaired and dangerous driving through fostering awareness-building programs targeted at young people. As you saw above, young men in particular are at the highest risk for impaired-driving fatalities. Effective programs would target the attitudes of young people (as you saw in the previous chapter, where attitude-changing programs such as Fourth R had an impact on recasting the culture of sexual assault among high school students).

Some organizations propose laws that would penalize the sale of alcohol to obviously intoxicated persons or minors who might subsequently cause death or injury as a result of alcohol-related crashes. While the idea might have a place in safe server training, it does nothing to *solve* the problem; it is only a temporary fix at best. But programs in schools and colleges that make young people more aware of the impact of even small amounts of alcohol in their blood (discussed below) combined with the promotion of ways for bystander interveners to stop people from driving after drinking would help to cultivate cohorts of nonoffenders for life.

A Model Program: Students against Destructive Decisions (SADD) Likely more could be done in schools to change the attitudes of teenagers toward speeding, distracted driving, and driving under the influence of alcohol and other drugs in relation to traffic crashes. One model that is being used in schools—and that makes good sense—is Students against Destructive Decisions. It was started as Students against Driving Drunk in 1981 by high school hockey coach Robert Anastas after two of his players were killed in a drunk-driving crash. As an educator and coach, he realized that the best way to help youth avoid drinking and driving was to get them involved in making their own good decisions.

A key element of his strategy requires students to sign a "contract for life," which requires teens to learn about the risks of drinking and driving and then to make a commitment not to do it. The teens also commit to calling a parent to pick them up from a party if they have been drinking, and parents commit to picking them up as well as to holding off on any discussions or punishment until the next day. The smart component here is that teens *proactively* make this decision; they are not *reactively* responding to rules or punishment. This program has spread across the United States and other countries. Its new name reflects its commitment to divert youth from a broad range of destructive behaviors.[34]

Unfortunately, none of the programs such as this that outreach to young adults to prevent drinking and driving has been the subject of clear evaluations—or the subject of significant funding. Still, there are lots of logical reasons to invest in them to prevent traffic crashes and serious injuries that involve teens.[35]

Notably, programs such as SADD could also go a step further by mobilizing peer bystanders to intervene when risky behavior is taking place on the roads. You saw in the previous chapter how Green Dot is effective at teaching young people to intervene before situations become dangerous. When young people speed, drive distractedly, drink and drive, or drive while high, it often occurs in the presence of friends and witnesses. Therefore, an awareness component that changes students' attitudes (and subsequently encourages them to intervene in risky behavior) would likely lead to fewer road fatalities and serious injuries.

TARGETING RISK FACTORS BEFORE POTENTIAL DANGEROUS DRIVERS HAVE A CHANCE TO OFFEND

Stricter Blood Alcohol Levels

The United States requires a relatively high level of drunkenness before charging an offender with driving under the influence (DUI). It uses 0.08 grams of alcohol per liter of blood as the federal legal benchmark for impairment. Still, a driver who tests at 0.08 blood alcohol concentration (BAC) or lower is nevertheless likely to be a danger on the road, even if not "legally" impaired. In fact, it is well established that driving abilities become rapidly more impaired for most drivers as the alcohol in the bloodstream rises over 0.04. For this reason, young or novice drivers as well as commercial drivers legally need lower blood alcohol limits. Such regulations already exist in many states and should be implemented in all the rest.

The research is irrefutable here. One US study found that at a 0.08 blood alcohol level, adult drivers in all age and gender groups were eleven times more likely to die in a car crash than their sober counterparts who had no alcohol in their systems. The results for sixteen- to twenty-year-old males were even more concerning: at a 0.08 blood alcohol concentration, these drivers were *fifty-two times more likely* than their sober counterparts to die in a fatal crash.[36] And remember, these drivers aren't technically breaking any laws, even though they are clearly endangering lives. So, while the legal blood alcohol limit remains at 0.08 for adult drivers, citizens and legislators alike must ask themselves, Why is such a proven impairment allowed on the roads when the lives of potential victims are at stake, even when it is a verified *fact* that a lower limit would save lives and spare serious injuries?

Many experts argue that it is high time to change the legal blood alcohol concentration limit in the United States. The World Health Organization has established 0.05 as the best practice, and this level is used widely in Europe. In the United States, the Centers for Disease Control and Prevention have a National Center for Injury Prevention and Control that has reviewed the science on impaired driving. It has recommended a number of sensible improvements, including a change to a 0.05 blood alcohol limit as well as mandatory blood alcohol testing of victims of serious injuries in crashes in order to get better data to inform lifesaving policy. So why are legislators ignoring this recommendation, when someone dies in an alcohol-related car accident every fifty-three minutes—especially if we consider that those legally testing between 0.04 and 0.08 are also showing dangerously impaired judgment?

Targeting "Problem People" to Prevent Drunk Driving

The reoffending pattern of drunk drivers is clear. When we compare those killed in fatal crashes, a staggering 25 percent of the drivers with levels of alcohol above the legal limits had a previous suspension, compared to only 11 percent of those with no alcohol at all. Worse, 7 percent had a previous DUI conviction, compared to 1 percent of those killed without any alcohol in their blood.[37]

Indeed, the known risk factors for drunk-driving fatalities point to a group of young men for whom the fatal crash was not their first offense. The statistics show that drunk drivers in fatal crashes are more likely to be males, age twenty-five to thirty-four—a risk factor that is well established across affluent democracies. What's more, they tend to have a very high blood alcohol level; in fact, 57 percent of them register over *twice* the legal limit.[38] This is a group of problem reoffenders who live risky lives on the road—and who pose a risk to potential victims as well as to themselves. This group of risky drivers requires more research, particularly to identify what can change their behavior. Still, this "sketch" of the average offender points directly to a population that needs to be targeted for prevention.

We may know their age (young), gender (male), and dangerous driving history (a long one), but we don't know much about the behavior of repeat road-crime offenders. One of the first studies in this vein was conducted in 2000 by the National Highway Traffic Safety Administration, which analyzed repeat drunk-driving offenders.[39] It showed them to be underprivileged and underachieving males with previous convictions for violent offenses. In fact, some—though not all—of their risk factors may be similar to the risk factors known to cause violent and criminal behavior in general. Importantly, we know that some road-crime offenders (i.e., drunk drivers, speeders, etc.) tend to be persistent repeat offenders not only of traffic offenses but also of other violent crimes. Interestingly, law enforcement has known about this connection for some time, and some smart policing strategies put this knowledge to work. In the proven policing strategies to suppress gun crime (discussed in chapter 2), law enforcement was trained to use traffic enforcement to catch offenders involved in violent crimes—and it works.

This link also seems to hold true for petty violent and property crime. A lot of what we know about this came out of England in the 1960s, when pioneer criminologist Terrence Willett compared people convicted of petty violent and property crime with people convicted of drunk and/or dangerous driving. His study demonstrated a close connection between the two.[40] That is, offenders who are involved in property crime are also involved in dangerous driving behavior.

Unfortunately, most researchers have overlooked the link between childhood experiences and driving behavior. We know that inconsistent and uncaring parenting, difficulties in school, and other risk factors predispose youth to assaults and theft, but we largely do not know whether those same experiences predispose youth to DUI or other reckless driving. It is disappointing that those concerned with reducing deaths on the road have not pursued this connection further. More research on this would certainly help save lives down the road by enabling the development of targeted prevention strategies.

HOW THE COURTS CAN PREVENT DRUNK DRIVERS FROM REOFFENDING

If we look at the experience of efforts to stop domestic violence using punishment, then we know that those offenders who have little to lose in life are not deterred, whereas those with a job and status are deterred by the punishment. Importantly, it is not the length of the penalty that is important but the existence of an arrest combined with some penalty. Yes, a misdemeanor arrest for an offender with a job and a family (that is, with something to lose) might push the offender to change his future behavior.

If we apply these lessons to drunk driving, then those drunk drivers with a job and status are likely to be deterred. But for those *without* anything to lose, the length of sanctions has no effect and may make matters worse through loss of employability and other collateral consequences, as you saw in part I. Therefore, sanctions that are primarily punitive and that have no preventive focus provide little protection to would-be victims and are expensive for taxpayers. They have little preventive benefit other than to detain people so that they cannot physically commit an offense while they are behind bars.

The toughest dangerous-driving laws on the books are (1) vehicular homicide, where a driver kills another person through the operation of a motor vehicle, either intentionally or negligently; (2) DUI felony, where driving under the influence becomes a felony offense based on a high number of prior convictions; and (3) DUI child endangerment, which allows for additional penalties for a drunk-driving conviction when a child is a passenger in the vehicle. Again, while prison time for these offenses might detain offenders, there is no real focus on *solving* the problem here.

Therefore, the smartest approach is to combine enforcement and treatment in order to effectively reduce reoffending; we already saw how this worked in the case of drug courts.

So why don't we create more alcohol and drunk-driving courts that specialize in these cases—and that have a real understanding of what type of judicial response will prevent reoffending? For instance, drunk-driving courts might deal with repeat offenders by keeping them in proven treatment programs and also by mandating the use of an ignition interlock device (discussed above) for a long period of time.

Although there is still a long way to go when it comes to eliminating road crimes, progress comes from compelling offenders who are amenable to treatment to take part in the treatment—and *not* through the mass incarceration of offenders.

MAYBE IT'S TIME TO TAKE A SMARTER LOOK AT ALCOHOL IN GENERAL

The previous sections focused on the "driving" part of the drinking and driving equation. Here, we'll start to look into the "drinking" part. We'll see how alcohol is a major factor in a slew of violent crimes and then consider how being smarter about alcohol will lead to reductions in victimizations across the board.

Excessive Alcohol Use and Increases in Violence

Alcohol is a well-established contributor to violence. In 40 percent of violent crimes, the perpetrator has consumed enough alcohol to be visibly drunk; the proportion of drunk offenders is much higher for sexual assault and homicide. What's more, abuse of alcohol by the perpetrator is cited as a factor in about two-thirds of all reported intimate partner violence.[41] And as you saw above, about one-third of traffic fatalities involve a driver who has consumed more (usually considerably more) than the legal limit of alcohol.

This correlation between alcohol and violence is a worldwide trend. For instance, the World Health Organization includes alcohol as one of seven key risk factors for violence.[42] What's more, the International Crime Victim Survey confirms that countries where more beer is consumed per capita have higher rates of assault.[43] Another important study conducted by the United Kingdom's drug advisory board ranked alcohol as the number one most harmful drug in terms of harm to others (e.g., street violence, sexual assault, traffic fatalities) and as the fourth most harmful to the user after crack cocaine, heroin, and methamphetamines.[44]

So more alcohol consumption equals more crime. And while the overuse of alcohol has many costs to victims, it also means increased costs for society in general. Monetarily, the health costs associated with binge drinking are significant and should not be ignored.[45] In fact, one Australian study detailed the costs of alcohol misuse and estimated that it equals at least twice the revenue brought in by their taxes on alcohol.[46] With this information in hand, shouldn't politicians start to consider smarter solutions for reducing the negative impacts that alcohol has on victims and on communities?

Smarter Management of Alcohol

Better managing the use of alcohol at the legislative level is one of the most effective (and cost-effective) ways to reduce violence. Strategies involving the smarter sale of alcohol, pricing of alcohol, and legal age of consumption are proven to actually stop alcohol-induced violence from occurring in the first place, which is much more appealing than having law enforcement simply react to this preventable violence after the fact and at great cost to taxpayers and victims. For instance, policies that promote the smarter sale of alcohol (e.g., bar staff training, alcohol licensing for premises where alcohol will be consumed, and enforcement of laws around the sale of alcohol) are shown to achieve as much as a 29 percent reduction in violence.[47]

The pricing of alcohol, as set by legislators, is another important tool that can be used to reduce crime. For example, one study that looked into the causes of the impressive crime drop in New York City during the 1990s found that it was partially associated with increases in the price of alcohol that led to fewer alcohol-induced crimes.[48]

Experts on violence, sexual assault, and alcohol all say that increasing the price of alcohol can reduce violence via less alcohol consumption. They recommend setting a minimum price per unit of alcohol as a deterrent from drinking excessively, and this strategy seems to work. One UK study concluded that a minimum price for a unit of alcohol of fifty pence (about eighty cents) could lead to around ten thousand fewer violent crimes a year.[49] That means fewer victims as well as fewer costs associated with the prosecution of (and incarceration for) these crimes.

While this seems like a good solution, we cannot ignore the possibility that increased alcohol prices (e.g., at bars, etc.) may encourage some users to shift to private consumption or to the use of illegal drugs such as cocaine. This area needs more study, especially in light of the fact that the prevalence of binge drinking seems to be on the rise. Indeed, purchasing alcohol from off-premises establishments (i.e., stores) and taking it off-site to drink privately seems to be associated with higher rates of violence, compared with purchasing alcohol from on-premises establishments (i.e., bars or restaurants) and consuming it there.

The International Crime Victim Survey confirmed the connection between the easy availability of alcohol and high rates of interpersonal violence.[50] One study in Cincinnati showed that assaults were nearly 30 percent higher when there was easy access to off-premises outlets. Another recent study in Richmond, Virginia, showed a relationship between ambulance calls and availability of alcohol on unrestricted premises.[51]

Many jurisdictions have legislation that forces on-premises establishments to shut down for the night at a certain time. The idea is that restricted hours will reduce how much people can drink. However, the wisdom behind this strategy is questionable. In the United Kingdom, fixed closing times for pubs have recently been abolished because cities were facing high rates of violence when many young adults (especially aggressive young males) were leaving bars at the same time. This move has been accompanied in some cases by the creation of medically supervised clinics, where persons who have been binge drinking can recover. We will have to wait for future evaluations to see what effect this has on levels of crime.

Legislation regarding the legal age at which alcohol can be purchased and consumed is another means for dealing with the destructive use of alcohol. In the United States, the legal drinking age was raised to twenty-one following the passage of the Federal Highway Act in 1984 that reduced federal funds for highways by 10 percent for those states that had not restricted access to alcohol for those under twenty-one. The most rigorous studies suggest that this accounts for about 11 percent fewer deaths of persons in this age range, which is well worth achieving.[52] However, the reasons for these reductions are confounded, since these gains are associated with other laws, such as those that require young persons to engage in longer driver training and those that prohibit young drivers from driving after a certain time of day, which also decrease injuries and fatalities at this age.[53] In contrast, countries across Europe allow alcohol consumption during the teenage years and in some cases are further liberalizing access to alcohol. Yet the United States has far worse rates of traffic fatalites due to alcohol-related road crimes. Any reduction in traffic fatalities must be celebrated, though more research into the reasons for Europe's advantage in fewer deaths among young people may help us discover additional smart actions.

Increasing Awareness about the Dangers of Drinking to Excess

It's true that implementing smarter strategies, such as restricting the sale of alcohol and increasing the price of alcohol, might not be popular at first, but the subsequent reductions in violent crime would certainly have measurable positive impacts on the lives of citizens. Still, the smartest (and more palatable) approach would be to increase awareness around the risks of alcohol misuse in order to encourage young people to make smarter decisions for themselves.

We know that discouraging the acts of drinking to excess (binge drinking) and drinking in public curbs violence more than other antidrug strategies. While these acts can be discouraged through legislation and law enforcement, they can also be prevented through education. Fortunately, we have evidence that points to some educational approaches that are proven to work, especially in terms of targeting young people. In fact, the World Health Organization has assembled proof of projects that have prevented alcohol-related violence.[54]

The Center for the Study and Prevention of Violence at the University of Colorado has endorsed three programs in its elite group of model programs that focus on tackling the abuse of alcohol and other drugs to reduce violence.[55] These programs have strong research to support the conclusions that they result in reductions in substance use and violence.

Model Programs: Life Skills Training, Towards No Drug Abuse, and Alcohol Screening and Intervention for College Students   We have already discussed Life Skills Training as a strategy to prevent violent offending in chapter 5, but it also aims to prevent alcohol and drug abuse in primary and secondary school by training students in life skills. The program brings together the influence of parents, peers, the media, community organizations, and health policies. It is delivered through classroom-based lessons that cover everything from the health consequences of alcohol and drug abuse to stress management.

In a study of three thousand youths across forty-two schools, Life Skills Training was proven to achieve between 20 and 40 percent reductions in alcohol and drug use. The costs were $175,000 per thousand adolescents—the equivalent of the annual cost of one police officer (with overtime) who would otherwise be *reacting* to the consequences of 20 to 40 percent more alcohol-induced violence down the road. Another project called Project Towards No Drug Abuse similarly targets late adolescence and has been proven to impact violence, alcohol use, and drug use with similar results and low costs.

When it comes to college students, the program called Brief Alcohol Screening and Intervention for College Students is also widely recognized as being an effective (and therefore a "model") program to combat alcohol-related violence. Such programs may reduce sexual assaults around campus as well as violence more generally.

Increasing Awareness of Fetal Alcohol Syndrome

One area that requires increased education and awareness is fetal alcohol syndrome (FAS), which is caused by excessive alcohol consumption by mothers during pregnancy (especially during the first trimester). FAS leads to a number of mental deficiencies that limit the ability of children to learn or to regulate their impulses,[56] which unfortunately can increase their chances of committing crimes when they are grown. As there are no cures for FAS, prevention is important. The best prevention is information, education, and support for the mother to avoid drinking alcohol.

However, as most of the damage is done during the first three months of pregnancy, the mother may not be immediately aware that she is pregnant and may also have difficulty changing her habits.

CONCLUSION

Points to Note: Smarter Strategies to Prevent Violence on the Road and Alcohol-Related Violence

Every year in the United States, thirty thousand or more persons are killed in motor vehicle collisions; nearly one-third involve a driver known to be impaired. Both these rates are worse than in any other affluent democracy. Standards agreed on by the World Health Organization call for a central unit to plan and lead solutions.

Ways to reduce death on the road that are largely endorsed by the Centers for Disease Control and Prevention include a reduction of the legal blood alcohol limit to 0.05 from 0.08 and better enforcement of measures to control speed, to foster greater use of seat belts, and to discourage drivers from drinking and using smart phones. They also call for better data to support smarter reforms.[57]

MADD has a list of desirable laws for state legislation. Those states that have adopted these have fewer persons drinking and driving. MADD also calls for universal interlocks on ignitions. Much more education is needed, particularly in schools, to stop young people from drinking and driving and to mobilize interveners to foster safer driving. SADD is one logical way to encourage this. Programs proven to be effective in reducing alcohol abuse, such as Life Skills Training in schools and Alcohol Screening in colleges must become a universal part of the curriculum.

For offenders, the use of ignition interlocks has proven to be effective, at least for a period of time. Court-ordered intervention with proven alcohol abuse treatment is promising. But the best policy must include investment in pre-crime prevention to reduce the number of persistent offenders—some of whom also engage in violent offending and property crimes.

Alcohol plays a role in at least 40 percent of violent crime. There are several alcohol management strategies that legislators can

implement, including more informed policies on the sale and consumption of alcohol. The best approach is to educate and prevent
youth from using alcohol dangerously in the first place, which is
low-cost and effective.

Actions for Politicians to Prevent Violence on the Road and Alcohol-Related Violence

1. Legislators must create an office for reducing serious injuries and
   fatalities on the roads to establish and implement a plan to bring
   US highway injuries and fatalities down to the much lower rates of
   other affluent democracies within ten years.
2. Legislators must adequately fund promising prevention, including:
   a. Life Skills Training, Alcohol Screening in colleges, and SADD;
   b. Pre-crime prevention, as discussed in chapter 5; and
   c. Analysis of emergency department data to solve problem places.
3. Legislators must adopt laws to implement:
   a. Actions that MADD has identified as effective, including igni-
      tion interlock for convicted drunk drivers;
   b. Requirements for courts to use proven reoffending reduction
      treatments;
   c. Reduction in the legally acceptable blood alcohol limit to 0.05;
      and
   d. Improvements in safety standards for car production, such as a
      universal ignition interlock and protections for occupants and
      pedestrians.
4. Legislators must direct enforcement to focus on:
   a. Controlling speed, including extending the use of fixed cameras;
   b. Increasing the use of seat belts and child restraints while de-
      creasing the use of cell phones and smart devices;
   c. Ensuring that persons do not drive with blood alcohol levels in
      excess of the legal limit; and
   d. Selling and serving of alcohol consistent with laws and regula-
      tions.

This chapter has shown that smarter crime control must focus on a
culture of safety as good prevention, on design that reduces opportu-

nity and provides protection, on enforcement of regulatory standards when certainty of detection (rather than heavy punishment) is the key, and on efforts to deal with persistent offenders through pre-crime prevention and court-ordered treatment. The proposals are generally based on evidence, often from other countries. It calls for data to inform innovation and monitor progress. In sum, the proposals in this chapter are much more focused (and much less punitive and costly) than standard reactive crime control.

9

PREVENTING PROPERTY CRIME
IN COMMUNITIES, BY COMMUNITIES

INTRODUCTION

In 2011, victims suffered 3.6 million household burglaries, 628,000 car thefts, 560,000 robberies (i.e., thefts with violence), and a whopping 12.8 million other thefts.[1] Cumulatively, they suffered $22 billion in loss of property and quality of life, of which $6 billion was due to robbery alone.[2]

Believe it or not, these statistics are a "good news" story. Victims are much less at risk to these crimes today, as the rate of victimization is now 25 percent what it was in 1973 (when the National Crime Victimization Survey first started). As figure 9.1 shows, the risk to victims has dropped steadily over the past forty years for most property crimes.[3] I have included robbery with property crime for this chapter, as the pattern of its trends are so similar to other property crimes, even if on a different scale.

The impact on a victim of property crime is generally much less than for violent crime. However, if the property crime becomes a robbery because the offender uses violence, the impact is similar to that of violent crime and brings emotional trauma, loss of quality of life, and so on. Household burglaries can also cause trauma for many victims who react to the fear of a stranger in their private space. The nature of the

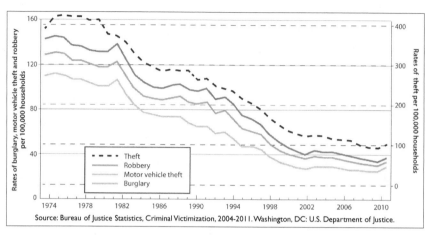

Figure 9.1   Rates of Property Crime: 2011 Rates Are Four Times Lower Than 1973 Rates

harm to victims of nonviolent property crime is often mitigated by insurance for the value of any property loss above a standard deductible. Yes, there may be red tape and frustration involved, but when it comes to electronic goods such as televisions and cell phones, it often means an upgrade. When the property stolen has emotional significance, like a wedding ring or a photo of a loved grandparent, however, it can create irreparable emotional pain.

As you saw in chapter 1, nearly half of all property crime goes unreported to police (with the exception of car theft, which is usually reported for insurance purposes). What's more, only about one-quarter (or less) of reported property crimes actually result in an arrest, and even fewer in the recovery of the stolen possessions. Still, taxpayers are paying an estimated $72 billion annually simply in reaction to these common property crimes for traditional policing, justice, and corrections, of which $41 billion is just for robbery.[4] Clearly, reaction isn't working well enough when it comes to fixing the problem of property crime—and average Americans are paying the price.

Let's look first at what *has* been achieved through the current systems of policing, courts, and corrections and then turn to more effective and cost-effective ways to stop property crime against individuals. Table 9.1 gives an overview of the highlights of what can be accomplished through three smart strategies: (1) improving social development; (2) reducing

Improving social development	Reducing Opportunity	Increasing neighborhood collaboration
Increased university enrollment	Residences secure by design	Cocoon neighborhood watch
Increased immigration	Car security	Neighbors problem solving
Reducing relative deprivation	Smart gadget revolution	
Comprehensive (combining these strategies)		

Table 9.1   What Stops Crime against Personal Property?

opportunity for property crime; and (3) building community and collaboration between neighbors, as well as (4) comprehensive strategies that combine these three strategies—all of which act *preventively* rather than only *reactively* toward stopping citizens from becoming victims of property crime.

HOW SOCIAL DEVELOPMENT LEADS TO FEWER PROPERTY CRIMES

Are Mass Incarceration and Policing Innovation Responsible for the Property Crime Drop?

It's hard to know definitively what is responsible for the downward trend in property crime that started in the 1970s. American criminologists have been debating this furiously and have offered different explanations based on looking exclusively at US data (although only for the past twenty years, and without considering global trends). Some say it was due to the use of mass incarceration with new, harsher penalties and longer jail time for thieves; others say it was due to more policing and hot-spots patrols.[5]

However, once we look over a longer period and use comparative data from other affluent democracies, it seems unlikely that the numbers of US property crime victims were reduced in any major way by the uniquely American versions of mass incarceration or innovations in policing. Indeed, an important book called *The International Crime Drop*, released in 2012, used internationally comparable victimization data and examples using national police data to show this.[6]

First, scientists demonstrated that the drop in property crime rates in the past two decades happened across most affluent democracies. The drop was usually between 40 and 50 percent—which is not so different from the drop in the United States if you start the clock at 1993, as many criminologists have. The scientists demonstrated this common trend using the International Crime Victim Survey, which compares national rates of property crime since 1989 (when this survey started). Though the survey uses relatively small samples in each country, the numbers become more reliable as they are collected across countries and over time. This survey is particularly powerful, as it goes directly to the public with a standard definition of the offenses and so avoids problems with reporting to police, police recording, and definitions that differ among countries.[7]

This conclusion is further confirmed by the steadily falling rates of burglaries, thefts, robberies, and car thefts. Figure 9.1 plots these trends over a time period much longer than the past twenty years, using data from the National Crime Victimization Survey.[8] If property crime rates were *really* impacted by the skyrocketing use of mass incarceration that started in the 1980s and its continued use at levels that amount to hyperincarceration in the 1990s and 2000s, then a drop in property crime would have been apparent in the 1980s, which it is not. The drop in the 1990s is similar to other affluent democracies.

Another scientific confirmation is presented in figure 9.2, which shows the rates of burglaries in the United States (as recorded by the police) to be average compared with other affluent democracies. Similarly, when researchers compare the international rates of common property crime (as measured by the International Crime Victim Survey), the US rates are average.[9] So despite the nationwide use of mass incarceration at a per capita rate that is seven times the average for other affluent democracies, there is no apparent additional benefit for potential victims of property crime brought about by the taxes expended on incarceration.

How Social Development Affects Property Crime

Any accurate explanations of crime drops must take into consideration changes in demographics as well as social situations and opportunities. It is well known that the composition of many affluent democracies has changed significantly since the 1970s. For instance, the swollen baby boom cohort passed through the high-risk age for residential burglary (fifteen to twenty-five years old) in the 1970s. So an initial part of the

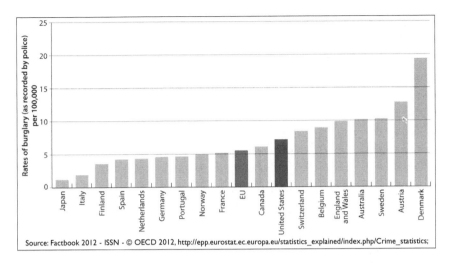

Source: Factbook 2012 - ISSN - © OECD 2012, http://epp.eurostat.ec.europa.eu/statistics_explained/index.php/Crime_statistics;

Figure 9.2   US Burglary Rates: Similar to Other Affluent Democracies

property crime decline can be explained simply by the reduced number of young males at high risk for committing burglary.

Two other rapid social changes were also mentioned by Andrew Karmen in his careful analysis of the crime drop in New York City in the 1990s, titled *New York Murder Mystery: The True Story Behind the Crime Crash of the 1990s*: higher enrollment in colleges, and increasing numbers of immigrants—both of which are good news for reducing crime.[10] And indeed, across the United States, there was a staggering 47 percent increase in the number of full-time enrollments in degree-granting universities from 1990 to 2010, and black students now make up an unprecedented 14 percent of US college students—close to their proportion in the population.[11] What's more, starting in the late 1980s, the number of new legal immigrants in the United States doubled, from around 500,000 a year to over a million.

Another scientist has confirmed these trends by noting that those cities that saw violence decreasing were those where there were more college graduates and immigrants.[12] Since some similar trends in education and immigration also occurred in other affluent democracies that experienced a comparable crime drop, it seems likely that these factors did contribute to reduced property crime rates in the United States—a far cry from assigning these trends to simple increases in police or the skyrocketing use of mass incarceration.

We know that unemployment for young single men can be a reason to drift into theft. But the data available are not able to show how higher unemployment rates are contributing (or not) to the continuing levels of theft. However, we know that the mapping of property crimes shows higher rates in areas that are disadvantaged (problem places), where many people are unemployed. This is a strong reason to implement the pre-crime prevention strategies from chapter 5 in problem places.

Another factor that must be mentioned is that many of the consumer goods that thieves would want to steal are becoming cheaper and more widely available—and therefore less attractive to would-be thieves. A classic reason for theft—known as "relative deprivation"—suggests that people steal because they feel deprived relative to others. Unfortunately, some easily accessible consumer items such as cell phones and tablets (which are also easily transportable—a key to theft) are now being stolen at high rates, perhaps because commercial groups such as Apple market these phones by trying to make people feel deprived if they do not own the latest technology. In sum, social development factors will continue to be important to understanding the causes of crime and to stopping harm to victims. While some *general* social trends have been helpful, they occur rightly for reasons other than a concerted effort to control crime. Nevertheless, *focusing* social development in problem places is certainly important to a good social return on investment in reducing crime.

REDUCING PROPERTY CRIME BY REDUCING OPPORTUNITY

In the 1970s, I was able to review a lot of burglary data and interview a number of burglars to find out how they selected the residences that they entered.[13] What I learned confirmed that the ease of the opportunity to commit the offense determines who falls victim to property crime.

Ron Clarke has expressed this idea through a simple theory called situational crime prevention in his book of the same name.[14] He cites examples of crime prevention being achieved through such avenues as smarter design of the built environment. He reduced the concept to some key ideas, including: (1) if it's harder for a would-be offender to commit a crime, the potential thief will be that much less likely to commit it; (2) if the chances are greater that a would-be offender will get caught, he will be that much less likely to commit the crime; and (3) if the rewards for committing the crime are less, he will be that much less likely to commit it. Note that Clarke does not say that the longer the punishment behind bars, the less likely the would-be offender will be to commit the offense. Although these three ideas may seem obvious, it is important to remember that the current reactive policing approach is typically *reacting* to crimes one at a time and is not operating in terms of the strategic protections that reduce the likelihood of offending.

To make it easier to use these strategies, which reflect the idea of "situational crime prevention," the Police Executive Forum has brought examples of situational crime prevention together with examples of problem-oriented policing (discussed in chapter 2) on a unique and rich website, popcenter.org.[15] Importantly, Clarke's strategies are used widely by private security companies—probably because they work to *protect* their clients from suffering losses in the first place instead of just being dispatched to try to enforce the law and pick up the pieces after a breach has happened. And security companies are motivated to keep their clients happy—that is, *not* robbed, burglarized, or caught up in the slow and expensive criminal justice process—otherwise, they would quickly go out of business. Indeed, if traditional policing adopted this sort of preventive approach to property crime, then their "clients"—the taxpayers who pay their salaries—would suffer many fewer losses.

Private security companies continue to grow, which likely reflects decreasing confidence in isolationist policing strategies that fail to prevent. Today, there are about three private security professionals for every one sworn police officer—a dramatic reversal from the 1960s. These companies provide services to stores, museums, high-ranking individuals, and others that have the money to minimize their concern over theft and crime. It is made even more accessible to them because security officers often cost less than police and indeed the financial loss from not employing the security officers. Interestingly, some of these private security companies are hired to protect government buildings. This in itself is a small testament to how traditional policing is expensive and often less than optimally effective.

Designing to Make Property Harder to Steal

While private security is far out of reach for many Americans, the good news is that there are some simple and cost-effective design components that can easily be implemented to protect residences from property crime.

A Model Example: Secure by Design   The Secure by Design program is one inspiring example of a built environment-based crime prevention initiative that has been proven to stop residential burglaries. Inspired by a little-known British project, police in Holland started to think outside the box and created a problem-based strategy to combat property crime. They developed building standards for new housing that would render properties unattractive to burglars and decrease opportunities for theft. The standards manual covers areas such as parking, grounds, locks, and entries. For construction companies to have their new buildings approved, they had to meet these standards.

The evidence shows that this approach was effective. In the original study, the houses that met Secure by Design standards had burglary rates that were 50 percent lower than for those that did not. This evidence prompted the nationwide implementation of the Secured Housing Label program in 1996, which requires all new housing to meet opportunity-reducing standards. Since this regulatory change, there has been a 26 percent reduction nationwide in burglaries of new homes as compared to older houses. Importantly, there was no evidence that the prevented burglaries were displaced to other homes; rather, the number of overall crimes was simply reduced.

Notably, these reductions in victimization were all enabled by a police force that shifted away from *reactive* policing to concentrate its abilities on finding solutions to *prevent* property theft from happening in the first place. Another important point is that the Secure by Design regulations also included standards regarding resident participation and responsibility. This is an important factor in reducing property crime, as we will discuss later in this chapter.

Designing Cars That Are Difficult to Steal   Car theft rose in the late 1980s and crashed in the 1990s. One of the most thorough analyses of the explanations for this downward trend was written by Shuryo Fujita and Michael Maxfield, who showed that the car alarms and electronic mobilizers that were increasingly being designed into new cars in the 1990s contributed significantly to these reductions. This drop coincided with fewer arrests of youth car thieves, meaning that these security devices make it harder for young offenders to steal cars to "joy ride."[16] However, these electronic security measures did not reduce professional car theft rates. The authors stressed that these security devices will eventually be defeated by thieves—and indeed, some of the new systems that use transponders can already be easily overcome by thieves who access simple information on the Internet.

This is an important lesson: situational crime prevention may be effective for a number of years, but where there are still potential offenders, they will eventually find a way around it. However, it is worth meeting the challenge to the best of our ability for the butterfly effect alone, for if young perpetrators who have the potential to become professional offenders are stopped before they can be dragged into the revolving door of criminal courts and incarceration, then many future victims will be spared.

Ways to Make Theft More Likely to Lead to Arrest

Over the past few decades, many innovations have attempted to replace the human element of guarding property through the development of electronic technologies. For instance, installing alarm systems is a popular approach intended to protect both personal and commercial property. Some of these alarms do nothing more than make a noise when triggered, while others are connected to a central security firm that then checks in with the owner to decide whether to call the police. Insurance companies will often provide a discount on insurance premiums to householders or business owners who have installed an alarm, presumably in the belief that alarms reduce burglaries. The findings of the International Crime Victim Survey support this belief, as it concluded that the increased use of burglar alarms was correlated with the drops in residential burglary in the 1990s and 2000s.[17]

Closed circuit television (CCTV) is another example of a technology meant to replace the human element of guarding property. Its popularity is based on the belief that it will lower crime rates by increasing the potential offenders' perceived risk of getting caught and convicted by way of capturing their identities on camera. While the theory seems foolproof, the evidence concludes that CCTV is likely better at *reactively* helping to solve a crime than at actually *preventing* it from happening in the first place.

Still, the United Kingdom has so bought into the mirage that CCTV will stop crime that it was spending more than 75 percent of its "crime prevention" budget on CCTV rather than targeted social development, which would have provided more sustainable reductions in crime. The evidence shows that CCTV likely does have some moderate success in terms of prevention in some very limited situations, although the results are mixed. For instance, there has been some success in preventing property crimes when cameras are placed in high-crime areas, such as parking lots susceptible to vehicle theft. For instance, in one major UK evaluation, CCTV was installed in the troublesome nightlife areas of the city of Newcastle, England. Using a simple before-and-after comparison, a 56 percent reduction in burglary and a 47 percent reduction in vehicle crime was found.

When a scientific review of the research was conducted by Brandon Welsh and David Farrington—two of the world's leading experts on crime prevention—they concluded that CCTV reduces crime by only about 4 percent overall, although it is more useful against thefts relating to cars and thefts on transit systems.[18] Indeed, CCTV's success in preventing crime is mostly restricted to property crime. It has only limited success in preventing violent crime, although it offers some assistance in identifying an offender *after* a violent victimization has occurred.[19] So while alarms and closed-circuit TVs do have something to contribute in terms of prevention, they are no replacement for the old-fashioned notion of community and the protective factor of having involved neighbors, as we shall see later in the chapter.

Riding the Smart Gadget Wave to Reduce Property Crime

Electronic technology is leaping forward so quickly that it is hard to know how it will be used in the future. Already, the addition of photo and video capacity to smart phones and the wide use of smart phones have changed the potential for perpetrators to be recorded when committing a crime such as a theft in a public or semipublic place. Smart phones will transform the ability of victims and witnesses of crime to call the police and seek assistance. They will also increase the information and data available for the crime control system.

But advances in technology can be a double-edged sword. Perhaps the most rapidly increasing type of personal theft involves smart phones. Cell phones are small, easily transportable, and (for the moment) easily resalable, which make them attractive items to steal. They can be sold on schoolyards, in bars, and even in open markets, where sellers do not have to prove that the phones were not stolen. The UK equivalent of the National Crime Victimization Survey shows the theft of cell phones to be skyrocketing; about 2 percent of cell phone owners are now victims of this kind of theft every year, and the trend is growing. From 2011 to 2012, the proportion of thefts that involved cell phones jumped from 30 percent to 45 percent.[20]

Unfortunately, some of these thefts become robberies as offenders use force or the threat of violence to get the phone. As long as the cell phone company can use the theft to convince the customer to upgrade and the manufacturer subsequently gets more new business, there is little incentive to design phones that are harder to steal, or at least harder to use after being stolen. So it will be important to insist on design standards that make the phones less attractive to thieves, and focusing on resale presents a clear path forward for legislators.

Various types of cybertheft are also increasing, though apparently more against big businesses such as credit card companies and banks than individuals. Technology has enabled some thieves to move from individual victims to companies such as banks and ATMs. For instance, in mere hours in 2013, $45 million in cash was stolen from ATMs across twenty-seven different affluent democracies.[21] While this type of sophisticated crime tends to victimize larger corporations rather than individual citizens, individual citizens are also at risk of having their banking information, credit card information, and personal identities misappropriated.

INCREASING COMMUNITY COLLABORATION TO PREVENT PROPERTY CRIME

While alarms may be effective, the best alarm is more "eyes on the street," such as an immediate neighbor who is present most of the time and who knows how to intervene without getting hurt, thus providing effective prevention at very low cost.

How Fostering Cohesive Communities Protects Residents

From my own research in the 1970s, I've gained the perspective that any human presence would likely prevent crime against the property under protection but likely will not have an impact on crime in the surrounding neighborhood.[22] So private security will often be a good investment in short-term protection for those who can afford it—namely, the wealthy. But for the average American, there are also cost-effective measures (i.e., watchdogs that alert people to strangers in the area, neighbors who have agreed to intervene and/or call the police) that might work even better by protecting the entire neighborhood.

Jane Jacobs drew attention to the notion of "community" and to the importance of "eyes on the street" in her 1961 book, *The Death and Life of Great American Cities*. Importantly, by "eyes on the street" she was referring to neighbors and community members, not police patrols. She also talked about the preventive effect of persons feeling some ownership over an area. She asserted that the combination of eyes and ownership would reduce both property and violent crime. Some of this has been integrated into the work of Greg Saville on combining situational and social crime prevention.

Consistent with Jane Jacobs's original ideas, today's experts have also stressed the importance of creating a space that is socially *cohesive* rather than just being defensible. They argue that the space needs to facilitate a sense of community and not just supervision. It is this sense of belonging that contributes to people's feelings of ownership over an area—which is a key to having people protect not just their own property, but the property of those around them as well.

This was proven in the 1990s, when Felton Earls concluded that a feeling of ownership contributed to lowering crime rates in neighborhoods in Chicago.[23] This finding came out of one of the largest criminological studies ever that focused on what predisposed young people to offend. He also concluded that factors such as growing up in an uncaring and inconsistent household were important, but he added that the rate of offending was also affected by the extent to which neighbors looked after their neighborhoods and intervened to stop unsavory activity (e.g., nuisance teenagers and persons selling drugs)—what he dubbed "collective efficacy."

This finding runs counter to the view that it's *police* who must tidy up "broken windows" and "clean up" crime on the streets—both of which reflect a very *reactive* role of policing. Instead of police trying to pick up the pieces after the fact, it calls for neighbors to take charge and prevent the victimizations from happening in the first place. The linchpin here is that neighborhoods must remain connected *communities* in the true sense of the word and combat the collective isolation that urban living so often brings. This has many implications for city planners, as it stresses that they must avoid breaking up cohesive neighborhoods. Insurance companies would also likely benefit many times over from investments in crime prevention that include efforts to encourage this collective efficacy.

A Model Example: The Original Neighborhood Watch That Worked One remarkable success story about mobilizing communities to reduce residential burglary took place in Seattle in the 1970s. Sophisticated research confirmed a whopping 50 percent reduction in burglaries. There are lessons to draw from this success—lessons that unfortunately have largely been ignored.

The first lesson is that it was the mayor of the city who led the project and set up a law and justice planning office that reported directly to him, not to the police chief. He got this office to analyze how much crime was happening in the city, where it was happening, and why it was happening. It also conducted opinion polls to find out which issues were disturbing the citizens of Seattle. The analysis was submitted to the city council, which endorsed the need to give priority to burglaries, sexual assaults, and robberies in small stores.

Here's where the situation gets unique. With this knowledge in hand, the office began to work out how to actually *solve* each of these three problems. They talked to experts, police officers, and social scientists, and then they came up with tailored solutions that focused on proactively stopping the crimes from happening in the first place.

For burglary, they concluded—rightly or wrongly—that it was enabled when residents (1) left their homes unattended for long periods during the day and on weekends; (2) failed to intervene when there were suspicious strangers in the neighborhood; (3) did not have proper locks on their front doors; and (4) had not marked an identification number on property that was easily transportable and salable, such as televisions.

They then brainstormed a crime prevention strategy to remedy these deficiencies. It is important to note that the remedy targeted the four risk factors (above) that were thought to have caused the crime.[24] The strategy relied on training and coaching residents on the following: (1) making their residences look as if someone were inside when they weren't at home, such as keeping a dog or installing timers that turn radios and lights on and off; (2) having their neighbors agree to confront suspicious persons and/or call police; (3) installing effective locks such as deadbolts; and (4) labelling televisions, radios, bicycles, and other easily transportable and salable goods with the owners' social security numbers.

With funding from the US federal government as part of its Omnibus Crime Control and Safe Streets Act of 1968, the city—not the police—hired a group of university students who went into some of the most at-risk neighborhoods to train residents how to take the precautions listed above. Importantly, part of their activity was also to convince residents to host small groups of their immediate neighbors to talk about these measures and to get to know one another—in other words, to create collective efficacy within their communities.

The planning office had the foresight to set up an independent evaluation of the program with the assistance of a statistician. The coaching activities were delivered only in certain randomly selected high-crime areas so that the results could be compared with those of other high-crime neighborhoods not receiving any training. The rigorous evaluation used police records as well as victimization surveys to assess changes over time. In the end, the evaluation concluded that the program had reduced burglary by 50 percent or more in the areas that had received the training and community building. Even more importantly, this happened without any displacement of crime to other areas.

The glowing results earned the program an award from the US Department of Justice, and a manual was produced on how to implement this strategy elsewhere. As it turns out, it was the human presence (the protective "cocooning" effect) that made the program such an enormous success. Later research (including my own 1970s analysis) shows that it was the first two preventive measures—the willingness of neighbors to intervene and the appearance of someone being at home—that actually deterred burglars from stealing.[25] The other two measures likely had minimal impact; after all, burglars can easily get around deadbolt locks, and stolen goods are often sold on the streets, where no one tends to care that they were stolen.

This impressive success story inspired a worldwide movement of Neighborhood Watch members—all of whom are ardent believers in crime prevention, but most of whom have not followed the most important lessons and so have not been so successful.[26] Usually, neither the city nor the police department hire staff to analyze their city's crime problems, centrally organize the initiative, ensure that meetings involve the immediate neighbors, or coach residents on how to protect their property. Unfortunately, too many police departments have taken over the program as a public relations measure more than a crime reduction measure. Often, the neighborhoods that are most at risk (i.e., those with the lowest levels of community connection) are those where neighborhood watch is used least.

COMBINING APPROACHES TO PROBLEM-SOLVE PROPERTY CRIME

So we know that social investment targeted to problem places stops crime. We know that making it harder to commit crime actually prevents crime. We know that encouraging neighbors to intervene safely stops crime. So how about combining all three?

A Model Example: Kirkholt Neighborhood Watch

In the late 1980s, a problem place called Kirkholt in the United Kingdom developed a similar program to Seattle's *original* community crime prevention program. The Kirkholt program is listed as "effective" by crimesolutions.gov. This initiative was led by Ken Pease, a university professor with a bent for inspiring people to think about solutions to repeat victimizations (i.e., the reality that many persons are victims of more than one offense in a year, and often the same type of victimization). In the case of burglary, he had noticed that many victims were revictimized once the owner had replaced the stolen item.[27] Interestingly, while the victims soon figure out that burglars target specific houses more than once, the police often do not, as they are organized to respond on a call-by-call basis rather than to analyze the pattern of calls.

The Kirkholt area was facing an extraordinarily high level of break-ins (often repeat victimizations) on a housing estate. Smartly, Pease began by searching for a specific diagnosis of the extent and the causes of the problem. He also inspired police, municipal officials, and probation officers to collaborate with him, and as they were involved from the beginning, they were motivated to follow through with his solutions. The team members shared their respective knowledge about who was committing the break-ins, in whose residences they were occurring, and what was being stolen. They then designed a response to each of these causes.

In particular, they noted that cash was often being stolen from electricity meters (which collected residents' money up front before providing the electricity). They noticed how little protection was provided by other residents because they were absent or did not feel any responsibility for break-ins to other persons' residences—that is, they had noticed how little collective efficacy there was.

Therefore, they hired staff and established a well-organized neighborhood watch that mobilized neighbors in order to provide a protective, cocooning effect. They strengthened some physical security weaknesses by installing locks and lights. They also removed the electricity meters (which was where the cash was sitting, waiting to be stolen). Another part of the plan involved the probation service providing high-risk offenders with more intensive rehabilitative programming. Clearly, the team had come up with a uniquely Kirkholt solution to its particular crime problem.

The result was a program that worked (particularly with persistent offenders and repeat victims) to achieve a 75 percent reduction in break-ins over a four-year period. They demonstrated the equivalent of four dollars in savings in police time alone for each dollar spent on the program.

Despite the importance of the careful analysis and response to risk factors, efforts to replicate Kirkholt failed, as replications once again overlooked the importance of analyzing the problem before coming up with the solution. What works is the *problem-solving process*, not necessarily the one-size-fits-all approach.

A Model Program: Tackling Car Theft in Winnipeg, Canada

Politicians can look north for another good example of how to effectively use in-depth analysis of a specific problem place to truly solve the property-crime problem. In 2004, the midsize Canadian city of Winnipeg had North America's highest rate of auto theft—more than 1,900 thefts per 100,000 people. The annual cost to the provincial insurance company was $40 million. What's worse was that many residents were injured by reckless auto thieves.

After failing to arrest their way out of the problem, Winnipeg's first pragmatic but positive step toward countering this plague was to establish a task force that brought together key players such as police, the insurance company, youth services, and a leading academic. Their in-depth diagnosis of the epidemic showed that most thefts were committed by young offenders and that virtually all the vehicles were stolen for joyriding.

The second step was to get a $40 million investment—yes, $40 million, for a city of only half a million—from the provincial insurance agency to implement a three-pronged plan that was tailored specifically to Winnipeg's auto-theft problem. The plan included (1) intensive community supervision of high-risk youth; (2) a program requiring compulsory vehicle immobilizers for the most at-risk vehicles; and (3) youth programming to address the root causes of the vehicle thefts.

The Winnipeg-made solution was hugely successful at combating that city's car-theft plague. Evaluations showed that thefts declined by 29 percent in 2007, 42 percent in 2008, and an impressive 76 percent by 2010. Taxpayer savings were estimated to be an average of at least $40 million a year, and at least ten thousand crimes have been prevented annually. This is one clear example of how preventive programs that take all facets of the root causes into account get tangible results and, in this case, achieve them much more quickly than liberally applying only reactive crime control policies that are limited to policing, and maybe courts and corrections.

CONCLUSION

Points to Note: Smarter Strategies for Reducing Property Crime

The United States, like other affluent democracies around the world, has experienced a significant decrease in property crime over the past forty years. However, what starts as a theft may become a robbery, causing significant harm to victims that cumulatively costs up to $40 billion annually in reactive crime control. It is unlikely that US policing innovations or the spike in mass incarceration (i.e., money spent on reactive crime control) were major contributors to this drop in property crime, as the drop also occurred in other affluent democracies whose politicians did not institute such changes.

Demographic changes in the 1970s might have contributed to the decline, as might other long-term social trends such as an increased proportion of young people enrolling in college and more legal immigrants entering the country. The wider access to items desirable to young men may also be decreasing the feeling of being deprived, which is known to be a risk factor.

To stop property crime in problem places, the strategies recommended in chapter 5 are important. Strategies that make arrest more likely, such as CCTV and lighting, also stop some crimes in some situations. Property crime is also stopped by strategies that make the crime harder to commit, such as locks, alarms, and new gadgets in residences and cars. Advances in technology that lead to smaller, increasingly attractive consumer items such as smart phones increase their theft, particularly when incentives to design out crime are not present.

Neighbors stop crime when they provide "eyes on the street" and a commitment to intervene. Comprehensive strategies that use a problem-solving approach and then combine targeted social development, opportunity reduction, and citizen mobilization reduce the numbers of victims of crime and save money for both taxpayers and insurance companies.

Key Actions for Politicians for Smarter Crime Control

1. Legislators should invest in pre-crime prevention in problem places, as outlined in chapter 5.

2. Legislators should advance standards for the construction of houses and the design of cars and other consumer products based on evidence about what limits the ease with which these crimes can be committed and stolen products resold.

3. Legislators should encourage systems that increase the chances of making an arrest, such as CCTV and lighting, but only where their use can be justified on a cost-benefit basis.

4. Legislators should encourage cities to take the lead in diagnosing and promoting multipronged solutions to common property crime that involve law enforcement, youth services, neighborhoods, insurance groups, and pragmatic academics focused on prevention.

5. Legislators should encourage insurance companies that have a financial interest in stopping property crime to invest in crime reduction that promotes community cohesion.

6. Legislators should revise penal codes to reduce the use of long periods of incarceration for nonviolent thefts (for instance, by making these crimes misdemeanors and by implementing other recommendations from chapter 3).

This chapter has confirmed that large reductions in property crime were achieved as demographics, favorable social trends, and more security measures were put in place. Compelling evidence shows that smart pre-crime prevention that tackles social risk factors in problem places and ease of committing property offenses will reduce the number of property crime victims and costs to taxpayers. Once again, reactive policing and skyrocketing mass incarceration are unlikely to have had a major impact. Pre-crime prevention is better than expensive punishment with or without cure.

III

AN AGENDA TO PUT SAFETY FIRST FOR VICTIMS AND TAXPAYERS

10

REINVESTING IN SMART PUBLIC SAFETY TO SPARE VICTIMS AND LOWER TAXES

INTRODUCTION

The previous chapters have shown that crime and violence are not inevitable but instead are preventable. They provide the evidence (and so the hope) that there *can* be many fewer victims suffering harm from such preventable crimes as street violence, violence against women, and drunk driving.

Part I calls for *smarter* crime control that retools law enforcement, justice, and corrections to use these resources more effectively, including policing that focuses fairly on problem places. It calls for a shift away from unfocused and *reactive* approaches to crime "control," particularly when these operate too often in isolationist mindsets and lead to massive overuse of incarceration. Part II calls for smarter prevention through investments in children and youth that are focused on problem places. It also calls for comprehensive strategies to stop handgun violence, prevent violence against women (starting in schools), and enforce traffic rules smartly. Overall, the shift toward proactive and so smarter crime control based on effective prevention must include a shift away from the *reactive* measures of mass incarceration and the misdirected war on drugs with their immense social and racial costs as well as financial waste.

This chapter reminds us what the book has shown about the challenge still posed by the harm caused to victims through crime and violence despite the massive overuse of incarceration. "Too many Americans go to too many prisons for far too long and for no good law enforcement reason" is the quote from Attorney General Holder, but I prefer "Too many Americans go to too many prisons for far too long and for no good public safey reason."

It reminds us of the compelling knowledge that demonstrates how preventing crime *is* possible—knowledge that is endorsed by many of the world's leading and respected agencies dedicated to health and saving lives. It gives an overview of the important crime-reduction strategies that were identified in the different chapters and then shows how smart investment in these cost-effective strategies will save victims billions of dollars in harm and taxpayers billions of dollars in misdirected taxes.

This chapter reviews some sustainable ways to get these *smart* enforcement and cost-effective prevention strategies implemented where they are needed—in problem places, where problematic life situations too often lead to offending. Importantly, political vision and leadership within cities is a key to the successful implementation of these strategies. City and local school, housing, social services, and law enforcement administrations must engage in the development and implementation of a smarter plan in order for it to succeed.

The chapter concludes with a draft budget showing how to make the necessary reinvestment—the paradigm shift—away from costly and ever-expanding *reactive* crime control toward sustainable, proactive, and cost-effective crime *prevention*. It shows how the costs of making this shift can be covered through reallocating, not raising, taxes. In sum, it shows how legislators can choose to save victims' lives and spare them considerable pain, all while lowering taxes and saving taxpayers from misspent public funds.

THE CHALLENGE

The United States has rates of most common violent and property crime that are similar to those of other affluent democracies and that are indeed declining at similar rates (at least for the past twenty years). But these crimes still cause injury, pain, and huge loss of quality of life for victims, particularly victims of violence—estimated at $450 billion annually, or about 3 percent of the GDP.

The United States has particular areas where it is failing dismally compared with other affluent democracies. There is a persistent barrage of young men shooting each other with illegal handguns in some major cities; the proportion of young black men being shot is ten times higher than young white men. The country has a drunk-driving fatality rate twice that of the European Union and *six times* that of the United Kingdom. It has rising rates of drug overdoses that are believed to exceed those of other affluent democracies.

But it also has better data and more research on crime than any other democracy. It has a wealth of proven strategies that stop violence before it happens, although few of these are used. It also has the best data of any affluent democracy on violence against women, but not yet the breadth of proven solutions to stop this violence that are already available for other crimes.

For more than a century, the main response to crime control in the United States (as in other affluent democracies) has led to a system of policing, courts, and so-called corrections. Today, this system costs US taxpayers a staggering $260 *billion* annually just to operate—about 30 percent more per capita than countries such as the United Kingdom or Canada. While the United States has always had a reputation for being the most overzealous jailer in the Western world, in the past forty years it has expanded its highly punitive system from the 1970s to such an extent that by 2010 it was incarcerating about seven times more people than other affluent democracies. It even eclipses Russia by a factor of two and China by a factor of *seven*. This growth in prisons has led to one in nine young adult black men being behind bars at any given moment—a rate six times that of white men. Michelle Alexander has likened this to a system of new Jim Crow laws.

This imbalance has been fed in part by a supposed war on drugs, where taxpayers are spending $30 billion annually to arrest more persons for drug possession than for any other offense; they are also spending $20 billion annually to incarcerate these people—all while US rates of fatalities for illicit drug and opioid overdoses have shot past the yearly numbers for homicide and suicide or for traffic fatalities. This picture of the United States using more government expenditures to limit the freedom of some people in this democracy, which apparently champions small government and individual freedom, is ironic at best.

What this $260 billion goes toward every year is a *reactive* crime control system that focuses on "picking up the pieces" after a crime has already been committed—and after many persons have already been victimized. This system does not work toward reducing the number of victimizations that happen; rather, it punishes a generally small group of disadvantaged young men, who will be returned to problem places after having done the time for the crime and who will bring with them a long list of "collateral consequences" that will make it more likely they will do more time for more crimes—or maybe just for abusing alcohol and other drugs to kill the hopelessness.

PROVEN SOLUTIONS

The things mentioned above amount to a sorry misspending of money, lives, and pain and suffering—especially since we know how to stop much of this crime from happening in the first place. We now have the science to know what negative life experiences and "risk factors" lead more persons to offend. We know that "problem places" breed crime, and we know how this crime can be prevented by pre-crime prevention targeted to help those growing up in problem places. Much of this world-class science has come out of the United States and is available in plain English from websites promoted by US governmental departments and agencies, such as the Department of Justice and the Centers for Disease Control and Prevention. Unfortunately, the United States seems to be the affluent democracy with both the most severe problems and ironically the most knowledge about which cost-effective solutions would fix these problems. It is also the country doing the *least* to use that knowledge to stop Americans from becoming victims of crime or paying too much in taxes.

What Is Effective in Law Enforcement, Courts, and Corrections?

As you saw in chapter 2, US policing is resourced at levels little different from other affluent democracies. However, the law enforcement system has become reactive because too many of its resources are focused on emergency calls for service. Though populist politicians want to put more "boots" on the street, smarter policing that stops violence is about being more strategic. Mapping technology enables policing to focus on crime "hot spots"—what are better called "problem places." Police knowledge of these places has helped to focus enforcement on some of the precursors to violence, such as getting illicit handguns off the street through misdemeanor arrests. Police-led programs that use "focused deterrence" to make members of street gangs feel that they are likely to be put behind bars were associated with reductions in violence—by 40 percent or so—in some projects, but the reductions have been modest when applied nationally by law enforcement only. Multiple examples of "problem-oriented" policing, when implemented more than superficially, illustrate small gains that have been made to solve local problems of theft and assault.

But the same smart policing techniques have also been (mis)used in projects to confront street drug crime, which does not cause harm to victims. Police officers are disproportionately focused on "low-hanging fruit," arresting young black males involved in retailing drugs on the street; by targeting these less serious offenders, they can more easily make their arrest quotas. Still, young white men continue dealing drugs behind closed doors because they have been harder to catch—even though they are dealing more. Further, the mapping technology has led to the use of stop-and-frisk in problem places to catch less serious drug dealers, but it often gets misdirected against too many young black males who are innocent.

Chapter 3 showed how criminal courts are a part of a production line with a revolving door, where the judge sentences the convicted offender to incarceration. With many courts facing no less than 75 percent of their felony offenders who have been arrested before, the system is not working to save victims from harm. But judges could still be part of smart solutions to stop victimization if they focused on problem solving and using quick but short sanctions to keep offenders in treatment programs proven to work. This is particularly important for domestic violence and offenses related to abuse of alcohol, such as drunk driving. Drug courts have proven some effectiveness without excessive use of incarceration, but criminal courts should limit this role to the drug use that is linked to crimes that *do* cause harm to victims.

Overall, the lesson from looking at courts is that the most effective innovations use them much less. So the promising practices are diversions away from criminal courts to restorative justice, or referral to community mental health services, or attendance at community-based drug and alcohol treatment centers. The "legalization" of some drugs, such as marijuana, as has happened recently in Colorado and Washington, gets these cases away from the criminal courts and allows the whole law enforcement and criminal justice complex to focus on smart and proven ways to stop harm to victims.

Chapter 4 looked at how corrections (i.e., local jails and federal and state prisons) provide a limited benefit to potential victims by temporarily incapacitating offenders during the time they are behind bars. There is a time-limited benefit of incarceration to potential victims, as offenders tend to be less likely to reoffend as they get beyond age thirty. But this limited benefit comes at a huge cost to taxpayers—and to the already problematic communities from which, and to which, these offenders come and go.

Despite its name, the "corrections" system does not have an impressive record of correcting: approximately 40 percent of youth and 60 percent of adults get caught again and returned behind bars within three years of release. Extensive research has shown that it is possible to reduce these reoffending rates by 20 percent if everything is done right, using techniques that change attitudes, deal with alcohol and drug abuse, and work to mitigate the risk factors associated with reoffending.

Help to stay engaged with a job and a family, if they can be organized after release, is equally correcting. Still, the collateral consequences of prison time (e.g., loss of family cohesion, loss of employability, loss of standing within the community, loss of the right to vote) make staying away from crime after release even harder. In this vein, one of the most promising recent shifts in crime policy in the United States is the 50 percent decrease in the number of young offenders behind bars and the decrease in the New York City jail population. This change for youth will keep at-risk youth from suffering these collateral consequences and will also give them increased access to the interventions that will help them resist crime in the future.

What Is Effective and Cost-Effective in Prevention?

In part II, you saw considerable evidence that prevention is both an effective and a cost-effective way to reduce crime. As you saw in chapter 5, a number of strategies invest in problem places by providing help to families to focus on early childhood development and reduce child maltreatment, thereby reducing youth and adult crime. Many programs that outreach into problem places to families, children, and youth in their homes, schools, and communities are scientifically proven to reduce youth violence as well as violence later in life. The return on investments is huge. President Obama uses a figure of seven dollars saved for each dollar invested, but many other respected authorities show even better returns.

Guns are used in sensational (and fortunately rare) mass shootings. But, as chapter 6 showed, the majority of serious harm to crime victims from guns comes from the ubiquitous handgun crime that happens every day in the United States with little media attention in several but not all major cities—and mostly only in problem places. Smart policing projects have had some success in reducing urban handgun homicides, but the consensus outside the isolationist criminal justice mindset emphasizes comprehensive urban violence prevention that combines the critical components of analysis and investments in social development with the problem-based enforcement aspects from the Boston strategy—that is, they go beyond just smart enforcement, because you cannot simply arrest your way out of these crimes. Several cities and even some hospital emergency departments show whopping reductions in gun homicides. The sustained success of these strategies depends on the creation of a permanent responsibility center to lead the shift in the cities.

Implementing gun laws focused on safety, as proposed by the Brady Center, is associated with general reductions in homicide (and suicide) and will at least not exacerbate the high-profile mass shootings that are fortunately still rare even in the United States.

Chapter 7 looked at how reducing violence against women must use proven strategies that change male attitudes in high schools and colleges. Successful strategies can also mobilize collective action through using friends and others as interveners, encouraged by male role models such as sports icons. There must be significant changes in the way police respond to victims to increase the proportion of female victims that have the confidence to come forward to the police and so be empowered in their intimate relationships. More data is needed annually to keep the attention of politicians on actions that do or do not reduce the violence. Additional research would also contribute some insights about where interventions should be focused in order to most effectively tackle the problem. When it comes to truly eliminating violence against women, other risk factors such as the prevalence of guns and alcohol abuse must also be addressed.

As chapter 8 showed, traffic fatalities (including drunk-driving fatalities) have been reduced significantly over the past decade, but they still leave the US rates of traffic fatalities and drunk driving at several times those of other affluent democracies. Among the contributors to this success are improvements in car design such as air bags. More research is needed about how to reduce distracted driving associated with smart phone use, but solutions will likely be technology based rather than enforcement based. In terms of reducing dangerous driving such as speeding and drunk driving, the United States is lagging behind other Western countries—likely because the efforts at focused deterrence are less stringent than in other countries. Fortunately, its successful approaches do not overly rely on mass incarceration for the majority of offenders.

Chapter 8 also looked at the many ways to reduce alcohol's negative influence, including increasing the price of alcohol through taxes and focusing treatment on problem drinkers.

Rates of property crimes such as burglary have been dropping steadily since 1970, in part because of the demographic shift. Chapter 9 showed that further drops in property crime over the past twenty years are being somewhat driven by secure neighborhood design and improved security gadgets that might defeat efforts by young offenders, such as alarms and fancy ignition locks. One of the strategies proven to be the most effective at prevention is mobilizing neighbors to be guardians and interveners who contribute to "collective efficacy," which is a hallmark of cohesive communities.

Community-Based Solutions: The Critical Role of the City in Controlling Crime

When we think about solving problems such as garbage or public transit, we think about the city. But when we think about dealing with crime or other life-and-death issues, we mistakenly think too often about the police department and corrections. This thinking must change if we are going to stop people from being victimized by violence and crime. When cities were facing cholera and typhoid epidemics in the 1800s, it wasn't emergency room doctors or senators who solved the disease problem; rather, it was *cities* that took the knowledge about waterborne illnesses and implemented programs that cleaned up the water to prevent illness in a sustained and affordable manner. Likewise, many experts on crime (including me) are certain that cities hold the keys to long-lasting and affordable crime reduction.

We must start thinking of cities (more than police) as the first line of defense against crime. It is through cities that cost-effective measures can be implemented and maintained to reduce the number of crime victims—and at an affordable price for taxpayers. As you saw in part I, a city's problem places generate a majority of the common crime problem. And as you saw in part II, initiatives in schools and outreach to youth account for many of the effective solutions to these same problems. We've also seen how a sense of community belonging and ownership helps to keep crime low. For reasons like this, in the 1990s, the United States Conference of Mayors (USCM) agreed that municipalities are strategically positioned to bring together those who can change the conditions that generate crime and called on the financial and technical support of other levels of government to help them do so.[1]

Yes, police will continue to play a major role, as they have the enforcement powers necessary to reduce some of the risk factors, but their role will be within a division of labor that includes smart policing but shifts priorities and resources to actions that can be taken by schools, youth development agencies, and public health nurses. Other levels of government will also remain involved, as they have the necessary financial and technical support. But it's cities that can take the real lead in orchestrating strategies to bring about lasting effects, as they are the unit of government closest to the problems and solutions, and so they are most able to focus actions where they are needed. Cities can target social services to the families in need and ensure outreach to youth. They can ensure that parking areas are designed to reduce theft and violence. They can enforce building standards that keep houses safe from burglars. They can encourage community-based initiatives that lead residents in watching over their own neighborhoods with a sense of ownership.

But more importantly, they have the ability to make smart changes and to set up better partnerships that work to tackle the roots of crime. They can mobilize school boards, housing services, social services, sports programs, neighborhoods, citizens, and even businesses to tackle the risk factors that predispose kids, families, and neighborhoods to crime. They can multiply the number of early parenting programs, youth centers, mentoring initiatives, and more—that is, they can directly increase access to some of the most important resources in the violence prevention toolkit. What's more, they can help ensure that these programs get consistent funding and become permanent fixtures within the community. They can insist that the local police department become more problem oriented and can get the police, schools, and social services agencies to work together to deal with problems such as school dropouts and bullying. They can ensure that local services are available to support victims and foster the peaceful resolution of conflicts. Indeed, cities are in the best position to deliver the concrete actions that we know reduce crime.

To do this effectively, cities will need to have designated crime reduction offices that receive ample and consistent funding, probably from other orders of government. These offices must not be token public relations storefronts; rather, they must have influence to mobilize city heavyweights such as police leaders, school board commissioners, and city budget officers. In simple terms, there must be a permanent but small planning board with staff that manages a process of diagnosing the crime problems facing the city.[2] It is important to assemble this board to include representatives from the key agencies that can influence risk factors. For instance, the board must include school officials, social services representatives, hospital and mental health officials, recreation planners, employment counselors, and police designates. It will be important to include women as well as representatives from specific ethnic or neighborhood groups where crime is a particular problem.

Cities can fund these offices in part through a portion of municipal taxes. After all, cities want to keep a stable tax base for their residents and are therefore motivated to ensure both safer neighborhoods and affordable taxes. Cities must also tap into state and national funding to fund start-up projects and get initiatives off the ground—but it is important that the financial longevity of these programs be taken into consideration right from the start. Importantly, funds can be reallocated from policing and crime control budgets at other levels of government to sustain the shift, for as we saw earlier, crime prevention is a smart investment that has great dividends for taxpayers.

Cities must look after the priorities of their taxpayers. They must consider whether an investment now in tackling the situations that put youth, families, women, road users, and neighborhoods at risk of victimization can justify an investment in changing the way they utilize their taxes. Preventing crime before it happens is cost-effective and also cost-beneficial, as healthy kids and youth turn into productive adults later on. Safe communities also provide for a better quality of life for their residents and enhanced opportunities for economic development, investment, and tourism. Just as cities have plans for transportation, the environment, and public health, so too must they have a public safety plan that sets priorities on how our taxes should be used.

THE PARADIGM SHIFT

The Challenge of Getting Governments to Implement What Is Effective

So we know what strategies are effective and the importance of cities taking a leadership role in implementation. Now we need to turn our attention to *how* to shift the crime-control paradigm away from reactive law enforcement, courts, and corrections, and toward prevention-focused strategies that target the risk factors of crime. Smarter crime control is not about more or less policing or jails but about what is cost-effective in stopping victimization and husbanding taxes.

As mentioned previously, the recent reforms to the juvenile justice system provide a promising example of how this shift can be accomplished. As crime rates go down, there are good reasons to cut back on funds going toward the reactive system. After years of having many more young offenders in custody per capita than any other affluent democracy, the United States has recently experienced a 50 percent drop in its juvenile incarceration rates (albeit to levels that are still high by international standards—but there is progress in avoiding the overuse of incarceration and saving taxpayers money).[3] So less crime, less reaction to crime makes sense for juveniles. Why not for adults?

An important study was done of five states that shifted their juvenile justice systems to programs that are proven to be effective. The organization, Advancing Evidence-Based Practice, had a team with two of the leading world experts analyze these states to see why they had shifted and how they had done it.[4] Why they'd shifted was relatively simple—it was always a response to crisis, such as a financial crisis or being sued by the Department of Justice over the poor conditions in their juvenile institutions. When it came to getting action, they had important things in common, as shown in table 10.1.[5]

The Annie E. Casey Foundation has a different "road map" for how to effectively shift the paradigm toward effective crime prevention.[6] I have shown two of its key ingredients in table 10.1 as well.[7] Other agencies highlight how law enforcement could effectively shift its own focus and use its influence to protect and increase funding for investments in programs that have been proven to reduce violence by investing in kids.[8] This was also a theme when police leadership made recommendations on how to put victims at the zenith of law enforcement.[9] In stark contrast, the Centers for Disease Control and Prevention don't even mention any role for police, courts, or corrections in terms of shifting the paradigm to prevent violence. This is consistent with the work of the World Health Organization (WHO), which approaches crime reduction in the same way as it approaches other public health strategies such as those dealing with tobacco and obesity. The WHO's "road map"

	Key Ingredient for Successful Shift from Reactive Crime Control to Effective and Smart Crime Reduction	Advancing Evidence based Practice	Annie E. Casey Foundation	World Health Organization
1	Political champion for change and high level task force to recommend plan for change	yes		yes
2	Have Law Enforcement support for funding and plan			
3	Invest in, and use for inspiration, what has been proven to be effective	yes	yes	yes
4	Promote support for, and response to, victims			yes
5	Limit use of custody		yes	
6	Provide technical assistance and funding for implementation	yes		
7	Invest in data on outcomes, such as trends in violence, including gender and race issues			yes

Table 10.1   What Shifts Policy from Overreaction to Stopping Violence?

for shifting from reaction to prevention is also included in table 10.1. It includes early childhood development and the main items from the Centers for Disease Control and Prevention, but it is more comprehensive.[10] I have grouped the WHO ingredients into five points.[11]

This table stresses the importance of a political champion that can set up a task force to propose a plan. To be cost-effective, the plan must use the evidence and proven programs from parts I and II of this book. Shifting from a reactive model to a proactive model requires a process of diagnosing the problem places as well as retraining professionals in the field. To ensure that taxes are available for this shift, deliberate efforts must be made to limit the use of incarceration. Politically, statistics that keep politicians focused on results are vital. The process must make victims a priority—not only by preventing them from being victims of crime, but also by ensuring that their needs are met with services and funds.[12]

Shifting to Investing in Prevention: A Ten-Year Action Plan

Using the WHO's suggestion to develop a ten-year national action plan, I propose that the United States should aim to reduce its rates of victims of violence, property crime, road crime, and drug overdoses by 50 percent over the next ten years. This is a modest and achievable goal, considering the knowledge and results we have seen in this book. However, meeting this goal will require a national paradigm shift toward preventive solutions. To realistically enable this shift, I propose that over five years an increasing proportion of taxes that are spent on reactive policing, courts, and corrections budgets be reinvested into effective prevention—until a ceiling of 20 percent has been transferred. This will allow those working in the current system to retool. It will also allow many of those hired into the explosion of mass incarceration twenty-five years ago to retire.

This 20 percent is the same amount of funding that the United Kingdom is successfully cutting from a much leaner police and prison system. So if the United Kingdom can do it, the United States can, too—particularly since US expenditures per capita are so much higher.

The paradigm shift must be accompanied by deliberate decarceration; this is something that the United States has experienced before, when large numbers of mentally ill patients were released from institutions in the 1950s, 1960s, and 1970s. So the lessons must be learned from that experience, particularly that it is possible to massively decarcerate but also that it will not work unless there is serious reinvestment in what works in community solutions.[13]

In table 10.2, I present the main prevention measures that would contribute to the goal of reducing victims of crime by 50 percent by 2025, if started in 2015. The reinvestments call for a total reallocation of $26 billion, which is only 10 percent of the total $260 billion spent each year in the United States.

I include in this table only strategies that were identified earlier in the book as proven to reduce crime—most by 20 percent or much more. Some of the targeted social development programs are based on the work of a number of rigorous scientific studies that constitute the "well-scrubbed lists of programs that have been proven to produce substantial reductions in recidivism [reoffending] and crime, while saving taxpayers more than $10 in future correctional costs for every dollar expended."[14] Some design initiatives (such as installing a quality deadbolt or a seatbelt) require minimal investment, but the potential cost savings in lives is obviously much more. Keep in mind that it is often not known whether these savings would be the same if the programs

		reinvestment from police protection and judicial functions in billions
	Prevention through targeted social development	
1.1	Preschool and early parenting	$4
1.2	Life skills for 6-12 year olds	$2
1.3	Outreach to street youth	$4
1.4	School Violence Prevention (relating to sex, alcohol, bullying, intervening ...)	$2
	Prevention through more effective police and justice	
2.1	Policing innovation (including focus on guns, traffic, alcohol and more)	$2
2.2	Reinvestment of courts and corrections in proven interventions	$2
	Prevention through advancing standards for property and traffic safety	
3.1	Designing prevention into goods (including housing, vehicles plus)	$2
	Prevention through effective implementation	
4.1	City role in spearheading prevention	$1
4.2	Data to measure both less harm to victims (fewer, less serious injuries, less violence against women) and less waste of taxes	$2
4.3	Provide incentives to States to decarcerate (but ensure investment in effective prevention)	$5
	Total	**$26**

Table 10.2   What Reinvestments Stop Violence Cost-Effectively?

were implemented on a larger scale; in some cases, economies of scale might lower implementation costs. Combining effective programs will decrease crime by more than one program on its own.

Prevention through Targeted Social Development I have included four priorities in this category in table 10.2, which were each discussed in chapter 5. The first is 1.1—parenting and preschool programs. They require real money, but when this is targeted to problem places and families, the programs work to reduce a variety of crime problems. For instance, they reduce child abuse (violence against children) by as much as 70 percent. Over time, they also reduce adolescent involvement in crime by 50 percent and possibly violence against women and crime on the road by an unknown, but not necessarily insignificant, amount. A common rate of return is seven dollars saved for each dollar invested—likely six dollars in reduction in harm to victims and one dollar in savings to taxpayers. Though the benefits are large, the programs are also relatively costly, so I am proposing an annual expenditure of $4 billion. This is still a minor cost when compared with what can be achieved through strategies in part I.

The second priority is 1.2—lifeskills training. These programs in schools have a relatively low cost, as they can be integrated into the school curriculum. These programs are effective at reducing delinquency and abuse of alcohol and other drugs. The impact is realized within two to three years of program delivery. The rate of return from simply reducing the harm from alcohol and other drug abuse is estimated at eighteen dollars for each dollar invested.[15] Due to the low cost, I am proposing an annual expenditure of $2 billion.

The third priority is 1.3—outreach to street youth. This must be focused on youth in problem places and contributes to large reductions in homicides and serious injuries. Because the economists typically estimate a young life lost at more than $5 million, it is easy to see that these programs would also exceed ten dollars for every dollar invested.[16] I am proposing an annual expenditure of $4 billion.

The fourth priority is 1.4—school violence prevention. These programs in schools have a relatively low cost, as they can be integrated into the school curriculum. These programs are effective at reducing chronic offending as well as violence against women and traffic fatalities. But we need more work done to estimate how long sexual violence training for boys lasts after they leave school and what impact it has on rape and intimate partner violence. Due to the low cost, I am proposing an annual expenditure of $2 billion.

Prevention through More Effective Law Enforcement, Courts, and Corrections   I have included four priorities in this category in table 10.2. The first is 2.1, which refers to police innovation to use police resources more smartly, as discussed in chapter 2. For instance, the smarter allocation of the $120,000 a year that will likely be spent on an additional police officer's salary and related costs that could better be spent elsewhere—would result in more cost-effective policing without any increase in police budgets. Particular programs targeted at certain problem places have only a marginal cost of reallocating a few officers to organize the effective activities. However, actions to remove handguns may require more reallocation over a longer period of time. Even so, as mentioned for youth outreach in 1.3, the cost of a young person's lost life is high. So if these reallocations are targeted, they will achieve a dividend that exceeds ten dollars for each dollar reallocated within the police budget. As shown in chapter 6, when these actions are combined with youth outreach, they have very impressive results.

Unfortunately, the exact dividend from the reallocation of police resources to better control speeding, the use of seat belts, drunk driving, and distracted driving has not been calculated. However, if the United States achieved a 75 percent reduction in overall road fatalities and serious injuries to reach the per capita level of the United Kingdom, it would save $180 *billion* in overall harm to victims—so there is likely also a twenty-dollar saving for every dollar reallocated here, particularly if technological innovations such as speeding cameras were used more. (Keep in mind that the total cost of policing in a year is $124 billion.) My proposed reinvestment of $2 billion is designed to get that $124 billion much better used. This is ultimately not an increase in police budgets, as some police leaders and researchers propose, but part of an overall shift from tactics that police do in isolation to policing as part of a more balanced and cost-effective use of taxes to reduce crime.[17]

The second priority, 2.2 is also about achieving innovation toward a more balanced and cost-effective crime reduction strategy for courts and corrections. The leading expert on corrections budgets, William Spelman, suggested that every 10 percent increase in the number of people incarcerated contributed only a 2 percent reduction in crime in the 1990s.[18] So a *50 percent increase* in the number of people incarcerated would equal only a 10 percent reduction in crime. In cost terms, that means that $41.5 billion (or 50 percent of the incarceration budget of $83 billion) was required for an approximate 10 percent reduction in the total annual costs of crime. Contrast this sizeable expenditure with what can be achieved from investments in prevention through targeted social development, which spare victims from being victimized in the first place, and for one-seventh to one-tenth of the correctional costs!

The good news from chapter 4 is that corrections can see some substantial cost benefits in relation to reductions in reoffending. For instance, the Washington State Institute for Public Policy gives both cognitive-behavioral therapy and functional family therapy a prevention dividend of over twenty dollars for every dollar invested. These sizeable dividends can be achieved simply by reallocating resources. Where additional resources are needed is in investing in alternative correctional programs within the community (e.g., restitution) and in encouraging more court alternatives such as diversion programs and drug and mental health courts. There is likely a prevention dividend, but the exact amount cannot be reliably estimated from the current analyses.

Prevention through Advancing Standards for Property and Traffic Safety In the third category in table 10.2, I have focused on industrial design. We have plenty of clear examples of where investments will have significant payoffs in terms of preventing crime and reducing serious injury or death. Safety and antitheft features for older motor vehicles and for housing must be brought up to date with the latest evidence. New housing units could be required to meet certain standards in terms of alarms, lighting, and locks. There is also a need to look into tighter controls on drunk driving by lowering the legal blood alcohol concentration limit from 0.08 to 0.05 in addition to the stricter enforcement already mentioned. Methods should also be implemented to inhibit smart phone use after the device has been stolen. All these require some funds to develop the standards, but once the resulting low-cost prevention strategies are implemented, they will have significant benefits.

Prevention through Planning and Training to Get Effective Implementation The fourth category in table 10.2 focuses on implementing smarter crime control. Successful programs that effectively (and cost-effectively) tackle the risk factors that lead to victimization will require an investment in mobilizing different agencies around a joint diagnosis of the problem in order to have a strategic plan.

The priority 4.1 comes from the earlier part of this chapter. Cities must play a leadership role in implementing and monitoring solutions—probably by bringing in consultants and trainers to assist in implementing the plan.

The priority 4.2 refers to better data to guide and assess implementation. An investment must also be made in getting more useful information from the computerized mapping technology used by police, but not only for police use. While it enables officials at different levels of city bureaucracy to see the geographic distribution of crimes recorded by police, the full potential of these maps is not fully realized, since police crime analysis units don't have a way of sharing these maps with the community agencies that can strategically use them to proactively tackle the causes of crime. This is something that needs to be remedied, as these maps confirm how the rates of offending and victimization are concentrated and related to other factors such as poverty, broken families, lack of sports facilities, and so on. Therefore, the agencies working with broken families or recreation need to be able to see this information in order to mobilize their services to strategically tackle the problems. Also, politicians must be able to see how resources should be added or reallocated to solve these problems.

Because so many of the crimes that occur behind closed doors (e.g., child abuse and violence against women) do not come to the attention of police, it is important for cities to invest in means other than these police maps to make this information evident to community safety planners. Data from child protection agencies, for instance, give some indication of where child abuse is happening. This information can be supplemented by school-based surveys that measure bullying and violence at home. Furthermore, surveys of women may help to indicate the extent of the violence they suffer. Focus groups can supplement these systematic data, as can hospital emergency rooms, with the result being a more complete picture of how communities should target their crime prevention efforts.

Priority 4.3 goes for a federal role in shifting the paradigm. Much of the overuse in incarceration and law enforcement was encouraged by incentives from the federal government. Now is a time for federal assistance with funding and sharing of knowledge and training to help shift to more cost-effective protections for victims and avoid waste of taxes. Ultimately, the federal (and in some cases state) government can provide incentives to states and local governments to decarcerate and retool with investments that work to improve public safety.

SMARTER CRIME CONTROL MAKES FISCAL SENSE

In table 10.3, I give some estimates to provide an order of magnitude for the savings to victims and to taxpayers. The totals certainly should help legislators consider seriously what has been set out in this book. Even if another economist calculated these estimates as only half of what I believe the evidence supports, the argument for reinvestment now still remains highly compelling.

The table schematically sets out areas where the effective prevention measures would save costs to victims or taxpayers because of the reinvestments listed in table 10.2. Most of the savings to victims of a 50 percent reduction in violence and fatalities are reductions in loss of quality of life, but they also include other related costs, such as

	What savings flow to potential victims of crime?	Savings and tax flows (approximate order of magnitude)	
A.1	50% reduction in homicides and DWI fatalities	$57	
A.2	50% reduction in rapes	$66	
A.3	50% reduction in child abuse	$62	
A.4	50% reduction in crashes (excluding DWI fatalities)	$87	
A.5	50% reduction in assaults	$28	
	Savings in quality of life to victims	**$300**	
	What savings flow to taxpayers?		
B.1	Reinvestment needed to reduce crime by 50% (see table 10.2)	–$26	
B.2	20% cut in law enforcement, judicial functions and corrections (crime drop dividend)	$52	$26
C.1	50% reduced costs of medical care with crime drop dividend	$6	$6
D.1	Cut mass incarceration to 1990 levels for non-drug crime	$4	
D.2	Decriminalise recreational use of marijuana	$9	$13
E.1	Excise tax on alcohol	$4	
E.2	Excise tax on marijuana	$9	$13
F.1	Cut incarceration to 1980 level from 1990 level	$28	
F.2	Cut incarceration to 1970 level from 1980 level	$3	
F.3	Cut incarceration to European level from 1970 level	$12	$42
G.1	*Decriminalise other illicit drugs (Portugal model)*	$33	
	Savings available for other priorities of taxpayers every year	**$100**	

Table 10.3   What Savings Flow to Crime Victims and Taxpayers?

hospital emergency care and loss of work productivity. The table also shows the taxes needed for the reinvestment in table 10.2 as a cost to taxpayers before showing the considerable savings and tax revenue that can be generated in the name of reducing violence, and where programs that are not cost-effective can be cut, including a more assertive reduction in mass incarceration down to levels that are more in line with the historical use of incarceration in the United States (before the 1980s), possibly even matching incarceration levels in the European Union.

Averted Loss of Quality of Life and Some Tangible Costs for Victims

To restate the US attorney general using what I have shown in this book, "too many Americans are victims of violence too often for no good reason because his department knows what stops violence." In table 10.3, I have presented the potential savings to victims of violence around the five categories for which I presented costs of harm (in figure 1.4 in chapter 1). These are estimates of the pain avoided by victims of crime in the first box rather than savings to taxpayers, to be discussed in the second box later.

The estimated costs to victims include medical costs and lost productivity as well as intangible costs (i.e., the loss of quality of life for which a civil court would award damages). The five categories were homicide and drunk driving deaths, rape, child abuse, and assault. They do not include the sixth category of illicit drugs as this did not include any costs to victims.

This book has identified ways to effectively reduce these violent crimes and has proposed in table 10.2 ways to reinvest 10 percent of reactive expenditures to achieve a target of a 50 percent reduction over the next ten years. So the resulting savings that would flow as improvements in quality of life for potential victims are 50 percent of these totals.[19] In table 10.3, the first category schematically shows where these savings in harm to victims would be achieved. Each item, A.1 to A.5, uses the groupings from figure 1.4 and assumes a 50 percent reduction in each of the groupings. The reductions would be achieved by the reinvestments that were presented in table 10.2.

These savings are estimated at a whopping and exciting $300 billion in reduced harm and quality of life to potential victims.

What Savings Flow to Taxpayers?

In the second box in table 10.3, I have presented the savings that would flow to taxpayers around six categories. B1–B2 itemize the net flow discussed in table 10.2. C1 is the saving emanating from table 10.2 to medical costs. E1–E2 cover potential tax revenue from alcohol and marijuana. D, F, and G show the reductions in tax costs associated with various reductions in mass incarceration and associated criminal justice costs.

This table shows accumulated savings of $100 billion from items B.1 to F.3 only (excluding G.1). About half of this saving would be achieved through the combination of reinvestment in cost-effective violence prevention (B.1, B.2, and C.1), cutting mass incarceration to 1990 levels (D.1), decriminalizing recreational use of marijuana (D.2), and increasing excise taxes on alcohol and marijuana (E.1 and E.2). I will discuss these further.

Using a Dividend from the Drop in Crime Rates to Reinvest in Smart Public Safety (Table 10.2) and a Bonus to Taxpayers

The first point to make from looking at figure 1.5 is that expenditures on the policing, courts, and corrections complex have increased almost every year since 1982 and likely for a decade or so before that. However, property crime has been dropping steadily since 1972 (see figure 9.1)— in fact, to 25 percent of its level in 1972. Violent crime is a bit more complicated, but it is also at 27 percent of the level of 1993.

So with much lower crime rates, there are good reasons to reduce expenditures on reactions that do not have a good justification in terms of reducing numbers of crime victims. Attorney General Holder repeats that "too many Americans go to too many prisons for far too long and for no good law enforcement reason." I would substitute "public safety" for "law enforcement" because chapters 3 and 4 show that incarceration is not reducing the numbers of crime victims.

Further reductions in mass incarceration are being achieved without any detrimental effect on the numbers of crime victims. Within the

United States, we have seen in chapter 4 how reductions in youth incarceration in many states and how reductions in New York City jail populations have gone along with lower crime rates. Also, the international comparisons in chapter 9 for property crime confirmed that US use of mass incarceration had not decreased those rates more in the United States than no mass incarceration did in other affluent democracies.

It is not so clear from chapter 2 whether reductions in expenditures on policing can be achieved without any impact on rates of victimization. Certainly, cuts in unfocused policing can be achieved without an impact on crime rates, but if police agencies find a fairer balance between response to necessary emergency calls and targeted smarter policing, those budgets can be justified in the short term until investment occurs in the many programs that are much more cost-effective even than smart policing.

The UK government is on course to achieve a 20 percent cut in policing and prison expenditures. This impressive cut is occurring even though the United Kingdom did not overspend to the extent that this book shows US policy makers have done. So the first saving to US taxpayers must be an across-the-board cut—I have used 20 percent from the current reactive expenditures on policing, courts, and corrections. This might be achieved by focusing on incarceration through retirements and attrition over a five-year period.

However, to realize more extensive and sustainable savings, it will be important to reinvest some of these initial savings in those cost-effective programs identified in part II of this book. In table 10.2, I have selected those reinvestments where the social return on reductions in numbers of victims is not only large—often a 50 percent reduction in harm to victims—but size of the benefit is achieved for a relatively small cost. The data to support these assertions is strongest in chapters 5, 6, and 9 but likely will be equally strong as the research is completed for chapters 7 and 8.

Reduced Medical Costs

The next section, C.1, shows savings in medical costs to governments—and thereby to taxpayers. It is difficult to arrive at a precise estimate today of these costs. Estimating from the sources used in chapter 1 that rely on decreases in violent crime and increases in costs of medical care. I have used an approximate cost of medical care of $12 billion annually for victims of crime. So a 50 percent cut in crime would save $6 billion of taxpayers' money.

Reduced Expenditures on Mass Incarceration

D.1 assumes both a further cut over B.2 and a reduction in the need for mass incarceration as crime continues to decrease because of the investments in table 10.2. With a 50 percent reduction in crime, it should be possible to cut expenditures on policing, courts, and corrections by 50 percent as well.

It is smart to keep police at current levels but to shift their focus much more to smarter, preventive strategies. For instance, they could apply problem-solving methods to reduce crime in problem places; they could also focus on reducing traffic fatalities, where they can have an important impact on saving lives.

In contrast, corrections provides only a small benefit in terms of incarceration itself, as shown in chapter 4, and this can be realized much more cost-effectively through targeted social development and pre-crime prevention, as shown in chapter 5. Further, the drop in both property and violent crime suggests that considerable savings could come from reducing incarceration by the same amount. For instance, New York City achieved a large reduction in incarceration while its crime rate was dropping.[20]

The item D.2 refers to the important dividend that would come with drug decriminalization. Colorado and Washington have become the first jurisdictions in the United States and the world to outright decriminalize the use of marijuana for recreational purposes by regulating, taxing, and controlling marijuana in a way similar to alcohol.[21] If this legislation goes ahead without federal interference, then it will have significant impact on the costs of reactive crime control. Jeffrey Miron is an expert in the field, and he has identified $9 *billion* in savings relating to a nationwide paradigm shift in terms of marijuana.

Income from Disincentives

E.1 and E.2 refer to possible tax revenues. Miron also estimated an inflow of public money if marijuana were to be taxed nationwide at levels similar to those currently for alcohol and tobacco. He estimated this figure to be $9 billion from taxes on marijuana alone. These estimates assume that all states will impose an equal tax; otherwise, buyers may avoid buying in those states where the taxes are higher.[22]

In relation to E.2 for alcohol, in chapter 8, we saw that one way to reduce violence is to reduce the use of alcohol and that one way to reduce the use of alcohol is to increase the price. Indeed, in New York City, a tax increase on hard liquor was identified as one of the contributors to the sizeable reductions in violence in that city in the 1990s.[23] The alcohol industry grosses around $137 billion in the United States each year. An additional 3 percent tax introduced gradually over two or three years would generate another $4 billion a year.[24]

I have not included in the table a reference to the taxes on regained lost productivity, but likely this would be significant—but only after the economy has absorbed the additional labor.[25]

Reducing Mass Incarceration to Successive Levels

It is clear from the research that mass incarceration could be reduced much more than proposed in item B.2 and D.1 in table 10.3 without any significant impact on crime rates. Large reductions in incarceration, in association with investments in children and youth in problem places, is much more likely to sustain community safety and reduce the negative collateral consequences (and subsequent cycle of reoffending) brought about by mass incarceration and the elements of racial bias in the system.[26]

What's more, police have recorded that property-crime rates have dropped to 1960s levels and violent crime rates to 1970s levels. Generally, the rate of common crime in the United States today is on par with the rates of common crimes in other affluent democracies that have incarceration rates at the European level. So why not adjust US incarceration levels to be more in line with these trends? For instance, in 1970 in the United States, 300,000 persons were in state and federal prisons and 200,000 in local jails. That equalled an incarceration rate of 200 per 100,000—which is roughly double the average rate today for Western Europe. As you saw in chapter 4, however, by 1990, the US incarceration rate had roughly *doubled* to 1.1 million in a span of twenty years.

Today, another twenty years hence, it has roughly doubled *again*. So the 50 percent reduction in today's incarceration levels in D.1 would put the United States at roughly its 1990 levels. A further reduction to 1980 levels would save another $28 billion (F.1). Reducing US rates to 1970 levels would save $3 billion (F.2) and to European levels would save an additional $15 billion (F.3).

In the twentieth century, affluent democracies have given prison amnesties from time to time just to reduce incarceration overflow and expenditures, sometimes by as much as 50 percent.[27] Further, the decarceration of mental hospitals in the United States decimated the numbers held forcibly in those hospitals. The fact that governments did not invest in the programs to manage the mentally ill in the community is more a lesson on the importance of balancing decarceration with smart investments than on not decarcerating. So item F.1 is simply to reduce incarceration to the level of 1980. Item F.3 would reduce the rate to the average level of European countries. Governments could get to these levels by taking a page from the amnesties; this would simply entail a decision that governments can no longer afford these levels, particularly when they impact so disproportionately on blacks.

Keep in mind that to avoid the negative consequences from emptying mental hospitals, this substantial decarceration would be accompanied by a range of effective prevention measures that are proven to reduce street violence, violence against women, and traffic fatalities due to dangerous and impaired driving, and these programs are *proven* to reduce crime to a much greater extent than any slight increase associated with the loss of the prison incapacitation effect.

Decriminalizing Other Illicit Drugs

The last item in table 10.3 deals with the significant cost savings associated with the decriminalization of some illicit drugs besides marijuana. Portugal has decriminalized (not legalized) illicit drugs such as cocaine and heroin. Canada and Switzerland have some degree of legalization to decriminalize some illicit drugs, including through heroin prescriptions and safe injection sites for heroin and cocaine. Miron estimates a $33 billion reduction in costs associated with reducing reactive crime control for decriminalizing drugs such as these for personal use. He also estimates an inflow of an additional $38 billion if the illicit drugs were taxed at similar levels to alcohol and tobacco.[28] However, in none of the Canadian or European examples is there an excise tax on these drugs. It is also not realistic to tax most hard drug users, who are homeless and unemployable. So at best, the savings would be only the $33 billion saved by unburdening the reactive policing, courts, and corrections systems. To avoid double counting, I have placed this in italics as some of these savings are achieved through decarceration. When this decriminalizing of illicit drugs takes place, this will provide some additional savings.

CONCLUSION

Crime and violence have been decreasing in the United States as they have in other affluent democracies, but they still inflict enormous but preventable loss and pain on too many victims. Every year, taxpayers fund a $260 billion reactive crime-control industry, but far too little of this money is spent on actually *preventing* the victimizations from happening in the first place. Rather, exorbitant amounts of public money are spent on reacting afterward—on "picking up the pieces," so to speak.

This book has identified many actions that stop crime before it inflicts harm. These initiatives were structured and evaluated mainly in the United States, by American experts, and are endorsed by respected US authorities like the Department of Justice—which ironically stops short at the moment of actually implementing them itself or providing significant funds to states and local government to stop violent crime.

We know that investing in proven development programs for children and adolescents would provide rich dividends of less crime and violence as well as a high return on investment of approximately ten dollars saved for every dollar spent. Most of this ten dollars is reduced harm to victims—very important to me. But at least one dollar is the reduced need for the enforcement and criminal justice complex. This one-dollar savings to taxpayers will be realized only if there are, in fact, reductions in budgets for law enforcement, justice, and corrections.

General programs integrated into the school system would also reduce violence and property crime, and they would importantly shift male attitudes and behaviors away from sexual violence and the abuse of alcohol. Outreach to youth in street gangs has also provided good results in terms of reduced gun violence and increased education levels. So investments in proven programs such as these would reduce crime and violence significantly.

For the traditional law enforcement system to contribute to more effective prevention, police officers need to stop working in isolation and stop merely *reacting* to crime after the fact. Instead, they need to partner with other community agencies to lend proactive solutions to crime problems. They also need to be trained to focus on (1) reducing guns to stop crime in problem places; (2) reducing speeding and impaired driving; and (3) targeting the abuse of alcohol. It is likely that these shifts in focus could be accomplished simply by reallocating personnel, even with reductions because crime is down.

For corrections to make a more effective contribution, a number of programs can be implemented. These programs, including cognitive-behavioral therapy and family functioning services, are known to result in strong reductions in reoffending. While these prison-based programs must be funded, there is room for big reductions in mass incarceration as a whole. Indeed, the US levels of incarceration can be brought closer to incarceration rates in other affluent democracies without jeopardizing potential victims of violence. This system needs to stop disproportionately incarcerating black males for less serious offenses while continuing to fail at stopping the high rates of homicides among the young black population.

The United States must also reduce the numbers of persons driving drunk and focus on ways to enforce speeding, dangerous driving, and distracted driving standards. Safety on the roads can be further increased by lowering the legal blood alcohol concentration level limit. There is also room for designing crime out of our lives through more rigorous construction standards that make buildings resist burglary, more collective efficacy among our neighborhoods, and more innovations in terms of electronic smart gadgets that can reduce the opportunity for theft.

Cities have a major interest in the safety of their taxpayers and the sound husbanding of taxes for this purpose. They are key players in ensuring that the paradigm shift from policing and incarceration to violence prevention is focused on the problem places where it is needed most. More data must be collected to ensure that actions are targeted where they are most needed. If we are to see a major shift, then the federal government must get involved to provide incentives for states to shift toward more effective prevention of crime and victimization.

These are all concrete examples of the paradigm shift that is ultimately needed to reduce the harm, pain, and losses that victims and their families suffer every day in the United States by $300 billion or more. This shift will not only alleviate lost quality of life on the part of victims, but it also represents huge cost savings in the tangible costs of crime, including productivity losses and emergency room costs. The spread of laws to decriminalize the recreational use of marijuana can also contribute to reduced costs, as can implementing excise taxes in order to discourage the abuse of alcohol and to control marijuana use.

These savings alone to taxpayers of as much as $100 billion justify significant reductions in mass incarceration, which must be achieved over a number of years to allow correctional officers hired in the boom years to retire and others to retool. They give us good reason to stop misspending taxpayers' money on expensive *reactions* to crime—and to stop spending on what we know does not work to protect the lives of victims.

This book shares the knowledge with taxpayers, potential victims, politicians, and the media on how smarter crime control can provide safer communities for us and our children in the United States or across the world of affluent democracies. It provides cautions for less affluent democracies about what to avoid and what to do to make communities safe while controlling expenditures smartly on violence prevention.

PRINCIPAL SOURCES

Alexander, Michelle. *The New Jim Crow: Mass Incarceration in the Age of Colorblindness*. New York: New Press, 2010.

All-Party Parliamentary Group on Drug Policy Reform. "Towards a Safer Drug Policy: Challenges and Opportunities Arising from 'Legal Highs.'" Working paper, All-Party Parliamentary Group on Drug Policy Reform, London, 2013.

American Bar Association. "National Inventory of the Collateral Consequences of Conviction." http://www.abacollateralconsequences.org/CollateralConsequences/map.jsp. Accessed March 19, 2013.

Annie E. Casey Foundation. "Juvenile Detention Alternatives Initiative Resources." Annie E. Casey Foundation, http://www.aecf.org/KnowledgeCenter/PublicationsSeries/JDAIResources.aspx. Accessed March 11, 2013.

———. "No Place for Kids: The Case for Reducing Juvenile Incarceration." Working paper, Annie E. Casey Foundation, Baltimore, MD, 2011. http://www.aecf.org/OurWork/JuvenileJustice/JuvenileJusticeReport.aspx. Accessed March 20, 2013.

Audit Commission. *Misspent Youth . . . Young People and Crime*. London: Audit Commission for Local Authorities and National Health Service in England and Wales, 1996.

Austin, James F. "The Proper and Improper Use of Risk Assessment in Corrections." *Federal Sentencing Reporter* 16 (2004): 1–6.

Austin, James F., Todd Clear, Troy Duster, David F. Greenberg, John Irwin, Candace McCoy, Alan Mobley, Barbara Owen, and Joshua Page. "Unlocking

America: Why and How to Reduce America's Prison Population." Working paper, JFA Institute, Washington, DC, 2007.

Austin, James F., and Michael Jacobson. "How New York City Reduced Mass Incarceration: A Model for Change?" Working paper, Brennan Center for Justice at New York University School of Law, 2013. http://www.brennan-center.org/sites/default/files/publications/How_NYC_Reduced_Mass_Incar-ceration.pdf. Accessed February 27, 2013.

Baumer, Eric P., and Kevin T. Wolff. "Evaluating Contemporary Crime Drop(s) in America, New York City, and Many Other Places," *Justice Quarterly* (2012): 1–34.

Bellis, Mark A., Karen Hughes, Clare Perkins, and Andrew Bennett. "Protecting People, Promoting Health: A Public Health Approach for Violence Prevention for England." Working paper, North West Public Health Observatory, Liverpool, October 2012.

Bennett, Trevor, Katy Holloway, and David Farrington. "The Effectiveness of Neighborhood Watch." *Campbell Systematic Reviews* 18 (2008).

Berman, Greg, and John Feinblatt. *Good Courts: The Case for Problem-Solving Justice*. New York: New Press, 2005.

Black, M. C., K. C. Basile, M. J. Breiding, S. G. Smith, M. L. Walters, M. T. Merrick, J. Chen, and M. R. Stevens. *The National Intimate Partner and Sexual Violence Survey (NISVS): 2010 Summary Report*. Atlanta, GA: National Center for Injury Prevention and Control, Centers for Disease Control and Prevention, 2011.

Blincoe, Lawrence J., Angela G. Seay, Eduard Zaloshnja, Ted R. Miller, Eduardo O. Romano, Stephen Luchter, and Rebecca S. Spicer. "The Economic Impact of Motor Vehicle Crashes 2000." Working paper, National Highway Traffic Safety Administration, Washington, DC, 2002.

Blumstein, Al, and J. Wallman, eds. *The Crime Drop in America*. Cambridge: Cambridge University Press, 2000.

Bonta, James, and Donald Andrews. "Risk-Need-Responsivity Model for Offender Assessment and Rehabilitation 2007–06." Working paper, Public Safety Canada, Ottawa, 2007.

Braga, Anthony, and David Weisburd. "The Effects of 'Pulling Levers': Focused Deterrence Strategies on Crime." *Campbell Systematic Reviews* 8, no. 6 (2012).

———. *Policing Problem Places: Crime Hot Spots and Effective Prevention*. New York: Oxford University Press, 2012.

Byrne, James. "Drunk Driving: An Assessment of 'What Works' in the Areas of Classification, Treatment, Prevention and Control." Working paper, Council of Productivity and Management, State of Maryland, Department of Parole and Probation, Drinking Driver Monitor Program. University of Massachusetts, Lowell, 2003.

Campbell, J. C., N. Glass, P. W. Sharps, K. Laughon, and T. Bloom. "Intimate Partner Homicide: Review and Implications of Research and Policy." *Trauma, Violence, and Abuse* 8, no. 3 (July 2007): 246–69.

Campbell, Kristine, Andrea M. Thomas, Lawrence J. Cook, and Heather T. Keenan. "Resolution of Intimate Partner Violence and Child Behavior Problems after Investigation for Suspected Child Maltreatment." *JAMA Pediatrics* 324 (2013): 1–7.

Carson, Ann, and William J. Sabol. "Prisoners in 2011." Working paper, Bureau of Justice Statistics, Washington, DC, December 2012.

Caulkins, Jonathan, and Sara Chandler. "Long-Term Trends in Incarceration of Drug Offenders in the United States." *Crime and Delinquency* 54, no. 4 (2006): 619–41.

Center for the Study and Prevention of Violence. "Blueprints Program." Model programs for preventing violence are available at http://www.colorado.edu/cspv/blueprints/ and http://www.blueprintsprograms.com/.

Centers for Disease Control and Prevention. "Safe Youth. Safe Schools." http://www.cdc.gov/Features/SafeSchools/.

———. "2010 Mortality Multiple Cause Micro-data Files. Table 10." http://www.cdc.gov/nchs/data/dvs/deaths_2010_release.pdf. Accessed February 17, 2013.

Center for Problem-Oriented Policing. http://www.popcenter.org/.

Chalk, Rosemary, and Patricia A. King, eds. *Violence in Families: Assessing Prevention and Treatment Programs*. Washington, DC: National Academy Press, 1998.

Chettiar, Inimai, and Ethan Nadelmann. "Justice Department Can Be Smarter about Sequester." *The Hill's Congress Blog* (blog). http://thehill.com/blogs/congress-blog/economy-a-budget/284953-justice-department-can-be-smarter-about-sequester#ixzz2M6tB6KkN.

Cissner, Amanda, Melissa Labriola, and Michael Rempel. "Testing the Effects of New York's Domestic Violence Courts: A Statewide Impact Evaluation." Working paper, Center for Court Innovation, New York, 2013. http://www.courtinnovation.org/sites/default/files/documents/statewide_evaluation_dv_courts.pdf.

Clarke, Ronald. *Situational Crime Prevention: Successful Case Studies*. Albany, NY: Harrow and Heston, 1997.

Clement, Marshall, Matthew Schwarzfeld, and Michael Thompson. "The National Summit on Justice Reinvestment and Public Safety: Addressing Recidivism, Crime, and Corrections Spending." Working paper, Council of State Governments Justice Center, New York, January 2011.

Cloud, David, and Chelsea Davis. "Treatment Alternatives to Incarceration for People with Mental Health Needs in the Criminal Justice System: The Cost-Savings Implications." Working paper, Vera Institute of Justice, New York, February 2013. http://www.vera.org/sites/default/files/resources/downloads/treatment-alternatives-to-incarceration.pdf.

Cohen, Mark A., and Alex R. Piquero. "New Evidence on the Monetary Value of Saving a High Risk Youth." *Journal of Quantitative Criminology* 25, no. 1 (March 2009): 25–49.

Coker, Ann L., Patricia G. Cook-Craig, Corrine M. Williams, Bonnie S. Fisher, Emily R. Clear, Lisandra S. Garcia, and Lea M. Hegge. "Evaluation of Green Dot: An Active Bystander Intervention to Reduce Sexual Violence on College Campuses." *Violence Against Women* 17 (2011): 777–96.

Community Guide. "Reducing Alcohol-Impaired Driving: Ignition Interlocks," October 1, 2010. Available at www.thecommunityguide.org/mvoi/AID/ignitioninterlocks.html.

Cooper, Alexia, and Erica L. Smith. "Homicide Trends in the United States, 1980–2008, Annual Rates for 2009 and 2010." Working paper, Bureau of Justice Statistics, November 2011. http://bjs.ojp.usdoj.gov/content/pub/pdf/htus8008.pdf. Accessed February 20, 2013.

Corso, P., J. Mercy, T. Simon, E. Finkelstein, and T. Miller. "Medical Costs and Productivity Losses Due to Interpersonal and Self-directed Violence in the United States." *American Journal of Preventive Medicine* 32, no. 6 (2007): 474–82.

Crooks, Claire V., David A. Wolfe, Ray Hughes, Peter G. Jaffe, and Debbie Chiodo. "Development, Evaluation and National Implementation of a School Based Program to Reduce Violence and Related Risk Behaviours: Lessons from the *4th R*." *IPC Review* 2 (March 2008): 109–36.

Cross, Brittany. "Mental Health Courts Effectiveness in Reducing Recidivism and Improving Clinical Outcomes: A Meta-Analysis." Master's thesis, University of South Florida, 2011.

Cullen, Francis T., Cheryl Lero Jonson, and Daniel S. Nagin. "Prisons Do Not Reduce Recidivism: The High Cost of Ignoring Science." *Prison Journal* 3 (2011) supplement.

Department for Transport. "Reported Road Casualties in Great Britain: 2011 Provisional Estimates for Accidents Involving Illegal Alchohol Levels, Statistical Release." Department for Transport, August 16, 2012. https://www.gov.uk/government/publications/reported-road-casualties-in-great-britain-2011-provisional-estimates-for-accidents-involving-illegal-alcohol-levels.

Dhani, Amardeep. "Police Service Strength: England and Wales, 31 March 2012." Statistical bulletin, Home Office, July 26, 2012. http://www.homeoffice.gov.uk/publications/science-research-statistics/research-statistics/police-research/hosb0912/hosb0912?view=Binary.

Donziger, Steven, ed. *The Real War on Crime: The Report of the National Criminal Justice Commission*. New York: Harper Perennial, 1996.

Dowden, Craig, and D. A. Andrews. "What Works in Young Offender Treatment: A Meta-Analysis." *Forum on Corrections Research* 11, no. 2 (1999).

Dugan, Laura, Daniel Nagin, and Richard Rosenfeld. "Explaining the Decline in Intimate Partner Homicide: The Effects of Changing Domesticity, Women's Status, and Domestic Violence Resources." *Homicide Studies* 3, no. 3 (August 1999): 187–214.

Durlauf, Steven, and Daniel Nagin. "Imprisonment and Crime: Can Both Be Reduced?" *Criminology & Public Policy* 10, no. 1 (2011): 13–54.

Elder, R. W., R. A. Shults, D A. Sleet, James L. Nichols, Stephanie Zaza, and Robert S. Thompson. "Effectiveness of Sobriety Checkpoints for Reducing Alcohol-Involved Crashes." *Traffic Injury Prevention* 3 (2002): 266–74.

Ellis, Tom, and Peter Marshall. "Does Parole Work? A Post-release Comparison of Reconviction Rates for Paroled and Non-paroled Prisoners." *Australian and New Zealand Journal of Criminology* 33, no. 3 (2000): 300–317.

European Monitoring Centre for Drugs and Drug Addiction. *State of Drugs Problem in Europe 2011: Annual Report*. Lisbon: European Monitoring Centre for Drugs and Drug Addiction, 2011.

European Transport Safety Council. "Police enforcement strategies to reduce traffic casualties in Europe." Working paper, European Transport Safety Council, Brussels, Belgium, 1999.

Farrington, David P. "Criminal Careers." In *The Cambridge Handbook of Forensic Psychology*, edited by J. M. Brown and E. A. Campbell, 475–83. Cambridge: Cambridge University Press, 2010.

Farrington, David P., and B. C. Welsh. *Saving Children from a Life of Crime: Early Risk Factors and Effective Interventions*. Oxford: Oxford University Press, 2007.

Federal Bureau of Investigation. "Table 1, Crime in the United States by Volume and Rate per 100,000 Inhabitants, 1992–2011." Federal Bureau of Investigation, http://www.fbi.gov/about-us/cjis/ucr/crime-in-the-u.s/2011/crime-in-the-u.s.-2011/tables/table-1.

Fisher, Bonnie. "Shifting the Paradigm: Primary Prevention on Campuses." PowerPoint presentation at the 5th Annual Campus Safety Summit, Dennison University, 2011. https://www.ohiohighered.org/files/uploads/CampusSafety/Fisher-August-2011-v5.ppt. Accessed February 26, 2013.

Fisher Bonnie, F. Cullen, and M. Turner. "The Sexual Victimization of College Women." Research paper, National Institute of Justice, Bureau of Justice

Statistics, Washington, DC, December 2000. https://www.ncjrs.gov/pdffiles1/nij/182369.pdf.

Fleegler, Eric W., Lois K. Lee, Michael C. Monuteaux, David Hemenway, and Rebekah Mannix. "Firearm Legislation and Firearm-Related Fatalities in the United States." *JAMA Internal Medicine* 173, no. 9 (2013): 1–9.

Florida, Richard. "A Growing Divide in Urban Gun Violence." *Atlantic Cities*, January 10, 2013. http://www.theatlanticcities.com/neighborhoods/2013/01/growing-divide-urban-gun-violence/4328/.

Garside, Richard, and Arianna Silvestri. "Justice Policy Review: Volume 2, 6 May 2011 to 5 May 2012." Working paper, Centre for Justice and Policy Studies, London, 2013.

Gendreau, Paul, Tracy Little, and Claire Goggin. "Meta-analysis of the Predictors of Adult Offender Recidivism: What Works?" *Criminology* 34, no. 4, (1996): 575–608.

Glaser, Dan. *The Effectiveness of a Prison and Parole System.* Indianapolis: Bobbs-Merrill, 1964.

Glaze, Lauren E., and Erika Parks. "Correctional Populations in the United States, 2011." Bulletin, Bureau of Justice Statistics, United States Department of Justice, November 2012.

Global Commission on Drug Policy. "Report of the Global Commission on Drug Policy." Working paper, Global Commission on Drugs, 2011. http://www.globalcommissionondrugs.org/wp-content/themes/gcdp_v1/pdf/Global_Commission_Report_English.pdf.

Goldblatt, Peter, and Chris Lewis, eds. "Reducing Offending: An Assessment of Research Evidence on Ways of Dealing with Offending Behaviour." Working paper, Home Office, Research and Statistics, 1998, London.

Gondolf, Edward. "Theoretical and Research Support for the Duluth Model: A Reply to Dutton and Corvo Transforming a Flawed Policy: A Call to Revive Psychology and Science in Domestic Violence Research and Practice." *Aggression and Violent Behavior* 11 (September 2006): 457–83. http://www.theduluthmodel.org/pdf/Theoretical%20and%20Research%20Support.pdf. Accessed February 12, 2013.

Greenwood, Peter W., Brandon C. Welsh, and Michael Rocque. "Implementing Proven Programs for Juvenile Offenders: Assessing State Progress." Working paper, Association for the Advancement of Evidence-Based Practice, December 2012. http://www.advancingebp.org/?page_id=18. Accessed April 16, 2013.

Harrendorf, Stefan, Markku Heiskanen, and Steven Malby, eds. "International Statistics on Crime and Justice." Working paper, European Institute on Crime Prevention and Criminal Justice, Helsinki, 2010.

Heaton, Paul. "Hidden in Plain Sight: What Cost of Crime Research Can Tell Us about Investing in Police." Working paper, Rand Corporation, 2010. http://www.rand.org/pubs/occasional_papers/OP279.html. Accessed April 14, 2013.

Heckman, James J., Seong Hyeok Moon, Rodrigo Pinto, Peter A. Savelyev, and Adam Yavitz. "The Rate of Return to the High/Scope Perry Preschool Program." Discussion Paper No. 4533, Institute for the Study of Labor, Bonn, October 2009. ftp://ftp.iza.org/SSRN/pdf/dp4533.pdf. Accessed February 14, 2013.

Henry, Kelli, and Dana Kralstein. *Community Courts: The Research Literature.* New York: Center for Court Innovation, 2011. http://www.courtinnovation.org/sites/default/files/documents/Community%20Courts%20Research%20Lit.pdf. Accessed February 2, 2013.

Her Majesty's Inspectorate of Constabulary. "How to Use the Crime and Policing Comparator." http://www.hmic.gov.uk/crime-and-policing-comparator/how-to/. Accessed January 9, 2013.

———. "What Is the Best Thing the Police Can Do to Reduce Crime?" http://www.hmic.gov.uk/pcc/what-works-in-policing-to-reduce-crime/what-is-the-best-thing-the-police-can-do-to-reduce-crime/. Accessed February 25, 2013.

Howell, J. C., and M. W. Lipsey. "Research-Based Guidelines for Juvenile Justice Programs." *Justice Research and Policy* 14, no. 1 (2012): 17–34.

Hughes, C. A., and A. Stevens. "What Can We Learn from the Portuguese Decriminalization of Illicit Drugs?" *British Journal of Criminology* 50 (2010): 999–1022.

Innes, Martin. "Doing More with Less: The 'New' Politics of Policing." *Public Policy Research* 18, no. 2 (June 2011): 73–80.

Institute of Medicine. "Clinical Preventive Services for Women: Closing the Gaps." Report brief, Institute of Medicine, National Academy of Sciences, 2011.

International Traffic Safety and Analysis Group. *Road Safety: Annual Report 2011.* http://www.internationaltransportforum.org/irtadpublic/pdf/11IrtadReport.pdf. Accessed February 18, 2013.

International Transportation Forum. "Towards Zero: Ambitious Road Safety Targets and the Safe System Approach." Report, Joint Transport Research Center, 2008. http://www.internationaltransportforum.org/jtrc/safety/targets/targets.html. Accessed January 7, 2013.

James, Doris J., and Lauren E. Glaze. "Mental Health Problems of Prison and Jail Inmates, Highlights." Bureau of Justice Statistics, September 2006. http://www.bjs.gov/content/pub/pdf/mhppji.pdf.

Justice Policy Institute. "Rethinking the Blues: How We Police in the US and at What Cost." Working paper, Justice Policy Institute, Washington, DC, 2012. http://www.justicepolicy.org/uploads/justicepolicy/documents/rethinkingtheblues_final.pdf. Accessed February 27, 2013.

Karmen, Andrew. *New York Murder Mystery: The True Story behind the Crime Crash of the 1990s.* New York: New York University Press (2000).

Kauder, Neal, and Brian Ostrom. *State Sentencing Guidelines: Profiles and Continuum.* Williamsburg, VA: National Center for State Courts, 2008.

Kelling, George, Tony Pate, Duane Dieckman, and Charles Brown. *Kansas City Preventive Patrol Experiment: A Summary Report.* Washington, DC: Police Foundation, 1974.

Kelling, George, and William Sousa. "Do Police Matter? An Analysis of the Impact of New York City's Police Reforms." Working paper, New York: Center for Civic Innovation at the Manhattan Institute, New York, December 2001.

Kennedy, David. *Don't Shoot: One Man, A Street Fellowship, and the End of Violence in Inner-City America.* New York: Bloomsbury, 2011.

Kennedy, David, Anthony Braga, Anne Piehl, and Elin Waring. "Reducing Gun Violence: The Boston Gun Project's Operation Ceasefire." Research report, National Institute of Justice, Washington, DC, 2001.

Kilpatrick, D. G., Heidi S. Resnick, Kenneth J. Ruggiero, Lauren M. Conoscenti, and Jenna McCauley. "Drug-Facilitated, Incapacitated, and Forcible Rape: A National Study." Working paper, National Institute of Justice, Washington, DC, July 2007. https://www.ncjrs.gov/pdffiles1/nij/grants/219181.pdf.

King, Ryan, and Jill Pasquarella. *Drug Courts: A Review of the Evidence.* Washington, DC: Sentencing Project, 2009.

Knapp, Kay. What Sentencing Reform in Minnesota Has and Has Not Accomplished. *Judicature* 68, no. 3 (October–November 1984): 181–89.

Kyckelhahn, Tracey. "Justice Expenditure and Employment Extracts, 2009—Preliminary." Bureau of Justice Statistics, May 30, 2012. http://www.bjs.gov/index.cfm?ty=pbdetail&iid=4335.

Labriola, Melissa, Sarah Bradley, Chris S. O'Sullivan, Michael Rempel, and Samantha Moore. "A National Portrait of Domestic Violence Courts." Working paper, Center for Court Innovation, New York, December 2009. https://www.ncjrs.gov/pdffiles1/nij/grants/229659.pdf. Accessed February 2010.

Labriola, Melissa, Michael Rempel, and Robert C. Davis. "Testing the Effectiveness of Batterer Programs and Judicial Monitoring: Results from a Randomized Trial at the Bronx Misdemeanor Domestic Violence Court." Working paper, Center for Court Innovation, National Institute of Justice, November 2005.

Landenberger, N. A., and M. A. Lipsey. "The Positive Effects of Cognitive Behavioral Programs for Offenders: A Meta-analysis of Factors Associated with Effective Treatment." *Journal of Experimental Criminology* 1 (2005): 451–76.

Latessa, Edward J., Lori B. Lovins, and Paula Smith. "Final Report: Follow-up Evaluation of Ohio's Community Based Correctional Facility and Halfway House Programs—Outcome Study." Working paper, Center for Criminal Justice Research, University of Cincinnati, February 2010. http://www.drc.ohio.gov/public/UC%20Report.pdf.

Lee, Stephanie, Steve Aos, Elizabeth Drake, Annie Pennucci, Marna Miller, and Laurie Anderson. "Return on Investment: Evidence-Based Options to Improve Statewide Outcomes—April 2012 Update." Working paper, Washington State Institute for Public Policy, April 2012. http://www.wsipp.wa.gov/pub.asp?docid=12-04-1201.

Levitt, Steven D. "Understanding Why Crime Fell in the 1990s: Four Factors That Explain the Decline and Six That Do Not." *Journal of Economic Perspectives* 18, no. 1 (Winter 2004): 163–90. http://pricetheory.uchicago.edu/levitt/Papers/LevittUnderstandingWhyCrime2004.pdf. Accessed April 14, 2013.

Lipsey, Mark W. "The Primary Factors that Characterize Effective Interventions with Juvenile Offenders: A Meta-Analytic Overview." *Victims & Offenders* 4, no. 2 (2009): 124–47.

Lipsey, Mark W., James C. Howell, Marion R. Kelly, Gabrielle Chapman, and Darin Carver. "Improving the Effectiveness of Juvenile Justice Programs: A New Perspective on Evidence-Based Practice." Working paper, Center for Juvenile Justice Reform, Washington, DC, December 2010.

Lonsway, Kimberly A., Victoria L. Banyard, Alan D. Berkowitz, Christine A. Gidycz, Jackson T. Katz, Mary P. Koss, Paul A. Schewe, and Sarah E. Ullman, with contributions from Dorothy Edwards. "Rape Prevention and Risk Reduction: Review of the Research Literature for Practitioners." VAWNET, National Online Resource Center for Violence Against Women, 2009. http://www.vawnet.org/applied-research-papers/print-document.php?doc_id=1655.

MacKenzie, Doris L. *What Works in Corrections: Reducing the Criminal Activities of Offenders and Delinquents*. Cambridge: Cambridge University Press, 2006.

MADD. "Rating the States' Drunk Driving Efforts." Mothers against Drunk Driving. http://www.madd.org/drunk-driving/campaign/state-report.html. Accessed February 16, 2013.

Mauer, Mark, and Kate Epstein, eds. "To Build a Better Criminal Justice System: 25 Experts Envision the Next 25 Years of Reform." Working paper, Sentencing Project, Washington, DC, 2011.

Mayor's Office for Policing and Crime. "Police and Crime Plan 2013–2016." Report, Mayor of London, March 2013.

Maxwell, Christopher D., Joel H. Garner, and Jeffrey A. Fagan. "The Effects of Arrest on Intimate Partner Violence: New Evidence From the Spouse Assault Replication Program." Research brief, National Institute of Justice, Washington, DC, July 2001.

McFarlane, Judith, Jacquelyn C. Campbell, and Kathy Watson. "The Use of the Justice System Prior to Intimate Partner Femicide." *Criminal Justice Review* 26, no. 2 (Autumn 2001): 193–208.

McGarrell, Edmund F., Natalie Kroovand Hipple, Nicholas Corsaro, Timothy S. Bynum, Heather Perez, Carol A. Zimmermann, and Melissa Garmo. "Project Safe Neighborhoods—A National Program to Reduce Gun Crime: Final Project." Working paper, National Institute of Justice, Washington, DC, 2009.

Miller, M., E. Drake, and M. Nafziger. "What Works to Reduce Recidivism by Domestic Violence Offenders?" Working paper, Washington State Institute for Public Policy, Olympia, January 2013.

Miller, T., and D. Hendrie. *Substance Abuse Prevention Dollars and Cents: A Cost-Benefit Analysis.* Rockville, MD: Center for Substance Abuse Prevention, Substance Abuse and Mental Health Services Administration, 2008.

Ministry of Justice. "Green Paper Evidence Report: Breaking the Cycle: Effective Punishment, Rehabilitation and Sentencing of Offenders." Working paper, Ministry of Justice, London, 2010.

Miron, Jeffrey, and Katherine Waldock. "The Budgetary Impact of Ending Drug Prohibition." White paper, Cato Institute, Washington, DC, 2010.

Mitchell, Ojmarrh, David B. Wilson, Amy Eggers, and Doris L. MacKenzie. "Assessing the Effectiveness of Drug Courts on Recidivism: A Meta-analytic Review of Traditional and Non-traditional Drug Courts. *Journal of Criminal Justice* 40 (2012): 60–71.

National Center for Health Statistics. *Health United States 2011: With Special Feature on Socioeconomic Status and Health.* Hyattsville, MD: National Center for Health Statistics, 2012.

National Crime Prevention Council. "Six Safer Cities: On the Crest of the Crime Prevention Wave." Working paper, National Crime Prevention Council, Washington, DC, 1999.

National Drug Intelligence Center. *The Economic Impact of Illicit Drug Use on American Society.* Washington DC: United States Department of Justice, 2011.

National Highway Traffic Safety Administration (NHTSA). "Traffic Safety Facts 2010: Alcohol-Impaired Driving." Fact sheet, National Highway Traffic Safety Administration, US Department of Transportation, Washington, DC, 2011. http://www-nrd.nhtsa.dot.gov/Pubs/811606.pdf.

————. "Traffic Safety Facts 2011: Alcohol-Impaired Driving." Fact sheet, National Highway Traffic Safety Administration, US Department of Transportation, Washington, DC, 2012. http://www-nrd.nhtsa.dot.gov/Pubs/811700. pdf. Accessed February 16, 2013.

National Institute of Justice. "Gun Violence Prevention." National Institute of Justice, March 28, 2010. http://www.ojp.usdoj.gov/nij/topics/crime/gun-violence/prevention/welcome.htm.

————. "'Swift and Certain' Sanctions in Probation Are Highly Effective: Evaluation of the HOPE Program." Accessed February 4, 2013. http://www. nij.gov/topics/corrections/community/drug-offenders/hawaii-hope.htm.

National Registry of Evidence-Based Programs and Practices. "About NREPP." NREPP. http://nrepp.samhsa.gov/AboutNREPP.aspx.

Naumann, R. B., A. M. Dellinger, E. Zaloshnja, B. A. Lawrence, and T. R. Miller. "Incidence and Total Lifetime Costs of Motor Vehicle-Related Fatal and Nonfatal Injury by Road User Type, United States, 2005." *Traffic Injury Prevention* 11 (2010): 353–60.

New York Civil Liberties Union. "Stop-and-Frisk Campaign: About the Issue." NYCLU, 2011. http://www.nyclu.org/issues/racial-justice/stop-and-frisk-practices.

Nutt, David J., Leslie A King, and Lawrence D. Phillips. "Drug Harms in the UK: A Multicriteria Decision Analysis on Behalf of the Independent Scientific Committee on Drugs." *Lancet* 376, no. 9752 (November 2010): 1558–65.

Organization for Economic Cooperation and Development, Road Safety Annual Report 2011, Paris, 2013. This is produced by the International Traffic Safety Data and Analysis Group (IRTAD), which is a permanent working group of the Joint Transport Research Centre of the OECD and the International Transport Forum. See www.irtad.net and http://internationaltransportforum.org/irtadpublic/pdf/09brochure.pdf.

Osher, Fred, David A. D'Amora, Martha Plotkin, Nicole Jarrett, and Alexa Eggleston. "Adults with Behavioral Health Needs under Correctional Supervision: A Shared Framework for Reducing Recidivism and Promoting Recovery." Working paper, Council of State Governments Justice Center, National Institute of Corrections, and Bureau of Justice Assistance consensus project, 2012.

Papachristos, Andrew V., Tracey L. Meares, and Jeffrey Fagan. "Attention Felons: Evaluating Project Safe Neighborhoods in Chicago." *Journal of Empirical Legal Studies* 4, no. 2 (2007): 223–72.

Patel, Deepali, and Rachel Taylor. *Social and Economic Costs of Violence: Workshop Summary*. Washington, DC: National Academies Press, 2012.

Patterson, Evelyn J. "The Dose-Response of Time Served in Prison on Mortality: New York State, 1989–2003." *American Journal of Public Health* 103, no. 3 (March 2013): 523–28.

Pew Center on the States. "State of Recidivism, One in 100: Behind Bars in America." Working paper, Pew Center on the States, Washington, DC, 2008.

———. "Time Served: The High Cost, Low Return of Longer Prison Sentences." Working paper, Pew Center on the States, Washington, DC., 2012.

President's Commission on Law Enforcement and Administration of Justice. *The Challenge of Crime in a Free Society: A Report.* New York: Avon, 1968.

Prinz, Ronald J., Matthew R. Sanders, Cheri J. Shapiro, Daniel J. Whitaker, and John R. Lutzker. "Population-Based Prevention of Child Maltreatment: The U.S. Triple P System Population Trial." *Prevention Science* 10 (2009): 1–12.

Prothrow-Stith, Deborah, and Howard Spivak. *Murder Is No Accident: Understanding and Preventing Youth Violence in America.* San Francisco: Jossey-Bass, 2004.

Reddy, Vikrant P., and Marc Levin. "The Conservative Case against More Prisons." *American Conservative*, March 6, 2013. http://www.theamericanconservative.com/articles/the-conservative-case-against-more-prisons/comment-page-1/#comment-1401741. Accessed March 7, 2013.

Region of Waterloo. "Violence Prevention." Region of Waterloo. http://regionofwaterloo.ca/en/safeHealthyCommunity/violenceprevention.asp.

Reinarman, C., P. Cohen, and H. Kaal. "The Limited Relevance of Drug Policy: Cannabis in Amsterdam and in San Francisco." *American Journal of Public Health* 94 (2004): 836–42.

Reuland, Melissa, Matthew Schwarzfeld, and Laura Draper. "Law Enforcement Responses to People with Mental Illnesses: A Guide to Research-Informed Policy and Practice." Working paper, Council of State Governments Justice Center, New York, 2009.

Richardson, E. G., and D. Hemenway. "Homicide, Suicide, and Unintentional Firearm Fatality: Comparing the United States with Other High-Income Countries, 2003." *Journal of Trauma and Acute Care Surgery* 70, no. 1 (2011): 238–43.

Roehl, Jan, Dennis P. Rosenbaum, Sandra K. Costello, James R. "Chip" Coldren Jr., Amie M. Schuck, Laura Kunard, and David R. Forde. "Strategic Approaches to Community Safety Initiative (SACSI) in 10 U.S. Cities: The Building Blocks for Project Safe Neighborhoods." Working paper, National Institute of Justice, Washington, DC, 2006, 72–73.

Rossman, Shelli B., Janeen Buck Willison, Kamala Mallik-Kane, KiDeuk Kim, Sara Debus-Sherrill, and P. Mitchell Downey. "Criminal Justice Interventions for Offenders with Mental Illness: Evaluation of Mental Health Courts in Bronx and Brooklyn." Working paper, Center for Court Innovations, New York, 2006.

Royal Society for the Prevention of Accidents. "Drinking and Driving." Working paper, Royal Society for the Prevention of Accidents, Birmingham, England, August 2012. http://www.rospa.com/roadsafety/info/drinking_and_driving.pdf.

Sarteschi, Christine M., Michael G. Vaughn, and Kevin Kim. "Assessing the Effectiveness of Mental Health Courts: A Quantitative Review." *Journal of Criminal Justice* 39, no. 1 (2011): 12–20.

Schweinhart, Lawrence, Jeanne Montie, Zongping Xiang, W. Steven Barnett, Clive R. Belfield, and Milagros Nores. "The High/Scope Perry Preschool Study through Age 40: Summary, Conclusions and Frequently Asked Questions." Working paper, High/Scope Educational Research Foundation, Ypsilanti, MI, 2005.

Scotland Violence Reduction Unit. "About the Violence Reduction Unit." VRU. http://www.actiononviolence.com/about-us.

Sentencing Project. "Total Corrections Population." http://www.sentencingproject.org/map/map.cfm#map. Accessed February 15, 2013.

Shapland, Joanna, Anne Atkinson, Helen Atkinson, James Dignan, Lucy Edwards, Jeremy Hibbert, Marie Howes, Jennifer Johnstone, Gwen Robinson, and Angela Sorsby. Does Restorative Justice Affect Reconviction? The Fourth Report from the Evaluation of Three Schemes." Working paper, Ministry of Justice Research Series, London, 2008.

Sherman, Lawrence, David Farrington, Brandon Welsh, and Doris MacKenzie. *Evidence Based Crime Prevention*. New York: Routledge, 2002.

Sherman, Lawrence W., and Heather Strang. "Restorative Justice: The Evidence." Working paper, The Smith Institute, London, 2007. http://www.iirp.edu/pdf/RJ_full_report.pdf.

Shults, R., D. Sleet, R. Elder, G. Ryan, and M. Sehgal. "Association between State Level Drinking and Driving Countermeasures and Self Reported Alcohol Impaired Driving." *Injury Prevention* 8, no. 2 (June 2002): 106–10. http://www.ncbi.nlm.nih.gov/pmc/articles/PMC1730839/. Accessed February 16, 2013.

Shults, Ruth, R. W. Elder, D. A. Sleet, J. L. Nichols, M. O. Alao, V. G. Carande-Kulis, S. Zaza, D. M. Sosin, and R. S. Thompson. "Reviews of Evidence Regarding Interventions to Reduce Alcohol-Impaired Driving." *American Journal of Preventive Medicine* 21(4 suppl.): 66–88. Available at http://www.thecommunityguide.org/mvoi/mvoi-AJPM-evrev-alchl-imprd-drvng.pdf. Accessed February 16, 2013.

Sivak, Michael, and Brandon Schoettle. "Towards Understanding the Recent Large Reductions in U.S. Road Fatalities." Working paper, University of Michigan Transportation Research Institute, Ann Arbor, MI, 2010.

Skogan, Wesley G., and Kathleen Frydl, eds. *Fairness and Effectiveness of Policing: The Evidence*. Washington, DC: National Academies Press, 2003.

Skogan, Wesley, and Susan Hartnett. *Community Policing: Chicago Style*. New York: Oxford University Press, 1997.

Skogan, Wesley G., Susan M. Hartnett, Natalie Bump, and Jill Dubois. "Evaluation of CeaseFire-Chicago." Working paper, National Institute of Justice, Washington, DC, 2008. See executive summary at "CeaseFire Evaluation Report," Institute for Policy Research, Northwestern University, 2010. http://www.northwestern.edu/ipr/publications/ceasefire.html. Accessed March 28, 2010.

Sloan, J. H., A. L. Kellermann, D. T. Reay, J. A. Ferris, T. Koepsell, F. P. Rivara, C. Rice, L. Gray, and J. LoGerfo. "Handgun Regulations, Crime, Assaults and Homicide: A Tale of Two Cities." *New England Journal of Medicine* 319, no. 19 (1988): 1256–62.

Spelman, William. "Crime, Cash, and Limited Options: Explaining the Prison Boom." *Criminology & Public Policy* 8, no. 1 (2009): 29–77.

———. "The Limited Importance of Prison Expansion." In *The Crime Drop in America*, edited by Alfred Blumstein and Joel Wallman, 97–129. Cambridge: Cambridge University Press, 2000.

Steadman, Henry J., and Michelle Naples. "Assessing the Effectiveness of Jail Diversion Programs for Persons with Serious Mental Illness and Co-occurring Substance Use Disorders." *Behavioral Sciences and the Law* 23 (2005): 163–70.

Strang, Heather, and Lawrence W. Sherman. "Restorative Justice to Reduce Victimization." In *Preventing Crime: What Works for Children, Offenders, Victims, and Places*, edited by Brandon Welsh and David Farrington, 147–60. New York: Springer, 2006.

Substance Abuse and Mental Health Services Administration. *Report to Congress on the Prevention and Reduction of Underage Drinking*. Washington, DC: US Department of Health and Human Services, May 2012. http://store.samhsa.gov/product/Report-to-Congress-on-the-Prevention-and-Reduction-of-Underage-Drinking-2012/PEP12-RTCUAD. Accessed February 16, 2013.

Telep, Cody W., and David Weisburd. "Crime and Disorder? What Is Known about the Effectiveness of Police Practices in Reducing Crime." *Police Quarterly* 15 (2012): 331.

Truman, Jennifer L., and Michael Planty. "Criminal Victimization, 2011." Bulletin, Bureau of Justice Statistics, US Department of Justice, Washington, DC, 2013.

Turner, Susan, James Hess, and Jesse Jannetta. "Development of the California Static Risk Assessment Instrument (CSRA)." Working paper, Center for Evidence-Based Corrections, University of California, Irvine, November 2009.

United Nations. *Global Study on Homicide, 2011*. Vienna: United Nations Office on Drugs and Crime, 2011. http://www.unodc.org/documents/data-and-analysis/statistics/Homicide/Global_study_on_homicide_2011_web.pdf.

———. *Handbook on the Crime Prevention Guidelines: Making Them Work*. Vienna: United Nations Office on Drugs and Crime, 2010. http://www.unodc.org/documents/justice-and-prison-reform/crimeprevention/10-52410_Guidelines_eBook.pdf.

United Nations Entity for Gender Equality and the Empowerment of Women. *Handbook for National Action Plans on Violence against Women*. New York: UN Women, 2012.

United Nations Habitat, Safer Cities Program. http://www.unhabitat.org/categories.asp?catid=375. Accessed August 18, 2013.

United Nations General Assembly. Resolution 40/34, "Declaration of Basic Principles of Justice for Victims of Crime and Abuse of Power." November 29, 1985. http://www.un.org/documents/ga/res/40/a40r034.htm.

Van Dijk, Jan, Andromachi Tseloni, and Graham Farrell, eds. *The International Crime Drop: New Directions in Research*. Houndmills: Palgrave Macmillan, 2012.

Van Stelle, Kit R., Janae Goodrich, and Jason Paltzer. "Treatment Alternatives and Diversion (TAD) Program: Advancing Effective Diversion in Wisconsin, Advancing Fiscally Sound, Data-Driven Policies and Practices to Enhance Efficiencies in the Criminal Justice System and to Promote Public Safety, 2007–2010 Evaluation Report." Working paper, University of Wisconsin, Population Health Institute, December 2011.

Vennard, J., D. Sugg, and C. Hedderman. "Changing Offenders' Attitudes and Behaviour: What Works?" Home Office Research Study 171, Part I. London: Home Office, 1997.

Vera Institute of Justice. "Further Work in Criminal Justice Reform." Working paper, Vera Institute of Justice, New York, 1977. https://www.ncjrs.gov/pdffiles1/Digitization/44645NCJRS.pdf.

Waller, Irvin. *Less Law, More Order: The Truth about Reducing Crime*. Westport, CT: Praeger Imprint Series, 2006; Ancaster, Ontario: Manor House, 2008.

———, ed. *Making Cities Safer: Action Briefs for Municipal Stakeholders*. Action Briefs no. 3. Ottawa: University of Ottawa Institute for the Prevention of Crime, March 2009.

———. *Men Released from Prison*. Toronto, Ontario: University of Toronto Press, 1974/1978.

———. *Rights for Victims of Crime: Rebalancing Justice*. New York: Rowman and Littlefield, 2010.

————. "What Reduces Residential Burglary: Action and Research in Seattle and Toronto." In *The Victim in International Perspective*, edited by Hans Joachim Schneider, 479–92. New York: De Gruyter, 1982.

Waller, Irvin, and Janet Chan. "Prison Use: A Canadian and International Comparison." *Criminal Law Quarterly* 17, no. 1 (December 1974): 47–71. Also in *Correctional Institutions*, 2nd ed., edited by L. T. Wilkins and D. Glazer, 41–60. Philadelphia: Lippincott, 1977.

Waller, Irvin, and Norm Okihiro. *Burglary, the Victim and the Public*. Toronto: University of Toronto Press, 1978.

Waller, Irvin, Daniel Sansfaçon, and Brandon Welsh. *Crime Prevention Digest II: Comparative Analysis of Successful Community Safety*. Montreal: International Centre for Prevention of Crime, 1999.

Walmsley, Roy. "World Prison Population List." International Centre for Prison Studies. http://www.idcr.org.uk/wp-content/uploads/2010/09/WPPL-9-22.pdf. Accessed February 3, 2013.

Weatherburn, Don, and Megan Macadam. "A Review of Restorative Justice Responses to Offending." *Evidence Base*, no. 1 (2013). http://journal.anzsog.edu.au/userfiles/files/EvidenceBase2013Issue1.pdf.

Webster, D. W., J. M. Whitehill, J. S. Vernick, and F. C. Curriero. "Effects of Baltimore's Safe Streets Program on Gun Violence: A Replication of Chicago's CeaseFire Program." *Journal of Urban Health* 90, no. 1 (February 2013): 27–40.

Welsh, Brandon, and David Farrington, eds. *Preventing Crime: What Works for Children, Offenders, Victims, and Places*. New York: Springer, 2006.

Western, Bruce. *Punishment and Inequality in America*. New York: Russell Sage Foundation, 2006.

Whitehill, Jennifer, D. W. Webster, S. Frattaroli, and E. M. Parker. "Interrupting Violence: How the CeaseFire Program Prevents Imminent Gun Violence through Conflict Mediation." *Journal of Urban Health* (February 26, 2013): 1.

Willett, Terrence. *Criminal on the Road: A Study of Serious Motoring Offences and Those Who Commit Them*. London: Tavistock, 1971.

Willis, C., S. Lybrand, and N. Bellamy. "Alcohol Ignition Interlock Programmes for Reducing Drink Driving Recidivism." *Cochrane Database of Systematic Reviews* no. 3 (2004).

Wolfe, D. A., C. V. Crookes, P. Jaffe, D. Chiodo, R. Hughes, W. Ellis, L. Stitt, and A. Donner. "A Universal School-Based Program to Prevent Adolescent Dating Violence: A Cluster Randomized Trial." *Archives of Pediatric and Adolescent Medicine* 163 (2009): 693–99.

Woolf, Steven H., and Laudan Aron, eds. *U.S. Health in International Perspective: Shorter Lives, Poorer Health*. Washington, DC: National Academies Press.

World Health Organization. *Global Status Report on Road Safety, 2013.* Geneva: World Health Organization, 2013.

————. *Preventing Intimate Partner and Sexual Violence against Women: Taking Action and Generating Evidence.* Geneva: World Health Organization, 2010.

————. "Preventing Violence: A Guide to Implementing the Recommendations of the World Report on Violence and Health." Working paper, World Health Organization, Geneva, Switzerland, 2004. http://www.who.int/violence_injury_prevention/media/news/08_09_2004/en/index.html.

————. *Violence Prevention: The Evidence.* Geneva: World Health Organization, 2009. http://www.who.int/violence_injury_prevention/violence/4th_milestones_meeting/publications/en/index.html. Accessed April 7, 2013.

————. *World Report on Violence and Health.* Geneva: World Health Organization, 2002.

Youth Justice Board, London. http://www.justice.gov.uk/about/yjb.

Zador, P. L. "Alcohol-Related Relative Risk of Fatal Driver Injuries in Relation to Driver Age and Sex." *Journal of Studies on Alcohol* 52, no. 4 (1991): 302–10.

NOTES

CHAPTER I: SMART PUBLIC SAFETY: GIVING PRIORITY TO VICTIMS AND TAXPAYERS

1. Steven H. Woolf and Laudan Aron, eds., *U.S. Health in International Perspective: Shorter Lives, Poorer Health* (Washington, DC: National Academies Press, 2013).

2. Sabrina Tavernise, "For Americans under 50, Stark Findings on Health Published," *New York Times*, January 9, 2013, http://www.nytimes.com/2013/01/10/health/americans-under-50-fare-poorly-on-health-measures-new-report-says.html?_r=1&, accessed February 20, 2013; National Research Council, *U.S. Health*.

3. Ernesto Zedillo, "Rethinking the 'War on Drugs': Insights from the US and Mexico," Vox, May 22, 2012, http://lnkd.in/x5E-7w, accessed August 11, 2013.

4. While death rates have been growing, opioids have increased the problem significantly. National Vital Statistics System, available at http://www.cdc.gov/nchs/nvss.htm.

5. Irvin Waller and Janet Chan, "Prison Use: A Canadian and International Comparison," *Criminal Law Quarterly* 17, no. 1 (1974): 47–71.

6. "Entire World—Prison Population Rates per 100,000 of the National Population," International Centre for Prison Studies, http://www.prisonstudies.org/info/worldbrief/wpb_stats.php?area=all&category=wb_poprate, accessed May 5, 2013.

7. One such survey is the National Crime Victimization Survey. The surveys are independent of law enforcement and so are not affected by police decisions to make their statistics look better—or worse. These surveys are independent of police decisions to allocate more or less resources to detectives or responses to 911 calls. The surveys go directly to adults in households in the same way as the census or annual surveys on unemployment do. Indeed, the Census Bureau identifies the representative sample and administers the survey for the US Department of Justice.

These surveys measure rates of victimization by common offenses such as residential burglaries, car thefts, assaults, robbery, and sexual assault. These surveys have been done every year since 1972—more than forty years. They are done on an impressive scale. In 2010, in the United States, nearly 150,000 individuals age twelve and older were interviewed in 84,000 households. Similar surveys are now commonplace in other industrialized countries. For instance, the Crime Survey for England and Wales is conducted annually on a sample of 60,000 households and has become the benchmark for measuring the success of British crime reduction strategies. Canada is behind the others as it only undertakes its survey every five years and on a comparatively small sample of 25,000 households. However, Canada has pioneered a similar survey to measure violence against women, which is beginning to be taken up in other countries. There is also an international crime victim survey that enables a comparison of rates between different countries but on national samples of only 2,000.

8. Irvin Waller, *Rights for Victims of Crime: Rebalancing Justice* (Lanham, MD: Rowman and Littlefield, 2010), 58–62.

9. Jennifer L. Truman and Michael Planty, *Criminal Victimization, 2011* (Washington, DC: US Department of Justice, Bureau of Justice Statistics, 2013).

10. See figure 7.1 in chapter 7.

11. M. C. Black, K. C. Basile, M. J. Breiding, S. G. Smith, M. L. Walters, M. T. Merrick, J. Chen, and M. R. Stevens, *The National Intimate Partner and Sexual Violence Survey (NISVS): 2010 Summary Report* (Atlanta, GA: National Center for Injury Prevention and Control, Centers for Disease Control and Prevention, 2011).

12. Ted Miller, Mark Cohen, and Brian Wiersema, *Victim Costs and Consequences: A New Look* (Washington, DC: US Department of Justice, National Institute of Justice, 1996).

13. In terms of productivity alone, a 2004 World Bank study shows that one in five of the workdays lost by women in established market economies are due to gender-based violence. See World Health Organization, *Economic Dimensions of Interpersonal Violence* (Geneva: World Health Organization, 2004). The economists have also looked at the pain and suffering that victims of crime

experience. They call this the "loss of quality of life." Their main measure was determined by research on the average awards made by juries in US civil courts for varying sorts of crimes. So economists calculated the damages for pain and suffering as being what victims who went to civil court were compensated (as determined by a jury of their peers). An alternative way of estimating these costs uses what people would be prepared to pay to avoid the pain and suffering brought on by being victimized. The latter leads to much higher costs than used in this book, as shown in Mark A. Cohen and Alex R. Piquero, "New Evidence on the Monetary Value of Saving a High Risk Youth," *Journal of Quantitative Criminology* 25, no. 1 (March 2009): 32–36.

14. See Waller, *Rights for Victims*, 24–26, for argument and details. The estimates use updated bottom-up estimates from Cohen and Piquero, "New Evidence," 32–36, but use the latest statistics in this book for rape (1,000,000) from chapter 7 and drunk driving crashes (12,000 deaths and 275,000 crashes with injuries) from chapter 8.

15. "Cost of Child Abuse and Neglect Rival Other Major Public Health Problems," CDC Injury Center, http://www.cdc.gov/violenceprevention/child-maltreatment/economiccost.html, accessed April 30, 2013.

16. "Statistics," Mothers against Drunk Driving (MADD), http://www.madd.org/statistics/, accessed February 16, 2013; "Impaired Driving in the United States," National Highway Traffic Safety Administration, http://www.nhtsa.gov/people/injury/alcohol/impaired_driving_pg2/us.htm, accessed April 28, 2013.

17. The CDC estimate of $51 billion is taken from L. Blincoe, A. Seay, E. Zaloshnja, T. Miller, E. Romano, S. Luchter, et al., "The Economic Impact of Motor Vehicle Crashes, 2000" (Washington, DC: US Department of Transportation, National Highway Traffic Safety Administration [NHTSA], 2002).

18. *The Economic Impact of Illicit Drug Use on American Society* (Washington, DC: US Department of Justice, National Drug Intelligence Center, 2011).

19. World Health Organization, *Economic Dimensions*.

20. Cohen and Piquero, "New Evidence," 46.

21. Dan Keating, "Gun Deaths Shaped by Race in America," *Washington Post*, March 22, 2013, http://www.washingtonpost.com/sf/feature/wp/2013/03/22/gun-deaths-shaped-by-race-in-america/, accessed March 25, 2013; Alexia Cooper and Erica L. Smith, "Homicide Trends in the United States, 1980–2008: Annual Rates for 2009 and 2010" (report, US Department of Justice, Bureau of Justice Statistics, NCJ 236018, November 2011), http://bjs.ojp.usdoj.gov/content/pub/pdf/htus8008.pdf, accessed February 20, 2013.

22. Lauren E. Glaze, "Correctional Populations in the United States, 2010," report, US Department of Justice, Bureau of Justice Statistics, NCJ 236319, December 2011.

23. Michelle Alexander, *The New Jim Crow: Mass Incarceration in the Age of Colorblindness* (New York: New Press, 2010).

24. Alexander, *The New Jim Crow*.

25. Irvin Waller and Janet Chan, "Prison Use: A Canadian and International Comparison," *Criminal Law Quarterly* 17, no. 1 (December 1974): 47–71.

26. Alexander, *The New Jim Crow*.

27. "Felony Defendants in Large Urban Counties, 2006," Bureau of Justice Statistics, http://bjs.ojp.usdoj.gov/index.cfm?ty=tp&tid=231, accessed March 13, 2013.

28. William Spelman, "Crime, Cash, and Limited Options: Explaining the Prison Boom," *Criminology & Public Policy* 8, no. 1 (2009); William Spelman, "The Limited Importance of Prison Expansion," in *The Crime Drop in America*, ed. Alfred Blumstein and Joel Wallman (Cambridge: Cambridge University Press, 2000), 97–129.

29. "Growing Federal Prison Budget May Force Cuts in DOJ Programs: IG," The Crime Report, November 21, 2012, http://www.thecrimereport.org/news/crime-and-justice-news/2012-11-ig-report-on-prisons, accessed March 13, 2013.

30. "Justice Expenditure and Employment in the United States, 2009," US Department of Justice, Bureau of Justice Statistics.

31. In 2004, BJS reported 800,000 sworn police officers, which is a 73 percent rise.

32. Irvin Waller, *Less Law, More Order: The Truth about Reducing Crime* (Westport, CT: Praeger, 2006; Ancaster, Canada: Manor House, 2008), 7–9.

33. Most of those increases occurred after violent crime was dropping. That is, the less the violent crime, the more expenditures increased—not the reverse. You will see that the best estimates are that 27 percent of the overall reduction in crime can be ascribed to the 300 percent increase in inmates. See Spelman, "The Limited Importance," 123.

34. Allison Brennan, "Analysis: Fewer U.S. Gun Owners Own More Guns," CNN, July 31, 2012, http://www.cnn.com/2012/07/31/politics/gun-ownership-declining; "A Shrinking Minority: The Continuing Decline of Gun Ownership in America," Violence Policy Center, http://www.vpc.org/studies/ownership.pdf.

35. The PROMISE legislation is one interesting exception. See "The Legislation," Youth Promise Action, http://www.youthpromiseaction.org/about-bill.html, accessed April 30, 2013.

36. Waller, *Less Law, More Order*; Irvin Waller, Daniel Sansfaçon, and Brandon Welsh, *Crime Prevention Digest II: Comparative Analysis of Successful Community Safety* (Montreal: International Centre for Prevention of Crime, 1999); Peter W. Greenwood, *Changing Lives: Delinquency Prevention as Crime-Control Policy* (Chicago: University of Chicago Press, 2006).

37. National Research Council, Institute of Medicine, *Juvenile Crime, Juvenile Justice* (Washington, DC: National Academies Press, 2001), 3–4, 66–104.

38. National Research Council, *Juvenile Crime, Juvenile Justice*, 3–4.

39. David P. Farrington, "Criminal Careers," in *The Cambridge Handbook of Forensic Psychology*, ed. J. M. Brown, J and E. A. Campbell (Cambridge: Cambridge University Press, 2010), 480–81.

40. Waller, Sansfaçon, and Welsh, *Crime Prevention Digest II*; National Research Council, *Juvenile Crime, Juvenile Justice*.

41. World Health Organization, *Violence Prevention: The Evidence* (Geneva: World Health Organization, 2009), available at http://www.who.int/violence_injury_prevention/violence/4th_milestones_meeting/publications/en/index.html, accessed February 13, 2013; US Department of Justice, National Institute of Justice website, Solutions to Crime: What Works in Criminal Justice, Juvenile Justice, and Crime Victim Services, http://crimesolutions.gov, accessed March 11, 2013.

42. *Blueprints for Healthy Youth Development*, http://www.colorado.edu/cspv/blueprints/, accessed March 11, 2013.

43. Lawrence Sherman, David Farrington, Brandon Welsh, and Doris MacKenzie, *Evidence Based Crime Prevention* (New York: Routledge, 2002).

44. World Health Organization, *Violence Prevention: The Evidence*; World Health Organization, *World Report on Violence and Health* (Geneva: World Health Organization, 2002); World Health Organization, *World Report on Road Traffic Injury Prevention: Summary* (Geneva: World Health Organization, 2004); World Health Organization, *Preventing Intimate Partner and Sexual Violence against Women: Taking Action and Generating Evidence* (Geneva: World Health Organization, 2010).

45. Centers for Disease Control and Prevention, "Safe Youth. Safe Schools," http://www.cdc.gov/Features/SafeSchools/.

46. Committee to Review Research on Police Policy and Practices, Wesley Skogan and Kathleen Frydl, eds., National Research Council, *Fairness and Effectiveness in Policing: The Evidence* (Washington, DC: National Academies Press, 2004).

47. For other websites in the United States, see Crime Solutions, "Other Evidence-Based Program Libraries," http://www.crimesolutions.gov/about_otherlibraries.aspx, accessed August 11, 2013.

48. Peter W. Greenwood, Brandon C. Welsh, and Michael Rocque, *Implementing Proven Programs For Juvenile Offenders: Assessing State Progress*, Association for the Advancement of Evidence Based Practice, December 2012, http://www.advancingebp.org/?page_id=18, accessed April 16, 2013.

CHAPTER 2: POLICING: FROM OVERREACTION AFTER THE FACT TO STOPPING CRIME BEFORE IT HARMS

1. Apple Job Creation, http://www.apple.com/about/job-creation/, accessed April 22, 2013.

2. Brian A. Reaves, "Census of State and Local Law Enforcement Agencies, 2008," July 2011 bulletin,Bureau of Justice Statistics, Office of Justice Programs, US Department of Justice, http://bjs.ojp.usdoj.gov/content/pub/pdf/csllea08.pdf.

3. "Justice Expenditure and Employment Extracts, 2009—Preliminary," table 1, "Percent distribution of expenditure for the justice system by type of government, fiscal year 2009 (preliminary)," Bureau of Justice Statistics , Excel file name cjee0901.csv, http://bjs.ojp.usdoj.gov/index.cfm?ty=pbdetail&iid=4335, accessed February 19, 2013.

4. Committee to Review Research on Police Policy and Practices, Wesley Skogan and Kathleen Frydl, eds., National Research Council, *Fairness and Effectiveness in Policing: The Evidence* (Washington, DC: National Academies Press, 2004). Her Majesty's Inspectorate of Constabulary, Police and Crime Commissioners, What is the best thing the police can do to reduce crime?, http://www.hmic.gov.uk/pcc/what-works-in-policing-to-reduce-crime/what-is-the-best-thing-the-police-can-do-to-reduce-crime/, accessed February 25, 2013.

5. Committee to Review Research, *Fairness and Effectiveness*.

6. Committee to Review Research, *Fairness and Effectiveness*, 4–5.

7. "What is the best thing the police can do to reduce crime?" Her Majesty's Inspectorate.

8. They also stressed the shift from policing acted in an isolated manner to partnering with community agencies such as schools to tackle a multitude of risk factors and therefore prevent crimes from happening in the first place, as will be discussed in chapters 5 and 10.

9. Irvin Waller, *Rights for Victims of Crime: Rebalancing Justice* (Lanham, MD: Rowman and Littlefield, 2010), 58–59.

10. "Percent of Crimes Cleared by Arrest or Exceptional Means, 2009," Crime in the United States 2009, http://www2.fbi.gov/ucr/cius2009/offenses/clearances/index.html#figure, accessed February 18, 2013.

11. "Table 29: Estimated Number of Arrests United States, 2011," Crime in the United States 2011, http://www.fbi.gov/about-us/cjis/ucr/crime-in-the-u.s/2011/crime-in-the-u.s.-2011/tables/table-29, accessed April 22, 2013.

12. Committee to Review Research, *Fairness and Effectiveness*.

13. Jan Van Dijk, Andromachi Tseloni, and Graham Farrell, eds., *The International Crime Drop: New Directions in Research* (Houndmills: Palgrave Macmillan, 2012), 300–318.

14. Janet L. Lauritsen and Robin J. Schaum, "Crime and Victimization in the Three Largest Metropolitan Areas, 1980–98," Bureau of Justice Statistics Technical Report, March 2005.

15. For example, in 1990—one of the city's peak crime years—there were more than 2,200 murders, 100,000 robberies, and 120,000 burglaries recorded by the NYPD. By 2012, there were only 417 murders, 20,000 robberies, and 19,000 burglaries.

16. Eric P. Baumer and Kevin T. Wolff, "Evaluating Contemporary Crime Drop(s) in America, New York City, and Many Other Places," *Justice Quarterly* (2012): 1–34.

17. Andrew Karmen, *New York Murder Mystery: The True Story behind the Crime Crash of the 1990s* (New York: New York University Press, 2000), xi–xiii.

18. Karmen, *New York Murder Mystery.* We will explore the other factors identified in chapter 5.

19. George Kelling and William Sousa, *Do Police Matter? An Analysis of the Impact of New York City's Police Reforms*, Civic Report no. 22, Center for Civic Innovation at the Manhattan Institute, New York, 2001.

20. See more at "Bloomberg Touts Record Low Murder Rate as New Cops Sworn In," CBS New York, December 28, 2012, http://newyork.cbslocal.com/2012/12/28/bloomberg-boasts-record-low-murder-rate-as-new-cops-sworn-in/#sthash.oySDwLVi.dpuf.

21. *Police and Crime Plan 2013–2016* (London: Mayor's Office for Policing and Crime, 2013).

22. Definition taken from the Bureau of Justice Assistance of the US Department of Justice, which is the main provider of discretionary funds for innovations in policing and is supporting a network on smart policing.

23. George Kelling, now a professor of criminology at Rutgers University in New Jersey, has played a significant role in the research on the effectiveness of policing and is often associated with the policies of Giuliani and Bratton in New York City. Kelling started his college studies in theology and then turned to social work for his postgraduate degree.

24. See Lawrence Sherman, David Farrington, Brandon Welsh, and Doris MacKenzie, eds., *Evidence-Based Crime Prevention* (New York: Routledge, 2002), but also see chapter 9 in this book for more discussion of this and other effective ways to reduce property crimes.

25. Cody W. Telep and David Weisburd, "What Is Known about the Effectiveness of Police Practices in Reducing Crime and Disorder?" *Police Quarterly* 15, no. 4 (2012): 331.

26. Telep and Weisburd, "What Is Known," 331; "Five Things Law Enforcement Executives Can Do to Make a Difference," National Institute of Justice, http://nij.gov/five-things/, accessed March 26, 2013.

27. Anthony Braga and David Weisburd, *Policing Problem Places: Crime Hot Spots and Effective Prevention* (Oxford: Oxford University Press, 2012).

28. Braga and Weisburd, *Policing Problem Places.*

29. Braga and Weisburd, *Policing Problem Places*, 9–14.

30. Herman Goldstein, *Problem-Oriented Policing* (New York: McGraw-Hill, 1990).

31. Center for Problem Oriented Policing, www.popcenter.org.

32. John Eck and William Spelman, *Problem Solving: Problem-Oriented Policing in Newport News* (Washington, DC: Police Executive Research Forum, 1987), available at https://www.ncjrs.gov/pdffiles1/Digitization/111964NCJRS.pdf, accessed April 22, 2013; "History of Problem-Oriented Policing," Center for Problem-Oriented Policing, http://www.popcenter.org/about/?p=history, accessed April 22, 2013.

33. Wesley Skogan and Susan Hartnett, *Community Policing: Chicago Style* (New York: Oxford University Press, 1997), 219–30, 242–44.

34. Skogan and Hartnett. *Community Policing*, 219–30, 242–44.

35. A. Braga, and D. Weisburd, "The Effects of 'Pulling Levers' Focused Deterrence Strategies on Crime," *Campbell Systematic Reviews* 8, no. 6 (2012): 19.

36. Braga and Weisburd, "The Effects of 'Pulling Levers,'" 6.

37. "Stop-and-Frisk Campaign: About the Issue," New York Civil Liberties Union, http://www.nyclu.org/issues/racial-justice/stop-and-frisk-practices, accessed April 22, 2013.

38. "Program Profile: Kansas City (MO) Gun Experiment," Crime Solutions, http://crimesolutions.gov/ProgramDetails.aspx?ID=238, accessed July 8, 2013; law enforcement has known for some time that enforcing traffic laws, particularly in problem places, leads to persons who are committing other offenses. Researchers unfortunately have largely overlooked the reality that some of the risky traffic violators are also committing other, violent offenses. We will discuss this more in chapter 8.

39. "Program Profile: Problem-Oriented Policing in Violent Crime Places (Jersey City, NJ)," Crime Solutions, http://www.crimesolutions.gov/Program-Details.aspx?ID=227, accessed August 17, 2013.

40. Ronald Clarke, ed., *Situational Crime Prevention: Successful Case Studies*, 2nd ed. (Boulder, CO: Lynne Rienner, 1997).

41. To be discussed in chapter 5 as a joint strategy of targeted law enforcement and social development in problem places.

42. Notably, the decreases exceeded the regional trends by 15 percent in New Haven, Portland, and Winston-Salem, and by 30 percent in Indianapolis. See Jan Roehl, Dennis P. Rosenbaum, Sandra K. Costello, James R. "Chip" Coldren Jr., Amie M. Schuck, Laura Kunard, and David R. Forde, *Strategic Approaches to Community Safety Initiative (SACSI) in 10 U.S. Cities: The Building Blocks for Project Safe Neighborhoods* (Washington, DC: National Institute of Justice, 2006), 72–73.

43. "Program Profile: Phoenix (Ariz.) Repeat Offender Program," Crime Solutions, https://www.crimesolutions.gov/ProgramDetails.aspx?ID=66, accessed April 23, 2013; Sherman, Farrington, Welsh, and MacKenzie, *Evidence-Based Crime Prevention*; Allan Abrahamse, Patricia Ebener, Peter Greenwood, Nora Fitzgerald, and Thomas Kosin, "An Experimental Evaluation of the Phoenix Repeat Offender Program," *Justice Quarterly* 8, no. 2 (1991):141–68.

44. Waller, *Rights for Victims of Crime*, 55–76.

45. "Stop-and-Frisk Campaign," New York Civil Liberties Union.

46. "Stop-and-Frisk Campaign," New York Civil Liberties Union.

47. "What Is the School-to-Prison Pipeline?" American Civil Liberties Union, http://www.aclu.org/racial-justice/what-school-prison-pipeline, accessed May 5, 2013.

48. James F. Austin and Michael Jacobson, "How New York City Reduced Mass Incarceration: A Model for Change?" (report for Brennan Center for Justice at New York University School of Law, 2013).

CHAPTER 3: JUSTICE: COURTS THAT STOP CRIME OR DO NOT UNNECESSARILY INTERFERE

1. "Felony Defendants," Bureau of Justice Statistics, http://bjs.ojp.usdoj.gov/index.cfm?ty=tp&tid=231, accessed March 13, 2013.

2. "State Court Caseload Statistics," Bureau of Justice Statistics, http://bjs.ojp.usdoj.gov/index.cfm?ty=tp&tid=30, accessed February 18, 2013.

3. "Felony Defendants," Bureau of Justice Statistics, http://bjs.ojp.usdoj.gov/index.cfm?ty=tp&tid=231, accessed March 13, 2013; R. LaFountain, R. Schauffler, S. Strickland, and K. Holt, *Examining the Work of State Courts: An Analysis of 2010 State Court Caseloads* (Washington, DC: National Center for State Courts, 2012), available at http://www.courtstatistics.org/Other-Pages/~/media/Microsites/Files/CSP/DATA%20PDF/CSP_DEC.ashx, accessed April 22, 2013.

4. Irvin Waller, *Rights for Victims of Crime: Rebalancing Justice* (New York: Rowman and Littlefield, 2010), 61–62.

5. "Federal Prison Terms for Black Men 20% Longer Than Those for Whites," *The Crime Report*, February 16, 2013, http://ht.ly/hOXfn.

6. Greg Berman, "Message from the Director," Center for Court Innovation, http://www.courtinnovation.org/message-director, accessed February 19, 2013.

7. "What Are Problem-Solving Courts?" Bureau of Justice Assistance, https://www.bja.gov/evaluation/program-adjudication/problem-solving-courts.htm.

8. "Who We Are," Center for Court Innovation, http://www.courtinnovation.org/who-we-are, accessed February 2, 2013.

9. "Who We Are," Center for Court Innovations.

10. Kelli Henry and Dana Kralstein, *Community Courts: The Research Literature* (New York: Center for Court Innovation, 2011), available at http://www.courtinnovation.org/sites/default/files/documents/Community%20Courts%20Research%20Lit.pdf, accessed February 2, 2013.

11. Douglas B. Marlowe, interview by Center for Court Innovations, http://www.courtinnovation.org/research/douglas-b-marlowe-treatment-research-institute-university-pennsylvania?url=research%2F11%2Finterview&mode=11&type=interview&page=2, accessed February 2, 2013; Douglas B. Marlowe, "Research Update on Adult Drug Courts," National Association of Drug Court Professionals, http://www.nadcp.org/sites/default/files/nadcp/Research%20Update%20on%20Adult%20Drug%20Courts%20-%20NADCP_1.pdf, accessed April 23, 2013.

12. Ojmarrh Mitchell, David B. Wilson, Amy Eggers, and Doris L. MacKenzie, "Assessing the Effectiveness of Drug Courts on Recidivism: A Meta-analytic Review of Traditional and Non-traditional Drug Courts," *Journal of Criminal Justice* 40 (2012): 60–71.

13. Doris L. MacKenzie, *What Works in Corrections: Reducing the Criminal Activities of Offenders and Delinquents* (Cambridge: Cambridge University Press, 2006).

14. Marlowe, "Research Update on Adult Drug Courts"; "Drug Courts" (working paper, Washington State Institute for Public Policy), http://www.wsipp.wa.gov/rptfiles/1000.DrugCourt.pdf, accessed April 23, 2013; Ryan King and Jill Pasquarella, *Drug Courts: A Review of the Evidence* (Washington, DC: The Sentencing Project, 2009).

15. "'Swift and Certain' Sanctions in Probation Are Highly Effective: Evaluation of the HOPE Program," National Institute of Justice, http://www.nij.gov/topics/corrections/community/drug-offenders/hawaii-hope.htm, accessed March 2013.

16. "'Swift and Certain' Sanctions," National Institute of Justice.

17. *Drug Courts Are Not the Answer: Toward a Health-Centered Approach to Drug Use*, Drug Policy Alliance, http://www.drugpolicy.org/sites/default/files/Drug%20Courts%20Are%20Not%20the%20Answer_Final2.pdf.

18. Such as cognitive-behavioral and multisystemic therapies, which are discussed in chapter 4.

19. Mitchell et al., "Assessing the Effectiveness."

20. *Drug Courts Are Not the Answer*, Drug Policy Alliance, 17.

21. Andrew M. Mecca, "Blending Policy and Research: The California Outcomes Study," CNS Productions, http://www.cnsproductions.com/pdf/Mecca.pdf, accessed March 24, 2013.

22. Home page of California Alcohol and Other Drug Policy Institute, http://www.aodpolicy.org/, accessed March 24, 2013.

23. *Evaluation of the Substance Abuse and Crime Prevention Act: Final Report*, California Alcohol and Drug Programs, http://www.adp.ca.gov/SACPA/PDF/SACPAEvaluationReport_Final2007Apr13.pdf, accessed March 21, 2013.

24. "Archive: Substance Abuse and Crime Prevention Act," California Alcohol and Drug Programs, http://www.adp.ca.gov/SACPA/index.shtml, accessed March 21, 2013.

25. This issue is discussed more in chapter 4.

26. "Nation's Jails Struggle with Mentally Ill Prisoners," NPR, September 4, 2011, http://www.npr.org/2011/09/04/140167676/nations-jails-struggle-with-mentallyill-prisoners, accessed February 6, 2013.

27. Fred Osher, David A. D'Amora, Martha Plotkin, Nicole Jarrett, Alexa Eggleston, "Adults with Behavioral Health Needs under Correctional Supervision: A Shared Framework for Reducing Reoffending and Promoting Recovery" (working paper, Council of State Governments Justice Center, National Institute of Corrections, and Bureau of Justice Assistance consensus project, 2012), 4.

28. Doris J. James and Lauren E. Glaze, "Mental Health Problems of Prison and Jail Inmates, Highlights," Bureau of Justice Statistics, September 2006, http://www.bjs.gov/content/pub/pdf/mhppji.pdf.

29. Osher et al., "Adults with Behavioral Health Needs."

30. Brittany Cross, "Mental Health Courts Effectiveness in Reducing Recidivism and Improving Clinical Outcomes: A Meta-Analysis" (master's thesis, University of South Florida, 2011), http://scholarcommons.usf.edu/etd/3052/, accessed February 11, 2013; C. Sarteschi, M. Vaughn, and K. Kim, "Assessing the Effectiveness of Mental Health Courts: A Quantitative Review," *Journal of Criminal Justice* 39, no. 1 (2011): 12.

31. Stephanie Lee, Steve Aos, Elizabeth Drake, Annie Pennucci, Marna Miller, and Laurie Anderson, "Return on Investment: Evidence-Based Options to Improve Statewide Outcomes—April 2012 Update" (working paper, Washington State Institute for Public Policy, April 2012), http://www.wsipp.wa.gov/pub.asp?docid=12-04-1201, accessed February 13, 2013.

32. Recently, the government of England and Wales has committed to evaluate the implementation of these planned actions. See Department of Health, "Improving Health, Supporting Justice: The National Delivery Plan of the Health and Criminal Justice Programme Board," November 2009, Na-

tional Mental Health Development Unit, http://www.nmhdu.org.uk/silo/files/improving-health-supporting-justice.pdf, accessed July 11, 2013.

33. George Gascón, "The Courage to Change: How Prosecutors Can Lead on Public Safety," *Huffington Post*, March 19, 2013, http://www.huffington-post.com/george-gasc/the-courage-to-change-how_b_2903597.html, accessed March 21, 2013.

34. Kay Knapp, "What Sentencing Reform in Minnesota Has and Has Not Accomplished," *Judicature* 68, no. 3 (October–November 1984): 181–89.

35. Robert Weisberg, "How Sentencing Commissions Turned Out to Be a Good Idea," *Berkeley Journal of Criminal Law* 12 (2007): 179.

36. Susan Turner, James Hess, and Jesse Jannetta, "Development of the California Static Risk Assessment Instrument (CSRA)" (working paper, Center for Evidence-Based Corrections, University of California, Irvine, November 2009); "Risk/Needs Assessment 101: Science Reveals New Tools to Manage Offenders" (working paper, Pew Center on the States, Washington, DC, 2011).

37. David Cloud and Chelsea Davis, "Treatment Alternatives to Incarceration for People with Mental Health Needs in the Criminal Justice System: The Cost-Savings Implications: Research Summary" (working paper, Vera Institute of Justice, New York, February 2013), http://www.vera.org/sites/default/files/resources/downloads/treatment-alternatives-to-incarceration.pdf, accessed February 22, 2013.

38. Henry J. Steadman and Michelle Naples, "Assessing the Effectiveness of Jail Diversion Programs for Persons with Serious Mental Illness and Co-occurring Substance Use Disorders," *Behavioral Sciences and the Law* 23 (2005): 163–70.

39. Kit R. Van Stelle, Janae Goodrich, and Jason Paltzer, "Treatment Alternatives and Diversion (TAD) Program: Advancing Effective Diversion in Wisconsin, Advancing Fiscally Sound, Data-Driven Policies and Practices to Enhance Efficiencies in the Criminal Justice System and to Promote Public Safety, 2007–2010 Evaluation Report" (working paper, University of Wisconsin Population Health Institute, December 2011).

40. "More Local Teens Referred to Diversion Programs Compared to State Average," San Diego County NewsCenter, January 4, 2013, http://www.countynewscenter.com/news/more-local-teens-referred-to-diversion-programs-compared-state-average.

41. The Law Enforcement Assisted Diversion (LEAD) program is a diversion pilot program developed with the Seattle community to redirect low-level drug and prostitution offenders to community-based services instead of to jail and prosecution. LEAD's goal is to improve public safety by reducing the criminal behaviors of participants. This program has gotten good results,

but the offending behavior that is reduced does not have a direct impact on victims of crime.

42. "Diverting Individuals with Substance Use Disorders from Incarceration to Community Treatment Saves Billions, Prevents Crime" (fact sheet, Center for Health and Justice at TASC, November 2012), http://www.centerforhealthandjustice.org/FOJ%2003-13.pdf, accessed May 5, 2013.

43. Peter Neyroud, "Caution Reviews 'Uninterested in Effectiveness,'" Police Oracle, April 15, 2013, http://www.policeoracle.com/news/Comment-Caution-Reviews-Uninterested-In-Effectiveness_63412.html, accessed April 23, 2013.

44. Waller, *Rights for Victims of Crime*, chapters 5 and 6.

45. Heather Strang and Lawrence W. Sherman, "Restorative Justice to Reduce Victimization," in *Preventing Crime*, ed. Brandon C. Welsh and David P. Farrington (New York: Springer, 2006), 147–60.

46. "Why Restorative Justice?" Restorative Solutions, http://www.restorativesolutions.org.uk/page/92/Why-Restorative-Justice-.htm, accessed April 23, 2013.

47. Lawrence W. Sherman and Heather Strang, "Restorative Justice: The Evidence" (working paper, The Smith Institute, London, 2007), http://www.iirp.edu/pdf/RJ_full_report.pdf, accessed July 12, 2013.

48. Joanna Shapland, Anne Atkinson, Helen Atkinson, et al., "Does Restorative Justice Affect Reconviction? The Fourth Report from the Evaluation of Three Schemes" (working paper, Ministry of Justice Research Series, London, 2008).

49. Don Weatherburn and Megan Macadam, "A Review of Restorative Justice Responses to Offending," *Evidence Base*, no. 1 (2013), http://journal.anzsog.edu.au/userfiles/files/EvidenceBase2013Issue1.pdf, accessed March 24, 2013.

50. These are discussed in chapter 4.

51. "Drug Policy," Sentencing Project, http://www.sentencingproject.org/template/page.cfm?id=128, accessed April 23, 2013; see also Jonathan Caulkins and Sara Chandler, "Long-Term Trends in Incarceration of Drug Offenders in the United States," *Crime and Delinquency* 54, no. 4 (2006): 619–41.

52. Estimates are that the costs of illicit drug use (not only marijuana) on the court system are more than $50 billion annually, and another $50 billion is lost as a result of lost productivity. *The Economic Impact of Illicit Drug Use on American Society* (Washington, DC: US Department of Justice, National Drug Intelligence Center, 2011).

53. *State of Drugs Problem in Europe 2011: Annual Report* (Lisbon: European Monitoring Centre for Drugs and Drug Addiction, 2011), 42.

54. Keith Coffman and Nicole Neroulias, "Colorado, Washington First States to Legalize Recreational Pot," Reuters, http://www.reuters.com/article/2012/11/07/us-usa-marijuana-legalization-idUSBRE8A602D20121107, accessed March 24, 2013.

55. "Partisans Disagree on Legalization of Marijuana, but Agree on Law Enforcement Policies," Pew Research Center, April 30, 2013, http://www.pewresearch.org/daily-number/partisans-disagree-on-legalization-of-marijuana-but-agree-on-law-enforcement-policies/, accessed May 12, 2013.

56. C. Reinarman, P. Cohen, and H. Kaal, "The Limited Relevance of Drug Policy: Cannabis in Amsterdam and in San Francisco," *American Journal of Public Health* 94 (2004): 836–42.

57. Reinarman, Cohen, and Kaal, "Limited Relevance of Drug Policy."

58. Jeffrey Miron and Katherine Waldock, "The Budgetary Impact of Ending Drug Prohibition" (white paper, Cato Institute, Washington, DC, 2010).

59. "2013 National Drug Control Strategy," Office of National Drug Control Policy, http://www.whitehouse.gov/ondcp/2013-national-drug-control-strategy, accessed May 6, 2013.

60. Dee Cook, Mandy Burton, Amanda Robinson, and Christine Vallely, *Evaluation of Specialist Domestic Violence Courts/Fast Track Systems* (London: Crown Prosecution Service, 2004).

61. Melissa Labriola, Sarah Bradley, Chris S. O'Sullivan, Michael Rempel, and Samantha Moore, "A National Portrait of Domestic Violence Courts" (working paper, Center for Court Innovation, New York, December 2009), https://www.ncjrs.gov/pdffiles1/nij/grants/229659.pdf, accessed February 2010.

62. Amanda Cissner, Melissa Labriola, and Michael Rempel, "Testing the Effects of New York's Domestic Violence Courts: A Statewide Impact Evaluation" (working paper, Center for Court Innovation, New York, 2013), http://www.courtinnovation.org/sites/default/files/documents/statewide_evaluation_dv_courts.pdf.

63. To be discussed in chapter 6.

64. M. Miller, E. Drake, and M. Nafziger, "What Works to Reduce Recidivism by Domestic Violence Offenders?" (working paper, Washington State Institute for Public Policy, Olympia, January 2013).

65. Waller, *Rights for Victims of Crime*, 97–132.

66. Caulkins and Chandler, "Long-Term Trends."

67. "Letter to President Obama from Superstar Coalition re: Mass Incarceration and Drug Policy Reform," Drug Policy Alliance, April 9, 2013, http://www.drugpolicy.org/resource/letter-president-obama-superstar-coalition-re-mass-incarceration-and-drug-policy-reform, accessed April 23, 2013.

68. Drug Policy Alliance, "Superstar-Studded Coalition to President Obama: Let's Tackle Mass Incarceration and Drug Policy Reform Together," press release, April 9, 2013, http://www.drugpolicy.org/news/2013/04/superstar-studded-coalition-president-obama-lets-tackle-mass-incarceration-and-drug-pol, accessed April 23, 2013.

69. "WSIPP's Benefit-Cost Tool for States: Examining Policy Options in Sentencing and Corrections" (working paper, Washington State Institute for Public Policy, August 2010), http://www.wsipp.wa.gov/rptfiles/10-08-1201.pdf).

70. Bryan Stevenson, "Drug Policy, Criminal Justice and Mass Imprisonment" (working paper, Global Commission on Drug Policies, Geneva, Switzerland, January 2011), http://www.globalcommissionondrugs.org/wp-content/themes/gcdp_v1/pdf/Global_Com_Bryan_Stevenson.pdf, accessed April 23, 2013.

71. Samuel Blackstone, "Portugal Decriminalized all Drugs Eleven Years Ago and the Results Are Staggering," Business Insider, http://www.businessinsider.com/portugal-drug-policy-decriminalization-works-2012-7, accessed April 23, 2012.

72. C. A. Hughes and A. Stevens, "What Can We Learn from the Portuguese Decriminalization of Illicit Drugs?" *British Journal of Criminology* 50 (2010): 999–1022.

73. Hughes and Stevens, "What Can We Learn," 1010.

74. University of British Columbia, "Medically Prescribed Heroin More Effective, Less Costly Than Current Methadone Treatment: UBC Research," press release, March 12, 2012, http://www.publicaffairs.ubc.ca/2012/03/12/medically-prescribed-heroin-more-effective-less-costly-than-current-methadone-treatment-ubc-research/, accessed May 6, 2013.

75. "Switzerland Embraces Heroin-Assisted Treatment," World Radio Switzerland, March 10, 2009, http://worldradio.ch/wrs/news/video/switzerland-embraces-heroin-assisted-treatment.shtml.

CHAPTER 4: CORRECTING CORRECTIONS: AWAY FROM MASS INCARCERATION AND TOWARD STOPPING CRIME

1. US Attorney General's speech to the American Bar Association, August 12, 2013, in which Holder recognized many problems with incarceration, both in the federal system and nationally, as well as recognizing the need to focus on victim issues, such as violence against women, on racial bias in violent victimizations, on the problem communities to incarceration pipeline, on prevention, and much more. www.economist.com/comment/2121948#comment-2121948, accessed August 18, 2013.

2. President's Commission on Law Enforcement and Administration of Justice, *The Challenge of Crime in a Free Society: A Report* (New York: Avon, 1968).

3. Todd D. Minton, "Jail Inmates at Midyear 2010—Statistical Tables," Bureau of Justice Statistics, April 2011, http://www.bjs.gov/content/pub/pdf/jim10st.pdf.

4. Roy Walmsley, "World Prison Population List," International Centre for Prison Studies, http://www.idcr.org.uk/wp-content/uploads/2010/09/WPPL-9-22.pdf, accessed February 3, 2013; Irvin Waller and Janet Chan, "Prison Use: A Canadian and International Comparison," in *Correctional Institutions*, 2nd ed., ed. L. T. Wilkins and D. Glazer (Philadelphia: Lippincott, 1977), 41–60.

5. "Entire World—Prison Population Rates per 100,000 of the National Population," International Centre for Prison Studies, World Prison Brief, http://www.prisonstudies.org/info/worldbrief/wpb_stats.php?area=all&category=wb_poprate, accessed February 10, 2013.

6. "Entire World—Prison Population Rates."

7. "Time Served: The High Cost, Low Return of Longer Prison Sentences" (working paper, Pew Center on the States, Washington, DC, 2012).

8. Tracey Kyckelhahn, "Justice Expenditure and Employment Extracts, 2009—Preliminary," Bureau of Justice Statistics, May 30, 2012, http://www.bjs.gov/index.cfm?ty=pbdetail&iid=4335.

9. "State of Recidivism: The Revolving Door of America's Prisons" (working paper, Pew Center on the States, Washington, DC, 2011), 4.

10. "Justice Expenditure and Employment Extracts, 1980 and 1981 Data from the Annual General Finance and Employment Surveys," Bureau of Justice Statistics, March 1, 1985, http://www.bjs.gov/index.cfm?ty=pbdetail&iid=3527; Kyckelhahn, "Justice Expenditure and Employment Extracts 2009—Preliminary"; James J. Stephan, "Census of State and Federal Correctional Facilities, 2005," Bureau of Justice Statistics, October 1, 2008, http://www.bjs.gov/index.cfm?ty=pbdetail&iid=530, accessed May 12, 2013.

11. Michelle Alexander, *The New Jim Crow: Mass Incarceration in the Age of Colorblindness* (New York: New Press, 2010).

12. Evelyn J. Patterson, "The Dose-Response of Time Served in Prison on Mortality: New York State, 1989–2003," *American Journal of Public Health* 103, no. 3 (March 2013): 523–28; "Total Corrections Population," map, Sentencing Project, http://www.sentencingproject.org/map/map.cfm, accessed February 15, 2013.

13. David P. Farrington, "Criminal Careers," in *The Cambridge Handbook of Forensic Psychology*, ed. J. M. Brown and E. A. Campbell (Cambridge: Cambridge University Press, 2010), 475–83.

14. Alex Burger, "For Kids with Parents behind Bars, the Work of Black History Month Is Incomplete," *Blog of Rights* (blog), American Civil Liberties Union, February 28, 2013, http://t.co/BCuBGobnpq, accessed March 19, 2013.

15. Sentencing Project, "Total Corrections Population." This page provides detailed data for both the nation and individual states. It provides the incarceration statistics, rate of racial disparity, amount spent by the state, and numbers

disenfranchised. Louisiana is the state with the highest rate of incarceration, but it is Wisconsin that has the highest rate of black incarceration.

16. "National Inventory of the Collateral Consequences of Conviction," American Bar Association, http://www.abacollateralconsequences.org/CollateralConsequences/map.jsp, accessed March 19, 2013.

17. Alexander, *The New Jim Crow*; Bruce Western, *Punishment and Inequality in America* (New York: Russell Sage Foundation, 2006).

18. Steven Donziger, ed., *The Real War on Crime: The Report of the National Criminal Justice Commission* (New York: Harper Perennial, 1996).

19. Waller and Chan, "Prison Use."

20. "State of Recidivism," Pew Center on the States.

21. "State of Recidivism," Pew Center on the States.

22. Doris L. MacKenzie, *What Works in Corrections: Reducing the Criminal Activities of Offenders and Delinquents* (Cambridge: Cambridge University Press, 2006), 33–52, esp. 37.

23. William Spelman, "The Limited Importance of Prison Expansion," in *The Crime Drop in America*, ed. Alfred Blumstein and Joel Wallman (Cambridge: Cambridge University Press, 2000), 97–129.

24. Jan Van Dijk, Andromachi Tseloni, and Graham Farrell, eds., *The International Crime Drop: New Directions in Research* (Houndmills: Palgrave Macmillan, 2012).

25. "Time Served," Pew Center on the States.

26. "State of Recidivism," Pew Center on the States.

27. "Recidivism," Bureau of Justice Statistics, http://www.bjs.gov/index.cfm?ty=tp&tid=17, accessed February 9, 2013.

28. "State of Recidivism," Pew Center on the States. The appearance of low reoffending rates can be enhanced by using different definitions. For instance, if the estimate is based on those on parole during a calendar year and limiting reoffending to those reincarcerated instead of just arrested, the reoffending rate may only be 16 percent. See "Recidivism," Bureau of Justice Statistics. During 2007, a total of 1,180,469 persons on parole were at risk of reincarceration. This includes persons under parole supervision on January 1 or those entering parole during the year. Of these parolees, about 16 percent were returned to incarceration in 2007.

29. "Time Served." Pew Center on the States, 40.

30. Many of these refer to the small number of very active offenders (6 percent of the cohort) who accounted for a disproportionately large number of the arrests (52 percent) in a Philadelphia birth cohort. M. E. Wolfgang, R. M. Figlio, and T. Sellin, *Delinquency in a Birth Cohort* (Chicago: University of Chicago Press).

31. Mark A. Cohen and Alex R. Piquero, "New Evidence on the Monetary Value of Saving a High Risk Youth," *Journal of Quantitative Criminology* 25, no. 1 (March 2009): 25–49.

32. See figure 2.2 in chapter 2.

33. "State of Recidivism," Pew Center on the States, 4.

34. "State of Recidivism," Pew Center on the States, 4.

35. "Time Served," Pew Center on the States, 40.

36. James F. Austin, "The Proper and Improper Use of Risk Assessment in Corrections," *Federal Sentencing Reporter* 16 (2004): 4.

37. Susan Turner, James Hess, and Jesse Jannetta, "Development of the California Static Risk Assessment Instrument (CSRA)" (working paper, Center for Evidence-Based Corrections, University of California, Irvine, November 2009).

38. Tom Ellis and Peter Marshall, "Does Parole Work? A Post-Release Comparison of Reconviction Rates for Paroled and Non-paroled Prisoners," *Australian and New Zealand Journal of Criminology* 33, no. 3 (2000): 300–317.

39. Again, this has been proven for more than fifty years—see, for instance, Dan Glaser, *The Effectiveness of a Prison and Parole System* (Indianapolis: Bobbs-Merrill, 1964); Irvin Waller, *Men Released from Prison* (Toronto, Ontario: University of Toronto Press, 1974/1978).

40. "Risk/Needs Assessment 101: Science Reveals New Tools to Manage Offenders" (working paper, Pew Center on the States, Washington, DC, 2011.

41. MacKenzie, *What Works in Corrections*.

42. Mackenzie is a fellow and has been president of the Academy of Experimental Criminology. She was the author of the corrections chapter in the University of Maryland study of what works in preventing crime by Sherman et al. She has been involved in three Campbell Collaboration systematic reviews on the effectiveness of prison-based drug treatment, drug courts, and correctional boot camps.

43. MacKenzie, *What Works in Corrections*, 62.

44. Mark W. Lipsey, James C. Howell, Marion R. Kelly, Gabrielle Chapman, and Darin Carver, "Improving the Effectiveness of Juvenile Justice Programs: A New Perspective on Evidence-Based Practice" (working paper, Center for Juvenile Justice Reform, Washington, DC, December 2010).

45. Lipsey et al.'s meta-analysis found that cognitive-behavioral therapy was responsible for an average 25 percent drop in reoffending; the most effective configurations of this therapy produced reoffending rates as low as 19 percent—more than a 50 percent decrease. N. A. Landenberger and M. A. Lipsey, "The Positive Effects of Cognitive Behavioral Programs for Offenders: A Meta-analysis of Factors Associated with Effective Treatment," *Journal of Experimental Criminology* 1 (2005): 451–76.

46. Stephanie Lee, Steve Aos, Elizabeth Drake, Annie Pennucci, Marna Miller, and Laurie Anderson, "Return on Investment: Evidence-Based Options to Improve Statewide Outcomes—April 2012 Update" (working paper, Washington State Institute for Public Policy, Olympia, April 2012), http://www.wsipp.wa.gov/pub.asp?docid=12-04-1201, accessed February 13, 2013.

47. Annie E. Casey Foundation, "Reliance on Juvenile Incarceration Is Not Paying Off for States, Taxpayers or Kids, Report Finds: Evidence Supports Trend among States to Scale Back Costly, Often Abusive Youth Prison Systems," news release, October 4, 2011, http://www.aecf.org/Newsroom/NewsReleases/HTML/2011Releases/NoPlaceforKids.aspx, accessed March 21, 2013; Annie E. Casey Foundation, "Youth Incarceration Sees Dramatic Drop in the United States," news release, February 27, 2013, http://www.aecf.org/Newsroom/NewsReleases/HTML/2013/YouthIncarcerationDrops.aspx, accessed March 24, 2013.

48. J. C. Howell, and M. W. Lipsey, "Research-Based Guidelines for Juvenile Justice Programs," *Justice Research and Policy* 14, no. 1 (2012): 17–34.

49. MacKenzie, *What Works in Corrections*, 62.

50. MacKenzie, *What Works in Corrections*, 62.

51. Robert Weisberg, "California's De Facto Sentencing Commissions," *Stanford Law Review Online* 64, no. 1 (November 11, 2011), http://www.stanfordlawreview.org/sites/default/files/online/articles/64-SLRO-1.pdf, accessed March 16, 2013; Robert Weisberg, "How Sentencing Commissions Turned Out to Be a Good Idea," *Berkeley Journal of Criminal Law* 12, no. 2 (2007): 179–230.

52. "Funding of Realignment," California Department of Corrections and Rehabilitation, http://www.cdcr.ca.gov/realignment/Funding-Realignment.html.

53. Marshall Clement, Matthew Schwarzfeld, and Michael Thompson, "The National Summit on Justice Reinvestment and Public Safety: Addressing Recidivism, Crime, and Corrections Spending" (working paper, Council of State Governments Justice Center, New York, January 2011); "Public Safety Performance Project," Pew State and Consumer Initiatives, http://www.pewstates.org/projects/public-safety-performance-project-328068, accessed April 24, 2013.

54. "Public Safety in Texas," Pew State and Consumer Initiatives, http://www.pewstates.org/research/state-fact-sheets/public-safety-in-texas-85899432273, accessed April 24, 2013.

55. Vikrant P. Reddy and Marc A. Levin, "The Conservative Case against More Prisons," *American Conservative*, March 6, 2013, http://www.theamericanconservative.com/articles/the-conservative-case-against-more-prisons/, accessed March 25, 2013.

56. In 1970, the US incarceration rate was 200 per 100,000. Today it is 700 per 100,000. The total expenditures in the correctional silo are $83 billion. So (700 − 200) / 700 ° 83 = $60 billion.

57. Irvin Waller, *Rights for Victims of Crime: Rebalancing Justice* (New York: Rowman and Littlefield, 2010), chap. 5.

CHAPTER 5: PREVENTING YOUTH FROM BECOMING REPEAT OFFENDERS

1. Steven H. Woolf and Laudan Aron, eds., *U.S. Health in International Perspective: Shorter Lives, Poorer Health* (Washington, DC: National Academies Press, 2013), 77, 80.

2. Shawn D. Bushway, Hui-Shien Tsao, and Herbert Smith, "Has the U.S. Prison Boom Changed the Age Distribution of the Prison Population?" (paper presented at IRP Summer Research Workshop "Current Research on the Low-Income Population," Madison, WI, June 2011), http://www.irp.wisc.edu/newsevents/workshops/2011/participants/papers/6-BushwayTsaoSmith.pdf, accessed April 26, 2013.

3. Thomas H. Cohen and Tracey Kyckelhahn, "Felony Defendants in Large Urban Counties, 2006," Bureau of Justice Statistics, May 26, 2010, http://www.bjs.gov/index.cfm?ty=pbdetail&iid=2193, accessed March 13, 2013.

4. Some of the leading researchers working within the police silo also use this term. See, for instance, Anthony Braga and David Weisburd, *Policing Problem Places: Crime Hot Spots and Effective Prevention* (New York: Oxford University Press, 2012).

5. "Juveniles," Crime Solutions, http://www.crimesolutions.gov/topicdetails.aspx?id=5, accessed May 9, 2013.

6. Mark A. Cohen and Alex R. Piquero, "New Evidence on the Monetary Value of Saving a High Risk Youth," *Journal of Quantitative Criminology* 25, no. 1 (March 2009): 25–49.

7. Marshall Clement, Matthew Schwarzfeld, and Michael Thompson, "The National Summit on Justice Reinvestment and Public Safety: Addressing Recidivism, Crime, and Corrections Spending" (working paper, Council of State Governments Justice Center, New York, January 2011.

8. John Pawasarat and Lois M. Quinn, "Wisconsin's Mass Incarceration of African American Males: Workforce Challenges for 2013" (working paper, Employment and Training Institute, University of Wisconsin, Milwaukee, 2013), www4.uwm.edu/eti/2013/BlackImprisonment.pdf, accessed April 25, 2013.

9. "Remarks by the President in the State of the Union Address, White House, February 12, 2013," http://www.whitehouse.gov/the-press-office/2013/02/12/remarks-president-state-union-address, accessed April 7, 2013.

10. Lawrence Schweinhart, Jeanne Montie, Zongping Xiang, W. Steven Barnett, Clive R. Belfield, and Milagros Nores, "The High/Scope Perry Pre-school Study through Age 40: Summary, Conclusions and Frequently Asked Questions" (working paper, High/Scope Educational Research Foundation, Ypsilanti, MI, 2005).

11. Crime Solutions, www.crimesolutions.gov, accessed April 24, 2013. The site includes 246 programs, of which 72 have been identified as effective, including 44 about investing in children's families and schools, 11 about problem-oriented policing, and 17 that overlap with the reactive crime control measures discussed in chapters 2–4.

12. "Blueprints for Healthy Youth Development," http://www.colorado.edu/cspv/blueprints/, accessed April 24, 2013.

13. Stephanie Lee, Steve Aos, Elizabeth Drake, Annie Pennucci, Marna Miller, and Laurie Anderson, "Return on Investment: Evidence-Based Options to Improve Statewide Outcomes—April 2012 Update" (working paper, Washington State Institute for Public Policy, April 2012), http://www.wsipp.wa.gov/pub.asp?docid=12-04-1201, accessed February 13, 2013.

14. David Farrington, "Family Influences on Delinquency," in *Juvenile Justice and Delinquency*, ed. D. W. Springer and A. R. Roberts (Sudbury, MA: Jones and Bartlett, 2010), 203–22.

15. "National Child Abuse Statistics," Childhelp, http://www.childhelp.org/pages/statistics, accessed April 24, 2013.

16. CDC Online Newsroom, "Child Abuse and Neglect Cost the United States $124 Billion," press release, February 1, 2012, http://www.cdc.gov/media/releases/2012/p0201_child_abuse.html, accessed April 24, 2013.

17. National Research Council, Institute of Medicine, *Juvenile Crime, Juvenile Justice* (Washington, DC: National Academies Press), 2001.

18. Janet Currie and Erdal Tekin, "Does Child Abuse Cause Crime?" (NBER Working Paper 12171, National Bureau of Economic Research, Cambridge, MA, April 2006), http://www.nber.org/papers/w12171.

19. "National Child Abuse Statistics," Childhelp.

20. "Nurse-Family Partnership—Top Tier," Coalition for Evidence-Based Policy, February 2012, http://evidencebasedprograms.org/1366-2/nurse-family-partnership, accessed April 7, 2013.

21. Lee et al., "Return on Investment."

22. Top Tier Evidence, http://toptierevidence.org/, accessed April 24, 2013.

23. "Nurse-Family Partnership Model Program," Blueprints for Healthy Youth Development, http://www.blueprintsprograms.com/factSheet.php?pid=972a67c48192728a34979d9a35164c1295401b71, accessed April 24, 2013.

24. "Program Profile: Nurse–Family Partnership," Crime Solutions, https://www.crimesolutions.gov/ProgramDetails.aspx?ID=187, accessed April 24, 2013.

25. "The Benefits of Positive Parenting," http://www.triplep.net/glo-en/find-out-about-triple-p/benefits-of-triple-p/, accessed August 12, 2013; Ronald J. Prinz, Matthew R. Sanders, Cheri J. Shapiro, Daniel J. Whitaker, and John R. Lutzker, "Population-Based Prevention of Child Maltreatment: The U.S. Triple P System Population Trial," *Prevention Science* 10 (2009): 1–12.

26. "The Benefits of Positive Parenting," http://www.triplep.net/glo-en/find-out-about-triple-p/benefits-of-triple-p/, accessed August 12, 2013.

27. "Program Profile: Triple P—Positive Parenting Program," https://www.crimesolutions.gov/ProgramDetails.aspx?ID=80, accessed April 24, 2013.

28. "Triple P System," Top Tier Evidence, http://toptierevidence.org/programs-reviewed/triple-p-system, accessed April 24, 2013.

29. "Triple P System: Promising Program," Blueprints for Healthy Youth Development, http://www.blueprintsprograms.com/factSheet.php?pid=07fd89a40a3755e21a5884640f23eaf59b66df35, accessed April 24, 2013.

30. Schweinhart et al., *The High/Scope Perry Preschool Study*.

31. Reactive crime control costs $270 billion, compared with a loss to victims estimated at $450 billion.

32. Schweinhart et al., *The High/Scope Perry Preschool Study*.

33. James J. Heckman, Seong Hyeok Moon, Rodrigo Pinto, Peter A. Savelyev, and Adam Yavitz, "The Rate of Return to the High/Scope Perry Preschool Program" (Discussion Paper No. 4533, Institute for the Study of Labor, Bonn, October 2009), ftp://ftp.iza.org/SSRN/pdf/dp4533.pdf (accessed February 14, 2013).

34. "Program Profile: Perry Preschool Project," Crime Solutions, https://www.crimesolutions.gov/ProgramDetails.aspx?ID=143; "High/Scope Preschool: Promising Program," Blueprints for Health Youth Development, http://www.blueprintsprograms.com/factSheet.php?pid=5b384ce32d8cdef02bc3a139d4cac0a22bb029e8, accessed April 24, 2013.

35. "SNAP," Child Development Institute, http://www.childdevelop.ca/programs/snap%C2%AE, accessed April 6, 2013.

36. Leena K. Augimeri, David P. Farrington, Christopher J. Koegl, and David Martin Day, "The SNAP™ Under 12 Outreach Project: Effects of a Community-Based Program for Children With Conduct Problems," *Journal of Child and Family Studies* 16 (2007): 799–807.

37. "SNAP® (Stop Now and Plan): An Evidence Based Gender Specific Mental Health and Crime Prevention for Children and Families" (fact sheet, Social Finance Canada), http://socialfinance.ca/uploads/documents/SNAP_LabOnePager.pdf, accessed April 9, 2013.

38. "Program Profile: SNAP® Under 12 Outreach Project," Crime Solutions, http://www.crimesolutions.gov/ProgramDetails.aspx?ID=231, accessed May 9, 2013.

39. Friedrich Lösel and Andreas Beelmann, "Child Social Skills Training," in *Preventing Crime: What Works for Children, Offenders, Victims, and Places*, ed. Brandon Welsh and David Farrington (New York: Springer, 2006).

40. "2013 National Drug Control Strategy," Office of National Drug Control Policy, http://www.whitehouse.gov/ondcp/2013-national-drug-control-strategy, accessed May 9, 2013.

41. David M. Horn, "Bruised Inside: What Our Children Say about Youth Violence, What Causes It, and What We Need to Do about It: A Report of the National Association of Attorneys General" (report, National Association of Attorneys General, Washington, DC, 2000).

42. Juan Williams, "Race and the Gun Debate," *Wall Street Journal Online*, March 26, 2013, http://online.wsj.com/article/SB10001424127887323869604578366882484600710.html, accessed April 24, 2013.

43. Cameron McWhirter and Gary Fields, "Communities Struggle to Break a Grim Cycle of Killing," *Wall Street Journal Online*, August 18, 2012, http://online.wsj.com/article/SB10001424052702304830704577496501048197464.html, accessed April 24, 2013.

44. Williams, "Race and the Gun Debate."

45. "Program Profile: Functional Family Therapy (FFT)," Crime Solutions, http://www.crimesolutions.gov/ProgramDetails.aspx?ID=122, accessed July 17, 2013.

46. "Functional Family Therapy (FFT): Model Program," http://www.blueprintsprograms.com/factSheet.php?pid=0a57cb53ba59c46fc4b692527a38a87c78d84028, accessed April 24, 2013.

47. "The Clinical Model," Functional Family Therapy, http://www.fftinc.com/about_model.html, accessed April 6, 2013.

48. Damon Jones, Brian K. Bumbarger, Mark T. Greenberg, Peter Greenwood, and Sandee Kyler, "The Economic Return on PCCD's Investment in Research-based Programs: A Cost-Benefit Assessment of Delinquency Prevention in Pennsylvania" (working paper, Prevention Research Center for the Promotion of Human Development, March 2008), http://prevention.psu.edu/pubs/docs/PCCD_Report2.pdf, accessed April 6, 2013.

49. "Multidimensional Treatment Foster Care (MTFC): Model Program," Blueprints for Healthy Youth Development, http://www.blueprintsprograms.

com/factSheet.php?pid=632667547e7cd3e0466547863e1207a8c0c0c549, accessed April 26, 2013.

50. Horn, "Bruised Inside."

51. "Olweus Bullying Prevention Program: Promising Program," Blueprints for Healthy Youth Development, http://www.blueprintsprograms.com/factSheet.php?pid=17ba0791499db908433b80f37c5fbc89b870084b, accessed April 26, 2013.

52. Irvin Waller, Daniel Sansfaçon, and Brandon Welsh, *Crime Prevention Digest II: Comparative Analysis of Successful Community Safety* (Montreal: International Centre for Prevention of Crime, 1999).

53. Irvin Waller, *Less Law, More Order: The Truth about Reducing Crime* (Westport, CT: Praeger Imprint Series, 2006; Ancaster, Ontario: Manor House, 2008).

54. Cohen and Piquero, "New Evidence on the Monetary Value."

CHAPTER 6: SMARTER PREVENTION OF GUN VIOLENCE: TARGETING OUTREACH AND CONTROL

1. E. G. Richardson and D. Hemenway, "Homicide, Suicide, and Unintentional Firearm Fatality: Comparing the United States with Other High-Income Countries, 2003," *Journal of Trauma and Acute Care Surgery* 70, no. 1 (2011): 238–43; Steven H. Woolf and Laudan Aron, eds., *U.S. Health in International Perspective: Shorter Lives, Poorer Health* (Washington, DC: National Academies Press, 2013).

2. 6009 out of 8075 in 2010—"Murder Victims by Weapon, 2006–2010," Federal Bureau of Investigation, http://www.fbi.gov/about-us/cjis/ucr/crime-in-the-u.s/2010/crime-in-the-u.s.-2010/tables/10shrtbl08.xls, accessed April 21, 2013.

3. "Murder Victims by Weapon, 2006–2010"; "2010 Mortality Multiple Cause Micro-data Files, Table 10, Centers for Disease Control and Prevention, http://www.cdc.gov/nchs/data/dvs/deaths_2010_release.pdf, accessed February 17, 2013.

4. "PBS Commentator Mark Shields Says More Killed by Guns Since '68 Than in All U.S. Wars," Politifact, http://www.politifact.com/truth-o-meter/statements/2013/jan/18/mark-shields/pbs-commentator-mark-shields-says-more-killed-guns/, accessed April 27, 2013.

5. D. W. Webster, J. M. Whitehill, J. S. Vernick, and F. C. Curriero, "Effects of Baltimore's Safe Streets Program on Gun Violence: A Replication of Chicago's CeaseFire Program," *Journal of Urban Health* 90, no. 1 (February 2013): 27–40.

6. A. Braga and D. Weisburd, "The Effects of 'Pulling Levers': Focused Deterrence Strategies on Crime," *Campbell Systematic Reviews* 8, no. 6 (2012).

7. David Kennedy, *Don't Shoot: One Man, A Street Fellowship, and the End of Violence in Inner-City America* (New York: Bloomsbury, 2011).

8. See generally, for a leading perspective on the public health approach to gang violence in the United States, Deborah Prothrow-Stith and Howard Spivak, *Murder Is No Accident: Understanding and Preventing Youth Violence in America* (San Francisco: Jossey-Bass, 2004).

9. David Kennedy, Anthony Braga, Anne Piehl, and Elin Waring, "Reducing Gun Violence: The Boston Gun Project's Operation Ceasefire" (research report, National Institute of Justice, Washington, DC, 2001), 57–66.

10. Anthony A. Braga, David Hureau, and Christopher Winship, "Losing Faith? Police, Black Churches, and the Resurgence of Youth Violence in Boston," *Ohio State Journal of Criminal Law* 6 (2008): 141–72, available at http://moritzlaw.osu.edu/osjcl/Articles/Volume6_1/Braga-PDF.pdf, accessed May 7, 2013.

11. There does not appear to have been any coordination between Cure Violence and Project Safe Neighborhoods.

12. "Gary Slutkin, MD," Cure Violence, http://cureviolence.org/staff-member/gary-slutkin/, accessed April 27, 2013.

13. Wesley G. Skogan, Susan M. Hartnett, Natalie Bump, and Jill Dubois, "Evaluation of CeaseFire-Chicago" (working paper, National Institute of Justice, Washington, DC, 2008); see executive summary at "CeaseFire Evaluation Report," Institute for Policy Research, Northwestern University, 2010, http://www.northwestern.edu/ipr/publications/ceasefire.html, accessed March 28, 2010.

14. Tracey L. Meares, Andrew V. Papachristos, and Jeffrey Fagan, "Homicide and Gun Violence in Chicago: Evaluation and Summary of the Project Safe Neighborhoods Program" (research brief, Project Safe Neighborhoods Chicago, 2009), http://www.psnchicago.org/PDFs/2009-PSN-Research-Brief_v2.pdf.

15. "The Interrupters," Internet Movie Database," http://www.imdb.com/title/tt1319744/, accessed April 27, 2013.

16. Webster et al., "Effects of Baltimore's Safe Streets Program"; Jennifer Whitehill, D. W. Webster, S. Frattaroli, and E. M. Parker, "Interrupting Violence: How the CeaseFire Program Prevents Imminent Gun Violence through Conflict Mediation," *Journal of Urban Health* (February 26, 2013): 1.

17. Violence Reduction Unit, http://www.actiononviolence.com/, accessed April 8, 2013.

18. "CIRV," Violence Reduction Unit, http://www.actiononviolence.org.uk/content/cirv, accessed April 27, 2013.

19. "Peter Duncan Donnelly," University of St. Andrews Research Portal, https://risweb.st-andrews.ac.uk/portal/en/persons/peter-duncan-donnelly (7a6eaedc-2a24-4e32-baa3-37b6d96052d1).html, accessed April 27, 2013.

20. "Blueprint for Action: Preventing Violence in Minneapolis" (working paper, Prevention Institute, October 2011), http://www.preventioninstitute.org/component/jlibrary/article/id-314/127.html, accessed April 27, 2013.

21. "Preventing Youth Violence," Find Youth Info, http://www.findyouthinfo.gov/youth-topics/preventing-youth-violence, accessed April 27, 2013.

22. "A Call to Action: Los Angeles' Quest to Achieve Community Safety" (report, Advancement Project), http://www.advancementprojectca.org/?q=ACallToAction, accessed May 7, 2013.

23. Vikram Dodd, "US 'Supercop' Bill Bratton: British Police Should Make Fewer Arrests," *Guardian Online*, February 25, 2013, http://www.guardian.co.uk/uk/2013/feb/25/bill-bratton-british-police-fewer-arrests, accessed April 27, 2013.

24. "Summer Night Lights," GRYD Foundation, http://www.grydfoundation.org/about-our-programs/summer-night-lights, accessed August 12, 2013.

25. "Blueprint for Action."

26. Unity: Urban Networks to Increase Thriving Youth, http://www.preventioninstitute.org/unity.html, accessed April 6, 2013.

27. US Department of Justice, "Attorney General Eric Holder Expands National Forum on Youth Violence Prevention to Ten Cities," news release, September 19, 2012, http://www.justice.gov/opa/pr/2012/September/12-ag-1135.html, accessed April 27, 2013.

28. "Preventing Youth Violence."

29. California Cities Gang Prevention Network, http://www.ccgpn.org/, accessed April 27, 2013.

30. National Network for Safe Communities, http://www.nnscommunities.org/, accessed April 27, 2013.

31. "The Legislation," Youth Promise Action, http://www.youthpromiseaction.org/about-bill.html, accessed April 27, 2013.

32. Mark A. Bellis, Karen Hughes, Clare Perkins, and Andrew Bennett, "Protecting People, Promoting Health: A Public Health Approach for Violence Prevention for England" (working paper, North West Public Health Observatory, Liverpool, October 2012).

33. *Health United States 2011: With Special Feature on Socioeconomic Status and Health* (Hyattsville, MD: National Center for Health Statistics, 2012), esp. table 95, http://www.cdc.gov/nchs/data/hus/hus11.pdf, accessed April 3, 2013.

34. "Amsterdam Copies Cardiff's Approach to Reducing Violence," *BBC News*, December 11, 2012, http://www.bbc.co.uk/news/uk-wales-south-east-

wales-20669062; "Violence and Society Research Group," Cardiff University School of Dentistry, http://www.cardiff.ac.uk/dentl/research/themes/appliedclinicalresearch/violenceandsociety/index.html, accessed March 13, 2013.

35. "Prof Jonathan Shepherd at TEDxCardiff 2012," YouTube video, 19:33, posted by TEDxTalks, April 10, 2012, http://www.youtube.com/watch?v=RduvYOxSuSM, accessed March 13, 2013.

36. "Violence Intervention Program," University of Maryland Medical Center, http://www.umm.edu/shocktrauma/special_programs/violence_prevention_program_vip.htm, accessed May 16, 2013.

37. T. L. Cheng, D. Haynie, R. Brenner, et al., "Effectiveness of a Mentor-Implemented, Violence Prevention Intervention for Assault-Injured Youths Presenting to the Emergency Department: Results of a Randomized Trial," *Pediatrics* 122, no. 5 (2008): 938–46.

38. Bellis et al., "Protecting People, Promoting Health."

39. Philip Caulfield, "Gun Deaths to Surpass Deaths in Traffic Accidents," *New York Daily News*, December 19, 2012, http://www.nydailynews.com/news/national/gun-deaths-outpace-traffic-deaths-2015-report-article-1.1223721#ixzz2L9YWMeoH, accessed February 17, 2013.

40. Leon Neyfakh, "The Gun Toll We're Ignoring: Suicide," *Boston Globe Online*, January 20, 2013, http://www.bostonglobe.com/ideas/2013/01/20/the-gun-toll-ignoring-suicide/xeWBHDHEvvagfkRlU3CfZJ/story.html.

41. "Public Safety and Crime Prevention (2013)" (resolution, National League of Cities, 2013) http://www.nlc.org/Documents/Influence%20Federal%20Policy/NMP/6-PSCP-NMP-2013.pdf, accessed April 27, 2013.

42. Jan Van Dijk, "Closing the Doors," Stockholm Prizewinner's Lecture 2012, available at http://www.criminologysymposium.com/download/18.4dfe0028139b9a0cf4080001575/1348484090486/TUE13,+van+Dijk+Jan.pdf, accessed July 18, 2013.

43. Joseph Carroll, "Gun Ownership and Use in America" (Gallup poll, November 22, 2005), http://www.gallup.com/poll/20098/gun-ownership-use-america.aspx.

44. Data are based on the number of gun-related and non-gun-related homicides in Canada and the United States. These are set in the context of the numbers of handguns and other guns estimated to be present in these two countries. The data were accessed at http://www.rcmp-grc.gc.ca/cfp-pcaf/res-rec/comp-eng.htm on April 27, 2013, but this website no longer populates the table as of August 18, 2013. Figure 6.1 is still considered indicative of the accessibility effect.

45. J. H. Sloan et al., "Handgun Regulations, Crime, Assaults and Homicide: A Tale of Two Cities," *New England Journal of Medicine* 319, no. 19 (1988): 1256–62.

46. Irvin Waller, *Less Law, More Order: The Truth about Reducing Crime* (Westport, CT: Praeger Imprint Series, 2006; Ancaster, Ontario: Manor House, 2008), 42–43.

47. They pointed out that despite the spending on health care in the United States, Americans were more likely to "engage in certain unhealthy behaviors . . . that increase the risk of fatal injuries," according to the report—including those caused by car accidents, gun violence, and drug overdoses. Steven H. Woolf and Laudan Aron, eds., *U.S. Health in International Perspective: Shorter Lives, Poorer Health* (Washington, DC: National Academies Press, 2013).

48. This was thought up by my group while I was the director general of the research and statistics group for the solicitor general of Canada.

49. Brady Center to Prevent Gun Violence, www.bradycenter.org/.

50. Eric W. Fleegler, Lois K. Lee, Michael C. Monuteaux, David Hemenway, and Rebekah Mannix, "Firearm Legislation and Firearm-Related Fatalities in the United States," *JAMA Internal Medicine* 173, no. 9 (2013); 732–40, http://archinte.jamanetwork.com/article.aspx?articleid=1661390, accessed March 30, 2013.

51. "Wish List," Law Center to Prevent Gun Violence, http://smartgunlaws. org/wish-list/, accessed April 9, 2013.

52. Arkadi Gerney, Chelsea Parsons, and Charles Posner, "America under the Gun: A 50-State Analysis of Gun Violence and Its Link to Weak State Gun Laws" (working paper, Center for American Progress, Washington, DC, April 2013), http://www.americanprogress.org/wp-content/uploads/2013/04/AmericaUnderTheGun-3.pdf, accessed April 9, 2013.

53. "Attorney General Eric Holder Speaks at the 15th Annual National Action Network Convention," US Department of Justice, http://www.justice.gov/iso/opa/ag/speeches/2013/ag-speech-130404.html, accessed April 10, 2013.

54. James Alan Fox, "No Increase in Mass Shootings," *Crime & Punishment* (blog), August 6, 2012, Boston.com, http://boston.com/community/blogs/crime_punishment/2012/08/no_increase_in_mass_shootings.html, accessed April 27, 2013.

55. New York County Lawyers' Association, "New York County Lawyers' Association Issues Recommendations on Proposed Federal Gun Control Legislation," news release, New York, March 19, 2013, http://www.nycla.org/siteFiles/Publications/Publications1601_0.pdf, accessed April 10, 2013.

56. James Alan Fox, "Top 10 Myths about Mass Shootings," *Crime & Punishment* (blog), December 19, 2012, Boston.com, http://boston.com/community/blogs/crime_punishment/2012/12/top_10_myths_about_mass_shooti. html, accessed April 8, 2013.

57. "The Australian Gun Buyback," *Bulletins* 4 (Spring 2011): 1–4, http://www.hsph.harvard.edu/hicrc/files/2013/01/bulletins_australia_spring_2011.pdf, accessed April 8, 2013.

58. "The Australian Gun Buyback."

59. "The Facts on Guns and Domestic Violence" (fact sheet, Futures without Violence, San Francisco), http://www.futureswithoutviolence.org/userfiles/file/Children_and_Families/Guns.pdf, accessed April 6, 2013. For data on increased risk, see the cited study by J. C. Campbell, D. Webster, J. Koziol-McLain, et al., "Risk Factors for Femicide in Abusive Relationships: Results from a Multi-Site Case Control Study," *American Journal of Public Health* 93, no. 7 (July 2003): 1089–97.

60. J. C. Campbell, N. Glass, P. W. Sharps, K. Laughon, and T. Bloom, "Intimate Partner Homicide: Review and Implications of Research and Policy," *Trauma, Violence, and Abuse* 8, no. 3 (July 2007): 246–69.

61. "The Legislation," Youth Promise Action.

CHAPTER 7: PREVENTING VIOLENCE AGAINST WOMEN

1. M. C. Black, K. C. Basile, M. J. Breiding, S. G. Smith, M. L. Walters, M. T. Merrick, J. Chen, and M. R. Stevens. *The National Intimate Partner and Sexual Violence Survey (NISVS): 2010 Summary Report* (Atlanta, GA: National Center for Injury Prevention and Control, Centers for Disease Control and Prevention, 2011).

2. It is an "ongoing, nationally representative random digit dial (RDD) telephone survey that collects information about experiences of sexual violence, stalking, and intimate partner violence among non-institutionalized English and/or Spanish-speaking women and men aged 18 or older in the United States." Black et al., *Sexual Violence Survey*. Both the national intimate partner survey and this survey include completed forced penetration, attempted forced penetration, or alcohol/drug facilitated completed penetration. D. G. Kilpatrick, Heidi S. Resnick, Kenneth J. Ruggiero, Lauren M. Conoscenti, and Jenna McCauley, "Drug-Facilitated, Incapacitated, and Forcible Rape: A National Study" (working paper, National Institute of Justice, Washington, DC, July 2007), https://www.ncjrs.gov/pdffiles1/nij/grants/219181.pdf.

3. For example, hit with a fist or something hard, beaten, slammed against something.

4. B. Fisher, F. Cullen, and M. Turner, "The Sexual Victimization of College Women" (research paper, National Institute of Justice, Bureau of Justice Statistics, Washington, DC, December 2000), https://www.ncjrs.gov/pdffiles1/nij/182369.pdf.

5. Kilpatrick et al., "Drug-Facilitated, Incapacitated, and Forcible Rape."

6. Kilpatrick et al., "Drug-Facilitated, Incapacitated, and Forcible Rape," 2.

7. Kilpatrick et al., "Drug-Facilitated, Incapacitated, and Forcible Rape."

8. Laura Dugan, Daniel Nagin, and Richard Rosenfeld, "Explaining the Decline in Intimate Partner Homicide: The Effects of Changing Domesticity, Women's Status, and Domestic Violence Resources," *Homicide Studies* 3, no. 3 (August 1999): 187–214.

9. Laura Dugan, Daniel S. Nagin, and Richard Rosenfeld, "Do Domestic Violence Services Save Lives?" *NIJ Journal* 250 (2003).

10. Dugan et al., "Explaining the Decline."

11. World Health Organization, *World Report on Violence and Health* (Geneva, World Health Organization, 2002).

12. World Health Organization, Preventing Intimate Partner and Sexual Violence against Women: Taking Action and Generating Evidence (Geneva: World Health Organization, 2010), 21.

13. Black et al., Sexual Violence Survey.

14. "Strategies for Healthy Youth Relationships," Centre for Prevention Science, http://youthrelationships.org/, accessed April 2, 2010.

15. "Program Profile: Safe Dates," Crime Solutions, http://www.crimesolutions.gov/ProgramDetails.aspx?ID=142, accessed April 28, 2013.

16. D. A. Wolfe, C. V. Crookes, P. Jaffe, D. Chiodo, R. Hughes, W. Ellis, L. Stitt, and A. Donner, "A Universal School-Based Program to Prevent Adolescent Dating Violence: A Cluster Randomized Trial," *Archives of Pediatric and Adolescent Medicine* 163 (2009): 693–99.

17. "Program Profile: 4th R Curriculum," Crime Solutions, http://www.crimesolutions.gov/ProgramDetails.aspx?ID=109, accessed April 28, 2013.

18. World Health Organization, Preventing Intimate Partner and Sexual Violence against Women.

19. Irvin Waller, *Rights for Victims of Crime: Rebalancing Justice* (New York: Rowman and Littlefield, 2010).

20. Kilpatrick et al., "Drug-Facilitated, Incapacitated, and Forcible Rape."

21. Bonnie S. Fisher, "Shifting the Paradigm: Primary Prevention on Campuses" (PowerPoint presentation, 5th Annual Campus Safety Summit, Dennison University, 2011), https://www.ohiohighered.org/files/uploads/CampusSafety/Fisher-August-2011-v5.ppt, accessed February 12, 2013.

22. "Green Dot Strategy," Violence Interpretation and Prevention Center, University of Kentucky, 2010, http://www.uky.edu/StudentAffairs/VIPCenter/learn_greendot.html, accessed April 2, 2010. A few universities have been inspired by the University of Kentucky, but always with the focus that the challenge deserves; see "Right to Respect Campaign," University of Ottowa, http://www.respect.uottawa.ca/en/, accessed April 2, 2010.

23. "Ending Violence . . . One Green Dot at a Time," Changemakers, February 22, 2010, http://www.changemakers.com/stopviolence/entries/ending-violenceone-green-dot-time, accessed April 9, 2013.

24. Ann L. Coker et al., "Evaluation of Green Dot: An Active Bystander Intervention to Reduce Sexual Violence on College Campuses," *Violence Against Women* 17 (2011): 777–96.

25. White Ribbon Campaign, 2010, http://www.whiteribbon.ca/, accessed April 2, 2010.

26. Annie-Rose Strasser, "Another Football Player Accused of Rape, Another Community Blaming the Victim," ThinkProgress, March 20, 2013, http://thinkprogress.org/health/2013/03/20/1751831/rape-football-victim/, accessed March 21, 2013.

27. "Be More Than a Bystander," Ending Violence Association of British Columbia, http://www.endingviolence.org/Be+More+Than+a+Bystander, accessed March 21, 2013.

28. Jan van Dijk, John van Kesteren, and Paul Smit, Criminal Victimisation in International Perspective: Key Findings from the 2004–2005 ICVS and EU ICS (The Hague: Boom Legal Publishers, 2008).

29. Jane Doe, *The Story of Jane Doe: A Book about Rape* (Toronto: Vintage Canada, 2004).

30. Rebecca Campbell, Debra Patterson, and Lauren Lichty, "The Effectiveness of Sexual Assault Nurse Examiner (SANE) Programs: A Review of Psychological, Medical, Legal, and Community Outcomes," *Trauma, Violence, and Abuse* 6, no. 4 (2005): 313–29; Holly Johnson and Myrna Dawson, *Violence against Women in Canada: Research and Policy Perspectives* (Toronto, Ontario: Oxford University Press, 2010).

31. Eleanor Lyon, Shannon Lane, and Anne Menard, "Meeting Survivors' Needs: A Multi-state Study of Domestic Violence Shelter Experience" (working paper, National Institute of Justice, October 2008), available at National Online Resource Center on Violence against Women, http://www.vawnet.org/Assoc_Files_VAWnet/MeetingSurvivorsNeeds-FullReport.pdf, accessed April 18, 2010.

32. Ten thousand beds relative to 20,000 means that the daily shortfall is 50 percent. A daily rate of 20,000 is equivalent to 300,000 over a year, or a factor of 15. So the shortfall is 10,000 × 365/15, or 243,000.

33. Michelle Bachelet, "UN Women Welcomes Agreed Conclusions at the Commission on the Status of Women," press statement, New York, March 15, 2013, http://www.unwomen.org/2013/03/un-women-welcomes-agreed-conclusions-at-the-commission-on-status-of-women/, accessed March 16, 2013.

34. M. Miller, E. Drake, and M. Nafziger, "What Works to Reduce Recidivism by Domestic Violence Offenders? (working paper, Washington State Institute for Public Policy, Olympia, January 2013).

35. See also E. Gondolf, "Evaluating Batterer Counseling Programs: A Difficult Task Showing Some Effects and Implications," *Aggression and Violent Behavior* 9 (2004): 605–31.

36. An important component of the act is the requirement for the Office for Violence against Women to demonstrate to Congress how the funds are reaching their targets and assess their effectiveness in reducing violence and serving victims' needs. VAWA's concern with outcomes is taken very seriously, although the efforts to evaluate its impact have mostly been limited to process evaluations.

37. Rosemary Chalk and Patricia A. King, eds., *Violence in Families: Assessing Prevention and Treatment Programs* (Washington, DC: National Academy Press, 1998), 4–5; World Health Organization, *World Report on Violence and Health*.

38. Fisher et al., "The Sexual Victimization of College Women"; Kilpatrick et al., "Drug-Facilitated, Incapacitated, and Forcible Rape."

39. Waller, Rights for Victims of Crime, chap. 3.

CHAPTER 8: PREVENTING VIOLENCE ON THE ROAD AND ALCOHOL-RELATED VIOLENCE

1. "Motor Vehicle Safety," Centers for Disease Control and Prevention, http://www.cdc.gov/Motorvehiclesafety/index.html, accessed April 11, 2013.

2. "Traffic Safety Facts 2011 Data: Alcohol-Impaired Driving" (fact sheet, National Highway Traffic Safety Administration, US Department of Transportation, Washington, DC, 2012), http://www-nrd.nhtsa.dot.gov/Pubs/811700.pdf, accessed February 16, 2013. See estimates for injuries from MADD at "Drunk Driving," MADD, http://www.madd.org/drunk-driving/, accessed April 30, 2013.

3. "Traffic Safety Facts 2011 Data." See also the list of all Traffic Safety Fact Sheets at http://www-nrd.nhtsa.dot.gov/cats/listpublications. aspx?Id=A&ShowBy=DocType, accessed April 28, 2013.

4. "Statistics," MADD, http://www.madd.org/statistics/, accessed February 16, 2013; "Impaired Driving in the United States," National Highway Traffic Safety Administration, http://www.nhtsa.gov/people/injury/alcohol/impaired_driving_pg2/us.htm, accessed April 28, 2013.

5. "Traffic Safety Facts 2011 Data."

6. "Drinking and Driving: A Threat to Everyone" (fact sheet, Centers for Disease Control and Prevention, Washington, DC, October 2011), http://www.cdc.gov/vitalsigns/DrinkingAndDriving/index.html, accessed April 11, 2013.

7. World Health Organization, *Global Status Report on Road Safety, 2013* (Geneva: World Health Organization, 2013). See also related analysis such as the country profiles at http://www.who.int/violence_injury_prevention/road_safety_status/2013/en/index.html, accessed March 15, 2013; "Road Safety Vademecum: Road Safety Trends, Statistics and Challenges in the EU 2011–2012" (working paper, European Commission, DG for Mobility and Transport, Unit C).

8. World Health Organization, *Global Plan for the Decade of Action for Road Safety 2011–2020* (Geneva: World Health Organization, 2011), www.who.int/roadsafety/decade_of_action/plan/plan_english.pdf, accessed April 2, 2013.

9. Insurance Institute for Highway Safety, http://www.iihs.org/, accessed April 12, 2013.

10. "Research & Statistics," Insurance Institute for Highway Safety, http://www.iihs.org/research/default.aspx, accessed April 12, 2013.

11. European New Car Assessment Program, http://www.euroncap.com/home.aspx, accessed April 11, 2013.

12. World Health Organization, *Global Plan for the Decade of Action*.

13. World Health Organization, *Global Plan for the Decade of Action*.

14. "Road Safety Vademecum."

15. Michael Sivak and Brandon Schoettle, "Towards Understanding the Recent Large Reductions in U.S. Road Fatalities" (working paper, University of Michigan Transportation Research Institute, Ann Arbor, MI, May 2010), Http://deepblue.lib.umich.edu/bitstream/handle/2027.42/71390/102304.pdf;jsessionid=234A57E7D1FF12ABBF58968979E33151?sequence=1, accessed February 16, 2013; "Road Safety Vademecum," 11.

16. Sivak and Schoettle, "Towards Understanding the Recent Large Reductions."

17. "Winnable Battles: Motor Vehicle Injuries," Centers for Disease Control and Prevention, http://www.cdc.gov/WinnableBattles/MotorVehicleInjury/, accessed April 11, 2013.

18. In the United Kingdom, for example, this number is 6.5 percent of officers, and the numbers are likely comparable in the United States. "Police Enforcement Strategies to Reduce Traffic Casualties in Europe" (working paper, European Transport Safety Council, Brussels, Belgium, May 1999).

19. "Road Safety Vademecum," 10.

20. "Police Enforcement Strategies"; J. Mendivil, A. García-Altés, K. Pérez, M. Marí-Dell'Olmo, and A. Tobías, "Speed Cameras in an Urban Setting: A Cost-Benefit Analysis," *Injury Prevention* 18, no. 2 (April 2012):75–80.

21. "Police Enforcement Strategies."

22. "Q&A: Cellphones, Texting and Driving," Insurance Institute for Highway Safety, March 2013, http://www.iihs.org/research/qanda/cellphones.aspx, accessed April 12, 2013.

23. R. Shults, D. Sleet, R. Elder, G. Ryan, and M Sehgal, "Association between State Level Drinking and Driving Countermeasures and Self Reported Alcohol Impaired Driving," *Injury Prevention* 8, no. 2 (June 2002): 106–10, doi:10.1136/ip.8.2.106.

24. "Campaign to Eliminate Drunk Driving," MADD, http://www.madd.org/drunk-driving/campaign/, accessed February 16, 2013.

25. "Program Profile: Checkpoint Tennessee," Crime Solutions, http://www.crimesolutions.gov/ProgramDetails.aspx?ID=136, accessed April 11, 2013; "Program Profile: Maryland Ignition Interlock Program," Crime Solutions, http://www.crimesolutions.gov/ProgramDetails.aspx?ID=63, accessed April 11, 2013.

26. "Program Profile: Maryland Ignition Interlock Program."

27. "Reducing Alcohol-Impaired Driving: Ignition Interlocks," The Community Guide, http://www.thecommunityguide.org/mvoi/AID/ignitioninter-locks.html, accessed February 16, 2013.

28. C. Willis, S. Lybrand, and N. Bellamy, "Alcohol Ignition Interlock Programmes for Reducing Drink Driving Recidivism (Review)" *Cochrane Database of Systematic Reviews* no. 3 (2004).

29. "Police Enforcement Strategies."

30. "Program Profile: Checkpoint Tennessee."

31. "Program Profile: Checkpoint Tennessee."

32. "Road Safety Vademecum," 11.

33. "Traffic Safety Facts 2008: Young Drivers" (fact sheet, National Highway Traffic Safety Administration, US Department of Transportation, Washington, DC, 2009), http://www-nrd.nhtsa.dot.gov/Pubs/811169.pdf.

34. "SADD's Mission and Policies," SADD, http://sadd.org/mission.htm, accessed April 11, 2013.

35. Stephen Wallace, "A Lease on Life: Parents Play a Pivotal Role in Keeping Teens Safe during the Summer Driving Season," MADD, http://sadd.org/articles_lease.htm, accessed April 11, 2013.

36. Wallace, "A Lease on Life."

37. "Traffic Safety Facts 2011 Data."

38. "Traffic Safety Facts 2011 Data."

39. "Repeat DWI Offenders Are an Elusive Target," National Highway Traffic Safety Administration, March 2000, http://www.nhtsa.gov/About+NHTSA/Traffic+Techs/current/Repeat+DWI+Offenders+Are+An+Elusive+Target, accessed April 11, 2013.

40. Terrence Willett, *Criminal on the Road: A Study of Serious Motoring Offences and Those Who Commit Them* (London: Tavistock, 1971).

41. "Crime and Alcohol: Alcohol a Factor in 40 Percent of Violent Crimes," About.com, http://alcoholism.about.com/cs/costs/a/aa980415.htm, accessed

April 8, 2013. See also "Fact Sheet: Alcohol and Violence" (fact sheet, Violence Prevention Coalition of Greater Los Angeles), http://www.ph.ucla.edu/sciprc/pdf/ALCOHOL_AND_VIOLENCE.pdf.

42. World Health Organization, *Violence Prevention: The Evidence* (Geneva: World Health Organization, 2009), available at http://www.who.int/violence_injury_prevention/violence/4th_milestones_meeting/publications/en/index.html, accessed April 7, 2013; Mark A. Bellis, Karen Hughes, Clare Perkins, and Andrew Bennett, "Protecting People, Promoting Health: A Public Health Approach for Violence Prevention for England" (working paper, North West Public Health Observatory, Liverpool, 2012).

43. Jan van Dijk, John van Kesteren, and Paul Smit, *Criminal Victimisation in International Perspective: Key Findings from the 2004–2005 ICVS and EU ICS* (The Hague: Boom Legal Publishers, 2008).

44. David J. Nutt, Leslie A. King, and Lawrence D. Phillips, "Drug Harms in the UK: A Multicriteria Decision Analysis on Behalf of the Independent Scientific Committee on Drugs," *Lancet* 376, no. 9752 (November 2010): 1558–65.

45. Ellen E. Bouchery, Henrick J. Harwood, Jeffrey J. Sacks, Carol J. Simon, and Robert D. Brewer, "Economic Costs of Excessive Alcohol Consumption in the U.S., 2006," *American Journal of Preventive Medicine* 41, no. 5 (2011): 516–24.

46. Matthew Manning, Christine Smith, and Paul Mazerolle, "The Societal Costs of Alcohol Misuse in Australia," *Trends & Issues in Crime and Criminal Justice*, no. 454 (April 2013).

47. Bellis et al., "Protecting People, Promoting Health," 42.

48. Andrew Karmen, *New York Murder Mystery: The True Story behind the Crime Crash of the 1990s* (New York: New York University Press, 2000), 185–87, 265.

49. Bellis et al., "Protecting People, Promoting Health," 42.

50. "The Stockholm Prize in Criminology," Stockholm University, http://www.su.se/english/about/prizes-awards/the-stockholm-prize-in-criminology, accessed March 13, 2013.

51. William Alex Pridemore and Tony H. Grubesic, "Alcohol Outlets and Community Levels of Interpersonal Violence: Spatial Density, Outlet Type, and Seriousness of Assault," *Journal of Research in Crime and Delinquency* 50, no. 1 (February 2013): 132–59; Saba W. Masho, Diane L. Bishop, Torey Edmonds, and Albert D. Farrell, "Using Surveillance Data to Inform Community Action: The Effect of Alcohol Sale Restrictions on Intentional Injury-Related Ambulance Pickups," *Prevention Science* (February 24, 2013).

52. J. C. Fell, D. A. Fisher, R. B. Voas, K. Blackman, and A. S. Tippetts, "The Relationship of Underage Drinking Laws to Reductions in Drinking Drivers in

Fatal Crashes in the United States," *Accident Analysis and Prevention* 40, no. 4 (July 2008): 1430–40.

53. Patricia A. Cavazos-Rehg, Melissa J. Krauss, Edward L. Spitznagel, Frank J. Chaloupka, Mario Schootman, Richard A. Grucza, and Laura Jean Bierut, "Associations between Selected State Laws and Teenagers' Drinking and Driving Behaviors," *Alcoholism: Clinical and Experimental Research* (2012), doi:10.1111/j.1530-0277.2012.01764.x.

54. World Health Organization, *Violence Prevention: The Evidence*; Bellis et al., "Protecting People, Promoting Health."

55. "Blueprints for Healthy Youth Development," Center for the Study and Prevention of Violence, http://www.colorado.edu/cspv/blueprints/, accessed April 28, 2013.

56. "Fetal Alcohol Spectrum Disorders and Impulse Control Disorders," FAS Community Resource Center, http://come-over.to/FAS/FASD-ICD.htm, accessed April 28, 2013.

57. "Impaired Driving: Get the Facts," Centers for Disease Control and Prevention, http://www.cdc.gov/motorvehiclesafety/impaired_driving/impaired-drv_factsheet.html, accessed April 10, 2013.

CHAPTER 9: PREVENTING PROPERTY CRIME IN COMMUNITIES, BY COMMUNITIES

1. Jennifer L. Truman and Michael Planty, "Criminal Victimization, 2011" (bulletin, Bureau of Justice Statistics, US Department of Justice, Washington, DC, 2013).

2. This is calculated using estimates of victim costs from Mark A. Cohen and Alex R. Piquero, "New Evidence on the Monetary Value of Saving a High Risk Youth," *Journal of Quantitative Criminology* 25, no. 1 (March 2009): 25–49, multiplied by the incidence estimates from Truman and Planty, "Criminal Victimization, 2011."

3. Shuryo Fujita and Michael Maxfield, "Security and the Drop in Car Theft in the United States," in *The International Crime Drop: New Directions in Research*, ed. Jan Van Dijk, Andromachi Tseloni, and Graham Farrell (Houndmills: Palgrave Macmillan, 2012), 237.

4. This is calculated using estimates of victim costs from Cohen and Piquero, "New Evidence," multiplied by the incidence estimates from Truman and Planty, "Criminal Victimization, 2011."

5. See for instance, Franklin E. Zimring, *The City That Became Safe: New York's Lessons for Urban Crime and Its Control* (New York: Oxford University Press, 2011).

6. Van Dijk et al., *The International Crime Drop*, 300–318.

7. Van Dijk et al., *The International Crime Drop*.

8. "National Crime Victimization Survey," US Census Bureau, http://www.census.gov/history/www/programs/demographic/national_crime_victimization_survey.html, accessed May 11, 2013; Truman and Planty, "Criminal Victimization, 2011"; Shannan Catalano, "Criminal Victimization, 2004" (bulletin, Bureau of Justice Statistics, US Department of Justice, Washington, DC, 2005).

9. Van Dijk et al., *The International Crime Drop*.

10. Andrew Karmen, *New York Murder Mystery: The True Story behind the Crime Crash of the 1990s* (New York: New York University Press, 2000).

11. "Fast Facts: Enrollment," National Center for Educational Statistics, http://nces.ed.gov/fastfacts/display.asp?id=98, accessed April 28, 2013.

12. Richard Florida, "Thank Immigrants for Safe Cities," *New York Daily News*, April 29, 2013, http://www.nydailynews.com/opinion/immigrants-safe-cities-article-1.1328639, accessed April 29, 2013.

13. Irvin Waller and Norm Okihiro, *Burglary, the Victim and the Public* (Toronto: University of Toronto Press, 1978).

14. Ronald Clarke, *Situational Crime Prevention: Successful Case Studies* (Albany, NY: Harrow and Heston, 1997).

15. Center for Problem-Oriented Policing, http://www.popcenter.org/, accessed May 10, 2013.

16. Fujita and Maxfield, "Security and the Drop in Car Theft."

17. Jan van Dijk and Ben Vollaard, "Self-limiting Crime Waves," in *The International Crime Drop: New Directions in Research*, ed. Jan Van Dijk, Andromachi Tseloni, and Graham Farrell (Houndmills: Palgrave Macmillan, 2012), 250–67.

18. Brandon Welsh and David Farrington, eds., *Preventing Crime: What Works for Children, Offenders, Victims, and Places* (New York: Springer, 2006).

19. The Boston bombings in April 2013 provide a typical illustration of this irony. A mass of CCTV and cell phone footage recorded the two bombers and helped law enforcement identify and arrest them quickly, but it did little to stop the bombing in the first place. This was also true of the 9/11 perpetrators and the bombers in the London public transit system.

20. "About This Release," Office for National Statistics, http://www.ons.gov.uk/ons/dcp171776_309791.pdf, accessed May 10, 2013.

21. "Global Network of Hackers Steal $45 Million from ATMs," *Time*, May 9, 2013, http://business.time.com/2013/05/09/feds-in-nyc-hackers-stole-45m-in-atm-card-breach/, accessed May 10, 2013.

22. Waller and Okihiro, *Burglary, the Victim and the Public*.

23. Felton Earls, interview by Dan Hurley, "On Crime as Science (A Neighbor at a Time)," *New York Times*, January 6, 2004, C1.

24. Wesley G. Skogan and Kathleen Frydl, *Fairness and Effectiveness in Policing: The Evidence* (Washington, DC: National Academies Press, 2004), 246–51.

25. Irvin Waller, "What Reduces Residential Burglary: Action and Research in Seattle and Toronto," in *The Victim in International Perspective*, ed. Hans Joachim Schneider (New York: De Gruyter, 1982), 479–92.

26. Lawrence Sherman, David Farrington, Brandon Welsh, and Doris MacKenzie, eds., *Evidence Based Crime Prevention* (New York: Routledge, 2002).

27. Graham Farrell and Ken Pease, "Preventing Repeat Residential Burglary Victimization," in *Preventing Crime: What Works for Children, Offenders, Victims, and Places*, ed. Brandon Welsh and David Farrington (New York: Springer, 2006), 162–76.

CHAPTER 10: REINVESTING IN SMART PUBLIC SAFETY TO SPARE VICTIMS AND LOWER TAXES

1. Irvin Waller, *Less Law, More Order: The Truth about Reducing Crime* (Westport, CT: Praeger Imprint Series, 2006; Ancaster: Manor House, 2008); Irvin Waller, ed., *Making Cities Safer: Action Briefs for Municipal Stakeholders*, Action Briefs, no. 3 (Ottawa: University of Ottawa Institute for the Prevention of Crime, March 2009).

2. Bogotá, Colombia, cut its extraordinarily high murder rate by 50 percent over ten years applying these principles. It had leadership at the city level—in this case, through the leadership of three consecutive mayors. The city established a crime prevention planning office that reported to the mayor. The job of the office was to analyze the risk factors that caused violence and then recommend actions to tackle those risk factors. The success was brought about with the help of the police force, who used problem-oriented policing strategies to help mitigate the risk factors. Yes, the city could have reduced more crime with a targeted investment in social development to the problem places, but a 50 percent reduction in homicides in a high-violence city is worth celebrating.

3. "Reducing Youth Incarceration in the United States" (working paper, Annie E. Casey Foundation, February 2013), http://www.aecf.org/~/media/Pubs/Initiatives/KIDS%20COUNT/R/ReducingYouthIncarcerationSnapshot/DataSnapshotYouthIncarceration.pdf, accessed May 3, 2013.

4. Peter W. Greenwood, Brandon C. Welsh, and Michael Rocque, "Implementing Proven Programs for Juvenile Offenders: Assessing State Progress"

(working paper, Association for the Advancement of Evidence-Based Practice, Downington, PA, December 2012), http://www.advancingebp.org/wp-content/uploads/2012/01/AEBP-assessment.pdf.

5. For instance, each state: (1) set up high-level task forces to analyze the situation and make recommendations, and these task forces included family and children's services agencies, mental health agencies, schools, police, and probation; (2) had a champion who wanted to see the changes happen; (3) had a person who knew the literature on what had worked; (4) tested new programs to learn practical issues relating to implementation; (5) had coaching on the evidence-based strategies; (6) started with multisystemic therapy (MST) or functional family therapy (FFT) (programs identified in chapter 4 as effective); (7) set up special funding to encourage particular evidence-based programs; and (8) provided technical assistance to counties for needs assessment, program selection, and implementation.

6. "No Place for Kids: The Case for Reducing Juvenile Incarceration" (working paper, Annie E. Casey Foundation, Baltimore, MD, 2011), http://www.aecf.org/OurWork/JuvenileJustice/JuvenileJusticeReport.aspx, accessed March 20, 2013.

7. The steps include: (1) limiting the use of custody; (2) investing in alternatives to incarceration; (3) adopting promising practices; (4) changing the incentives; and (5) establishing smaller and more intensive centers.

8. Fight Crime: Invest in Kids, http://www.fightcrime.org/, accessed April 17, 2013.

9. Irvin Waller, *Rights for Victims of Crime: Rebalancing Justice* (New York: Rowman and Littlefield, 2010), chap. 3.

10. "Preventing Violence: A Guide to Implementing the Recommendations of the World Report on Violence and Health" (working paper, World Health Organization, Geneva, Switzerland, 2004), http://www.who.int/violence_injury_prevention/media/news/08_09_2004/en/index.html.

11. (1) Increasing the capacity for collecting data on violence; (2) researching violence—its causes, consequences, and prevention; (3) promoting the primary prevention of violence based on the evidence of what works; (4) promoting gender and social equality to prevent violence against women; (5) strengthening care and support services for victims; and (6) bringing it all together—developing a ten-year national action plan.

12. Waller, *Rights for Victims of Crime*.

13. The United States decarcerated the mentally ill over a relatively short period. It achieved this through federal incentives. In 1955, the state mental hospital population was 559,000 when the total US population was 166 million, or a rate of 339 per 100,000. The state prison population is a not-incomparable

1.5 million for 310 million, or a rate of 485 per 100,000. Beginning around 1955, states began to let patients out of mental hospitals, and the decrease was precipitous. By 1972, the number of patients had decreased by 50 percent, and by 2000, the number had decreased by 90 percent. So rapid decarceration has happened in the United States before, and it was encouraged by federal incentives. Unfortunately, the prevention drugs were not used appropriately for the mentally ill. So a rapid decarceration would require the investment in effective prevention that has been proposed above.

14. Greenwood et al., "Implementing Proven Programs"; Stephanie Lee, Steve Aos, Elizabeth Drake, Annie Pennucci, Marna Miller, and Laurie Anderson, "Return on Investment: Evidence-Based Options to Improve Statewide Outcomes—April 2012 Update" (working paper, Washington State Institute for Public Policy, April 2012), http://www.wsipp.wa.gov/pub.asp?docid=12-04-1201, accessed February 13, 2013. At this point, WSIPP uses a discounting method for early childhood programs that does not respect the sustained reductions in violence once these programs are routine.

15. T. Miller and D. Hendrie, *Substance Abuse Prevention Dollars and Cents: A Cost-Benefit Analysis* (Rockville, MD: Center for Substance Abuse Prevention, Substance Abuse and Mental Health Services Administration, 2008); see also "2013 National Drug Control Strategy," Office of National Drug Control Policy, http://www.whitehouse.gov/ondcp/2013-national-drug-control-strategy, accessed May 2, 2013.

16. Mark A. Cohen and Alex R. Piquero, "New Evidence on the Monetary Value of Saving a High Risk Youth," *Journal of Quantitative Criminology* 25, no. 1 (March 2009): 25–49.

17. Rand Corporation brought together three studies that showed a statistical correlation between increases in the numbers of police officers employed by a police agency and decreases in numbers of robberies, assaults, burglaries, and motor vehicle thefts. Using only these offenses, it showed that a $150 million increase in expenditures on policing averted between $111 and $214 million in total costs of crime. See Paul Heaton, "Hidden in Plain Sight: What Cost of Crime Research Can Tell us about Investing in Police" (working paper, Rand Corporation, 2010), http://www.rand.org/pubs/occasional_papers/OP279.html, accessed April 14, 2013.

18. William Spelman, *Criminal Incapacitation* (New York: Plenum Press), cited in Steven D. Levitt, "Understanding Why Crime Fell in the 1990s: Four Factors That Explain the Decline and Six That Do Not," *Journal of Economic Perspectives* 18, no. 1 (Winter 2004): 163–90, http://pricetheory.uchicago.edu/levitt/Papers/LevittUnderstandingWhyCrime2004.pdf, accessed April 14, 2013.

19. Waller, *Rights for Victims of Crime*, 24–26; Centers for Disease Control and Prevention, "Universal Motorcycle Helmet Laws Increase Helmet Use and Save Money, news release, June 15, 2012, http://www.cdc.gov/injury/pressroom/story_archive/motorvehicle.html, accessed April 16, 2013.

20. James F. Austin and Michael Jacobson, "How New York City Reduced Mass Incarceration: A Model for Change?" (working paper, Brennan Center for Justice at New York University School of Law, 2013), http://www.brennancenter.org/sites/default/files/publications/How_NYC_Reduced_Mass_Incarceration.pdf, accessed February 27, 2013.

21. Drug Policy Alliance, "Colorado and Washington State Make History, Become First U.S. States to Regulate, Tax and Control Marijuana Like Alcohol," press release, November 7, 2012, http://www.drugpolicy.org/news/2012/11/colorado-and-washington-state-make-history-become-first-us-states-regulate-tax-and-cont.

22. Jeffrey Miron and Katherine Waldock, "The Budgetary Impact of Ending Drug Prohibition" (white paper, Cato Institute, Washington, DC, 2010).

23. Andrew Karmen, New York Murder Mystery: The True Story behind the Crime Crash of the 1990s (New York: New York University Press, 2000).

24. "Alcohol Industry 101: Its Structure & Organization" (working paper, American Medical Association Office of Alcohol and Drug Abuse, Chicago, IL, 2004), http://www.alcoholpolicymd.com/pdf/AMA_Final_web_1.pdf.

25. P. Corso, J. Mercy, T. Simon, E. Finkelstein, and T. Miller, "Medical Costs and Productivity Losses Due to Interpersonal and Self-directed Violence in the United States," *American Journal of Preventive Medicine* 32, no. 6 (2007): 474–82; Deepali Patel and Rachel Taylor, eds., *Social and Economic Costs of Violence: Workshop Summary* (Washington, DC: National Academies Press, 2012).

26. Michelle Alexander, The New Jim Crow: Mass Incarceration in the Age of Colorblindness (New York: New Press, 2010).

27. Irvin Waller and Janet Chan, "Prison Use: A Canadian and International Comparison," *Criminal Law Quarterly* 17, no. 1 (December 1974): 47–71; also in *Correctional Institutions*, 2nd ed., edited by L. T. Wilkins and D. Glazer, 41–60 (Philadelphia: Lippincott, 1977).

28. Miron and Waldock, "The Budgetary Impact."

LIST OF FIGURES

LIST OF TABLES

INDEX

911 calls: as reactive policing, 17, 30, 36, 38, 41, 52; mapping of, 20, 41, 46-49, 53

academic training. *See* education
affluent democracies, 91, 137: comparison of burglary rates, 209; comparison of homicide rates, 5; comparison of incarceration rates, 7; comparison of police per capita, 30; comparison of traffic fatalities, 6, 183;
African American. *See* racial minorities
alarms, 16, 212-215, 222, 234, 243
alcohol: addiction, 64, 68, 75, 95, 123, 144-145; as a risk factor, 72, 95, 102, 111, 150, 196-197; blood levels, 185, 187-190, 192-194, 201-202; controlled access, 22, 39, 176, 187, 197-199, 250; effective interventions, 167-168, 185, 187-203;

fetal alcohol syndrome, 200-201; related violence, 150-151, 164, 181-203; *See also* road violence
Alexander, Michelle. *See* Jim Crow, New
Amsterdam, 73, 150
assault: costs of, 10-11, 245; rates of 8, 33, 34-35, 128, 139, 150-151, 197-198, 231; *See also* sexual violence; violence against children; violence against women; violent crime
assault weapon. *See* guns
Australia, 5-7, 30, 72, 118, 156-157, 183, 190, 197, 209
Austria, 5-7, 30, 209

Baltimore, 144, 151
Belgium, 5-7, 30, 209
best practices. *See* models, inspiring
Big Brothers, Big Sisters, 123-124, 132

black. *See* racial minorities

Blueprint in Action program. *See*
  Minneapolis

Blueprints, 22, 111-112, 117, 119-
  120, 122-125, 129, 133-135; *See
  also* crimesolutions.gov; models,
  inspiring

Bogotá, 310n2

boot camps, 99, 112, 290

Boston, 44-45, 47-48, 83, 140-144,
  149, 233; *See also* deterrence,
  focused; Operation Ceasefire

Braga, Anthony, 41, 139

Brazil, 173

budget for shift from reaction to
  prevention, ix-xii, 239-254

bullying, 9, 50, 128-131, 136, 169,
  236, 244; *See also* assault

Bureau of Justice Statistics (BJS), 8,
  16, 33, 55, 64

burglary: costs of, 205-206; rates of,
  9, 34-35, 55, 205-206, 208-109;
  strategies for, 44, 71-72, 208-221,
  234-235, 253;

California, 62-63, 65, 68-69, 73, 83-
  86, 95, 100, 131, 147-149

calls for service. *See* 911 calls

cameras, video. *See* Closed circuit
  television (CCTV)

Canada: crime rates, 5-6, 91, 152-
  154; effective programs, 78-79,
  83, 130-131, 152-54, 168-172, 221,
  251; justice system, 7, 15, 29-30,
  85, 183, 209, 229, 274n7;

capital punishment. *See* death
  penalty

Cardiff strategy, 150; *See also* emergency room admissions

cars. *See* road violence

cell phone: distracted driving, 185-
  187, 201-202, 234; theft, 206, 210,
  214-215, 222, 243

Center for the Study and Prevention
  of Violence, 22, 111, 199; *See also*
  blueprints

Centers for Disease Control and
  Prevention (CDC), 111, 118, 164,
  167, 238; traffic fatalities, 10, 185,
  189, 193, 201

Chicago, 20, 44, 142-144, 216-217

child abuse. *See* violence against
  children

China, 7, 229

chronic offenders, 19-20, 88, 93,
  108-109, 193-195; effective reduction strategies, 48, 188, 195-196;
  pre-crime prevention strategies,
  109-127, 144-145, 241; reinvesting
  from incarceration to pre-crime
  prevention, 131-134, 239-242,
  245-247; *See also* Youth PROM-
  ISE Act; reoffending

citizens, *See* cost-effective; crime
  reduction; politicians, actions for;
  taxpayers

city-based solutions, 14, 20, 146-149,
  217-219, 234-237, 244, 253; *See
  also* neighbourhood; problem
  places

Clarke, Ronald, 210-211; *See also*
  situational crime prevention

clearance rates, 34-35

Closed Circuit Television (CCTV),
  213-214, 222-223, 309n19

cognitive-behavioral therapy, 96-99,
  122, 176, 243, 253

Cohen, Mark, 275

Colorado state, 111, 117, 128, 155;
  legalization of marijuana, 73, 232,